PAUL AND THE CREATION
OF CHRISTIAN IDENTITY

PAUL AND THE CREATION OF CHRISTIAN IDENTITY

by

WILLIAM S. CAMPBELL

t & t clark

Published by T&T Clark
A Continuum imprint
The Tower Building, 11 York Road, London SE1 7NX
80 Maiden Lane, Suite 704, New York, NY 10038

www.continuumbooks.com

All rights reserved. No part of this publication may be reproduced or transmitted in any form or by any means, electronic or mechanical, including photocopying, recording or any information storage or retrieval system, without permission in writing from the publishers.

Copyright © William S. Campbell, 2008

First published in hardback as volume 322 of the Library of New Testament studies, 2006

This edition published, 2008

William S. Campbell has asserted his right under the Copyright, Designs and Patents Act, 1988, to be identified as the Author of this work.

British Library Cataloguing-in-Publication Data
A catalogue record for this book is available from the British Library

Typeset by CA Typesetting, www.publisherservices.co.uk
Printed on acid-free paper in Great Britain by MPG Books Ltd., Bodmin, Cornwall

ISBN-13: PB: 978-0-567-03367-3
ISBN-10: PB: 0-567-03367-8

This book is dedicated to all my students with whom I have shared the joy of learning – at Sunderland, Selly Oak, King's, and Lampeter.

'You are my letter of recommendation' (2 Corinthians 3.2).

CONTENTS

Preface xi
Abbreviations xiii

Chapter 1
INTRODUCTION 1
  1.1 Jewish Identity in the First Century CE 2
  1.2 Ethnic Issues in the Pauline Letters 6
  1.3 Paul and the Politics of Difference 9
  1.4 The Approach of this Study 10
  1.5 Terminology 12
  1.6 Plan of the Book 13

Chapter 2
PAULINE INTERPRETATION AND CHRISTIAN IDENTITY:
ASPECTS OF THE HISTORY OF RESEARCH 15
  2.1 F.C.Baur and His Legacy 15
  2.2 The Recovery of Paul in His Jewish Context 17
  2.3 Paul Among Jews and Gentiles 21
  2.4 Ernst Käsemann and the Righteousness of God in Paul 23
  2.5 Sanders' and Dunn's New Perspective 26
  2.6 Opposition to the New Perspective 29
  2.7 Conclusion 31

Chapter 3
PAUL'S THEOLOGIZING CONCERNING THE OTHER 33
  3.1 Paul, the Recipient and Sole Interpreter of a Divine Revelation? 33
  3.2 Solidarity and Mutuality within the Communities 35
  3.3 Paul's Relationship with other Leaders and their Missions 38
  3.4 The Antioch Incident: The Catalyst of the Perception
      of Incompatibility Between Faith in Christ and Life as a Jew ? 42
  3.5 A Non-Sectarian Reading of Paul 46
  3.6 Conclusion 50

Chapter 4
PAUL'S PECULIAR PROBLEM:
THE CREATION OF GENTILE IDENTITY IN CHRIST 54
  4.1 Paul, the Innovator 54

4.2 The Scriptures of Israel and the Formation of Gentile
   Identity in Christ   57
4.3 Abraham, the Father of Us All, the Locus of Shared
   Identity in Christ   61
4.4 In What Sense Were the Pauline Communities Distinct?   64

Chapter 5
THE TRIPARTITE CONTEXT:
PAUL'S MISSION BETWEEN STATE AND SYNAGOGUE   68
   5.1 'Christians', Jews and Civic Authorities in Interaction 69
   5.2 Paul's Goal for His Communities in the Promotion
       of Solidarity in Christ   72
   5.3 Paul's Interaction with the Situation at Rome   75
   5.4 The Function of the Pauline Legacy in the Formation of
       'Christian' Identity in Antioch   79
   5.5 The Significance of the Tripartite Context for the Formation
       of 'Christian' Identity   83
   5.6 Conclusion   84

Chapter 6
I LAID THE FOUNDATION : PAUL THE ARCHITECT OF CHRISTIAN IDENTITY? 86
   6.1 Paul's Own Self-Understanding and Identity   87
   6.2 The Relativization of All Things in Christ   89
   6.3 Ethnicity and Paul's Construction of Identity in Christ 93
   6.4 Paul's Foundational Design: Potential Models   96
   6.5 Conclusion   101

Chapter 7
PAUL'S ATTITUDE TOWARDS JEWISH IDENTITY IN ROMANS   104
   7.1 The Identity of Paul's Addressees in Romans   104
   7.2 The Identity of the Jew in Romans 2   107
   7.3 Judaism and Jewish Identity in Romans: Negative Aspects 109
   7.4 Judaizers in Romans?   111
   7.5 Judaism and Jewish Identity in Romans: Positive Aspects 113
   7.6 The Affirmation of Jewish Identity in Romans 14–15   114
   7.7 Conclusion   119

Chapter 8
SELF-UNDERSTANDING AND THE PEOPLE OF GOD: ISRAEL IN ROMANS   121
   8.1 Jews, Gentiles and Israel: The Implications of Paul's Terminology 121
   8.2 The Remnant in Paul: A Saving Remnant and a Sign of Hope 127
   8.3 The Church is not Israel (or New Israel)   129
   8.4 Paul's Eschatology is Based on Confirmation of the Promises,
       not Fulfilment   133
   8.5 God's Covenant is Irrevocable: The Identity of Israel is not
       Transferable   134

Chapter 9
CHRIST-DEFINED IDENTITY — 140
9.1 Christ-Defined Identity and Continuity with the Narrative of Israel — 140
9.2 Christ-Followers as New Creation — 141
9.3 Divergent Interpretations of Divine Action in History — 143
9.4 Individualism and Faith in Christ — 147
9.5 Continuity and Discontinuity in Personal Identity in Christ — 149
9.6 A Christ-Defined Identity and Antagonism to Judaism — 151
9.7 Corporate Identity in Christ — 153
9.8 The Identity of Jesus as Messiah of Israel — 155
9.9 Multiple Identities in Christ? — 156

Chapter 10
CONCLUSION: PAUL'S THEOLOGY AS A THEOLOGY OF TRANSFORMATION — 159
10.1 Theology or Theologizing? — 159
10.2 The Catalyst: Social Factors in the Concrete Context of Paul's Communities — 161
10.3 The Basis: Belonging to Christ — 163
10.4 The Process: the Interaction Between Relativization and Transformation — 165
10.5 Transformation in Paul: an Ongoing Process — 171

EPILOGUE — 174

Bibliography — 176
Index of References — 197
Index of Authors — 201

PREFACE

The topics addressed in this study have been a focus of interest for more than a decade. At the 1985 meeting of the International Association for the History of Religions in Sydney, Australia, I gave a paper entitled 'Religious Identity and Ethnic Origin'. This was revised and published under the same title as a chapter in my book *Paul's Gospel in an Intercultural Context: Jew and Gentile in the Letter to the Romans* (1991, reprinted 1992). I offered a short paper on 'Christian Identity in a Multicultural Society' at the postgraduate seminar of the Faculty of Education, King's College, London on my arrival there in October 1997. This was in essence a broad outline of the present work which, in the absence of sabbaticals, proceeded slowly by articles given at various conferences: at the SNTS Annual Meetings at Tel Aviv and Durham, at SBL International Meetings Cambridge and Groningen, at the British New Testament Conferences in Manchester and Birmingham. Summaries of some of the topics in certain chapters were also given at postgraduate and New Testament seminars at the Universities of Oxford and Manchester and at an international symposium at the University of Basel. I am grateful to my colleagues in the Department of Theology, Religious Studies and Islamic Studies at the University of Wales Lampeter for providing a congenial and supportive context in which many issues I address here were frequently touched upon in the past eight years. In a lively and flourishing department, with a diverse international and multi-faith staff and students, questions of identity whether social or religious cannot be evaded. It becomes essential to discover ways of asserting one's own distinctiveness in ways that do not negate the identity of the other who is and remains different. This is the main focus of my research. Although over the years I have learnt much on questions of identity from dialogue and friendship with Jews and Muslims, the basic issues of my research have continued to be with Jewish and gentile identity in Paul, as evidenced in my PhD thesis on Romans 9–11 (Edinburgh, 1972) written prior to any real personal contact with members of other faiths. As my research on this volume proceeded, I have become increasingly aware of the growing pace of change in New Testament and especially Pauline interpretation. It has proved a difficult task to maintain acquaintance with the abundance of new commentaries, monographs and articles in the area but I am conscious of my indebtedness to a diverse and dedicated community of learning of which I have been privileged to be a part in many contexts at home and abroad. Where I acknowledge the sources of my indebtedness, I trust I report these accurately without misrepresentation. A special word of thanks is due to Kathy Ehrensperger for sharing her insights on feminist approaches to Paul and for her interest in and support of this project.

Lampeter January 2006
William S. Campbell

ABBREVIATIONS

AusBR	*Australian Biblical Review*
BDF	Friedrich Blass, A. Debrunner and Robert W. Funk, *A Greek Grammar of the New Testament and Other Early Christian Literature* (Cambridge: Cambridge University Press, 1961)
Bib	*Biblica*
BibInt	*Biblical Interpretation: A Journal of Contemporary Approaches*
BJRL	*Bulletin of the John Rylands University Library of Manchester*
BR	*Bible Review*
BTB	*Biblical Theology Bulletin*
BWANT	Beiträge zur Wissenschaft vom Alten und Neuen Testament
BZ	*Biblische Zeitschrift*
CBQ	*Catholic Biblical Quarterly*
CRBS	*Currents in Research: Biblical Studies*
EncJud	*Encyclopaedia Judaica*
ExpTim	*Expository Times*
FRLANT	Forschungen zur Religion und Literatur des Alten und Neuen Testaments
HTR	*Harvard Theological Review*
IBS	*Irish Biblical Studies*
ICC	International Critical Commentary
Int	*Interpretation*
JAC	*Jahrbuch für Antike und Christentum*
JBL	*Journal of Biblical Literature*
JBV	*Journal of Beliefs and Values*
JES	*Journal of Ecumenical Studies*
JR	*Journal of Religion*
JSNT	*Journal for the Study of the New Testament*
JSNTSup	*Journal for the Study of the New Testament*, Supplement Series
JSOT	*Journal for the Study of the Old Testament*
JSOTSup	*Journal for the Study of the Old Testament*, Supplement Series
JSP	*Journal for the Study of the Pseudepigrapha*
JSPSup	*Journal for the Study of the Pseudepigrapha*, Supplement Series
JTS	*Journal of Theological Studies*
LCC	Library of Christian Classics
LSJ	H.G. Liddell, Robert Scott and H. Stuart Jones, *Greek–English Lexicon* (Oxford: Clarendon Press, 9th edn, 1968)
JSR	*Journal of Scriptural Reasoning*
LTQ	*Lexington Theological Quarterly*
NovT	*Novum Testamentum*
NovTSup	*Novum Testamentum*, Supplements
NRSV	New Revised Standard Version
NTS	*New Testament Studies*
RB	*Revue biblique*

RelS	*Religious Studies*
RevQ	*Revue de Qumran*
RevScRel	*Revue des sciences religieuses*
RSR	*Recherches de science religieuse*
RSV	Revised Standard Version
RV	Revised Version
SBL	Society of Biblical Literature
SBLASP	SBL Abstracts and Seminar Papers
SBLDS	SBL Dissertation Series
SBLSP	SBL Seminar Papers
SBLSS	SBL Semeia Studies
ScrB	*Scripture Bulletin*
SE	*Studia Evangelica I, II, III* (= TU 73 [1959], 87 [1964], 88 [1964], etc.)
SJT	*Scottish Journal of Theology*
SNTSMS	Society for New Testament Studies Monograph Series
SNTU	Studien zum Neuen Testament und seiner Umwelt
SR	*Studies in Religion/Sciences religieuses*
ST	*Studia theologica*
TS	*Theological Studies*
TynBul	*Tyndale Bulletin*
TNTC	Tyndale New Testament Commentaries
TZ	*Theologische Zeitschrift*
WBC	World Biblical Commentary
WUNT	Wissenschaftliche Untersuchungen zum Neuen Testament
ZNW	*Zeitschrift für die neutestamentliche Wissenschaft*

Chapter 1

INTRODUCTION

'For neither circumcision counts for anything nor uncircumcision' (1 Cor. 7.19). This is one of the statements of Paul that has given rise to his acclamation as the second founder of Christianity. Texts such as this are the basis for his being perceived as having successfully overcome the particularities of ethnic and national identities, and created in place of such a universal brotherhood of Christ-followers which rises above the limitations of natural descent and culture. In the last two decades, however, the discourse on identity, ethnicity, and diversity has offered significant new insights some of which appear to challenge what for almost two centuries has seemed to be incontrovertible, the concept of a universal Christian identity. Within this developing discourse there is a greater awareness that whilst there is also a growing recognition of fluidity and flexibility in identity construction, it is equally recognized that such construction emerges not in contrast or opposition to, but within and in interaction with, specific particularities.

Whether emergent Christian identity followed such patterns or whether it uniquely followed its own original design in contrast to any other social patterns is therefore in dispute. The issue is whether Christ-followers leave behind their cultural affiliation and enter a newly created universal society or whether, as Jews or Greeks, they continue to live within that same culture but under the transforming influence of Christ. According to the former view, a posited new universal Christian identity opposes particularity and difference for the superior value of oneness in Christ, generally interpreted as sameness. Christian universalistic claims, however, whilst being beneficial in a specific form, in the contemporary world both lend themselves as an accessory to an imperialistic conception of a dominating Western culture over e.g. African or Korean culture, and tend also towards an unwarranted sense of superiority of Christianity over other world faiths. In the history of the church, it is easy to see how, from the earliest days of the recognition of the church within the Roman Empire, these universalistic claims have facilitated the victimization of Jews whether Christ-followers or not, and all those who did not conform to such claims.

Since Christianity did not originate in a historical and cultural vacuum,[1] but was always contextualized in diverse situations, I find the universalistic reading

---

1. Cf. Chrysostom's references to the martyr Lucian who at his trial answered each inquiry whether to fatherland, vocation, or ancestor by repeating each time 'I am a Christian'. Chrysostom explains how this is so, 'the Christian does not have a city on earth but the Jerusalem above. The

of Paul is no longer convincing. Recent research demonstrates that identities are not fixed immutably throughout history, but that they are continuously under construction or, rather, reconstruction. Thus it is important to review our understanding of *historic Christian identity* in its social, cultural and theological dimension, and reflect upon this in the light of new evidence. I propose in this study to reconsider the role of Paul in the creation of Christian identity in the light of such new perspectives. We will therefore consider several important areas of discourse highlighted by these new perspectives which are of crucial significance for a fresh understanding of Paul.

1.1 *Jewish Identity in the First Century* CE

The New Testament uses various terms to describe Jews of the first century, which are translated as Hebrews, Israelites, Jews/Judeans. Our quest will focus primarily on the identity of these people. The people thus described lived in Judea or originated from there. Ἰουδαῖος as an adjective is found in Mk 1.5 and Jn 3.22 and thus, in this form, can be used to distinguish Jews from the people of other geographical areas; Ἰουδαῖος/Jew tends to be a term used when that sort of distinction is being evoked or implied.[2] It is employed by both Jews and non-Jews to refer to Jewish people to distinguish them from others. In this usage Ἰουδαῖος/Jew or Jews is normally simply a neutral term though there has been much research and debate concerning οἱ Ἰουδαῖοι/the Jews' in John's Gospel. Urban C. von Wahlde has proposed retaining the term 'Jew' in a national sense but to use 'Judean'instead for regional use.[3] The obvious advantage of translating Ἰουδαῖος as 'Judean' rather than 'Jew' is that some of the prejudice which in Christian history has tended to be attached to the term 'Jew' is somewhat circumvented.[4] It may thus be preferable to use the term 'Judeans', an option taken in some recent research which we must also consider despite Shaye D. Cohen's insistence that there remain occasions in the first century when the word Ἰουδαῖοι is best translated 'Jews' where it has a religious or political sense.[5]

Paul's use of the term 'Jew' whether in the singular or plural is most clearly demonstrated in Romans. Here there are frequent examples in conjunction with gentiles or Greeks and it might appear to a casual observer that Paul has no fixed usage but prefers a variety of options. This is not the case. He does differentiate between Jew and gentile, or Jew and Greek, but his favoured term for describing his own people as the recipients of the covenant, is 'Israel', also their chosen

---

Christian does not have an earthly vocation but acts for the commonwealth above. The Christian has the saints as relatives and fellow citizens'. We note here how all forms of ethnic and group identity are deliberately replaced by the term Christian as if Christians live in a social and political vacuum. Cf. Mitchell 2000: 233.
    2. Dunn 1998: 505.
    3. U.C. von Wahlde 2000: 49.
    4. Cf. Esler's comment on this, 2003a: 62 and 68.
    5. 1999: 69–106.

1. Introduction

self-designation.⁶ What is absent from Romans is a discussion in terms of Israel and gentiles,⁷ or Jews and Israel. The nearest Paul gets to the latter is in 9.6b, 'not all Israel are Israel'. What is clear from this, however we interpret its significance, is that Paul has great respect for the appropriate terminology and is generally consistent in his use of it.

It is now recognized that the term 'Jew' originates as a geographical and ethnic identifier. As Philip Esler has emphasized, the term Ἰουδαῖος/Jew in the first century context necessarily included a territorial dimension. He disagrees with Shaye D. Cohen's thesis that all instances of Ἰουδαῖοι (or the Latin version thereof '*Iudaei*') before 100 BCE should be translated 'Judean', since they have an 'ethnic-geographic' sense not conveyed by 'Jew', but that thereafter there are occasions when the word is best translated 'Jew', where it has a 'religious' or 'political' sense. Esler maintains that Cohen's argument and the data he cites indicate that Ἰουδαῖοι does not lose its territorial connotation so as to justify the translation 'Jews' until well into the third century CE, if not two or three centuries later.⁸ Following Fredrik Barth's approach to ethnicity which maintains that the sense of the separateness of a group is antecedent to the (changing) ways in which separateness is expressed, and that cultural features are needed to signify the boundary, Esler argues that the Judeans/Israelites were a distinct group in the Mediterranean world who continued to select cultural features that changed over time in response to challenges to their uniqueness. His view is that the use of the term 'Jews' suggests that people remain essentially the same over centuries – thus assisting in the stereotype of 'the eternal Jew'.⁹ Esler also considers the contemporary (first century) use of the term Ἰουδαῖοι, particularly the *Judean Antiquities* of Josephus. Here Ἑβραῖοι is most commonly used of the people in the patriarchal and Egyptian period, while 'Israelites' comes to be used most frequently of them after Joshua led them across the Jordan. But from the time Cyrus gives them permission to return to Ἰουδαία to rebuild the temple, they are referred to on most occasions as Ἰουδαῖοι thus making a link between the name of the people and its homeland containing the capital city and temple of their God unmistakable.¹⁰

Against this proposal, it could be argued that to allow too great a distance between 'Judeans' and contemporary Jews might also assist in denying to post-New Testament Jews the heritage of Israel. As we will note in subsequent discus-

---

6. But see also the reported discussion in Gal. 2 where Paul says to Cephas, 'If you, though a Jew, live like a gentile (ἐθνικῶς) and not like a Jew (Ἰουδαικῶς), how can you compel the gentiles to live like Jews (Ἰουδαΐζειν)?' Cf. Dunn.1998: 505–6.

7. As Dunn notes, the near exceptions to this rule, Rom. 9.30–31 and 11.25, arise because here it is primarily unbelieving Israel that is in view in contrast to the gentiles, 1998: 506 n. 39.

8. Esler 2003a: 68–71. Esler holds that the root of the difficulty with Cohen's argument is due to the weaknesses in his concept of ethnicity particularly in connection with his failure to adequately relate culture and identity as well as religion and ethnicity. He also argues against Cohen that the concept of religion as a separate distinct realm of human experience in the first century is an anachronism since this concept only originated with the Enlightenment. Cf. 2003a: 69–74.

9. 2003a: 62–3.

10. 2003a: 64.

sion in this book, there are echoes of such a view in the contemporary world where Jews are categorized with the rest of humanity in such a way as to ignore or positively deprecate their affiliation to an ancestral faith.[11]

Interesting also in relation to this is Esler's own recognition of the potential of the term 'Israelite' demonstrated in his question, 'How does the Barthian perspective on ethnicity help us to understand the identity of the people for whom "Israelites" is a designation not the subject of the same problems as "Jews"?'[12] Does this question not suggest that even if we prefer the term Judean, sometimes we also necessarily require some other term such as 'Israelite' to assist the process of communication? On the other hand, a problem with the word 'Israelite' is that it represents the first century Jews' own favoured self-understanding, their inner group self-definition rather than how they were perceived or described by others. Basic to the problems referred to by Esler, is that the term 'Jew' as used throughout Christian history has not tended to be simply the name of a people, but implies a hostile rather than neutral reference. There has been little attempt on the part of Christians to look at Jews from an *emic* rather than an *etic* perspective. From our consideration of the diverse terminology used to describe Jews in the first century, we have to acknowledge that there is no one word that encompasses the range of aspects of Jewish identity at this time.

We find ourselves broadly in agreement with Esler's constructivist stance on ethnicity in the ancient world. He cites with approval, Richard Jenkins' claim that,

> there is good cause to reject totally any strongly primordialist view. Too much ethnographic evidence exists of the fluidity and flux of ethnic identification, and of the different degrees to which ethnicity organizes social life in different settings, for any other position to be sensible, and the theoretical argument in favour of a constructivist view is too well founded.[13]

He likewise affirms J.M. Hall's conclusion concerning Greek ethnicity, 'there is…no doubt that ethnic identity is a cultural construct, perpetually renewed and renegotiated through discourse and social practice'.[14] However, I would wish to maintain, in light of the fact that there is now widespread recognition among social scientists that it is necessary to propose some reconciliation between the interactive and self-ascriptive approach of Barth and the continuing importance of primordial dimensions of ethnicity,[15] that when dealing with Israelites/Jews in

---

11. One other factor worth noting is that terminology differs between languages. Thus the German word 'Jude' is closer to Esler's proposal than the English term 'Jew'. The Italian, 'Ebrei' is also interesting in this connection. Esler points out that in view of the Third Reich slogan 'Juden raus' (Jews out) still a living memory in Europe, the change in German from 'Juden' to 'Judäer' might be strengthened in this context (2003: 376 n. 136).

12. 2003a: 62. Cf. also Richard Horsley 2004: 228-37. Horsley was one of the first to translate Ἰουδαῖοι as Judeans – according to Esler already in the early 1990s (Esler 2003: 66).

13. 1997: 46 cited by Esler 2003a: 62.

14. Hall 1997 cited by Esler 2003a: 47. Cf. Jonathan Watt's claim that 'Ethnicity tends to stress roots and shared biological past and the common ancestors (factual or fictional). The basis of personal identification is cultural (including religion) and ethnicity is a matter of self-ascription'. 2003: 285.

15. 2003a: 46.

1. Introduction

the first century more attention should be given to the primordial aspects of ethnicity. Esler notes in relation to the reception of Fredrik Barth's views 'we should recall that in 1969 he (Barth) acknowledged in regard to complex polyethnic societies that 'ethnic identity implies a series of constraints on the kinds of roles an individual is allowed to play, and the partners he may choose for different kinds of transactions'.[16] It is acknowledged that Barth underestimated the affective power of ethnic ties, and the extent to which ethnic actors (for example minorities) encounter external constraints on their behaviour.[17] Since the Jews were frequently a minority among gentiles and, at this period, under Roman imperial dominance, the primordial elements in their ethnic understanding must be strongly underlined. As Lee Levine notes,

> A Jewish community was an entity no less ethnic than religious in essence, and as such, its common history, origins, customs, cultures, and aspirations served to bind them together. When one combines an ethnic base and a well-defined religious component, the bonds forged – internally and with other communities can be formidable.[18]

Such aspects cannot fail to be recognized since these people successfully retained some ongoing sense of particular identity despite sojourns in Babylon and enforced Hellenization.[19] The identity of the Jews in the first century was indelibly influenced by the Maccabean Wars when life and death choices arising from resistance to or conformity with Hellenization were called for as a result of their faith. In this respect the Maccabean martyrs and the resultant theology/ideology arising from this[20] contributed enormously to Jewish self-understanding in relation to the Romans and in issues concerning loyalty to or apostasy from the community and its traditions.[21]

Hutchinson and Smith offer six cultural features commonly stressed by groups to provide a distinct identity: (1) a common proper name to identify the group, (2) a myth of common ancestry, (3) a shared history or shared memories of a supposed common past, (4) a common culture, including customs, language and religion, (5) a link with a homeland, (6) a sense of communal solidarity.[22] The Jewish community exhibits these features with great clarity at the commence-

---

16. 2003a: 47. Esler also notes that when Barth revisited this debate at the 1993 Amsterdam conference celebrating the twenty-fifth anniversary of his book, *Ethnic Groups and Boundaries*, he complained that this aspect of his work had been frequently overlooked.

17. See Esler 2003a: 46–7. "Ethnicity is made of neither stone nor putty; Cornell and Hartmann" 1998: 71.

18. Cf. 2003: 11.

19. For this reason, I am cautious to ascribe general views of ethnicity as fluid and flexible to the Judaism of the first century, despite its diversity; there is a risk that post-Pauline Christianity's developing self-understanding is thus not sufficiently differentiated from Judaism in this respect. Paul, despite much appearance of flexibility is firmly rooted in his Jewish symbolic universe. There is a risk of reading back later Christian perspectives into Paul (contra Buell 2005: 6–13).

20. Caligula's attempt to place a statue of himself in the temple reawakened the memories of the Maccabean crisis.

21. Thus Esler warns against generalizing concerning children and grandchildren of immigrants' apparent tendency (in the modern era) to feel less attached to the original homeland (2003: 376 n. 128).

22. Hutchinson and Smith, 1996: 6–7.

ment of the period of Christian origins. As Cornell and Esler have insisted, a shared history and a collective memory are basic to a group's identity which in its collective memory is situated at the centre of the narrative. According to Cornell, such narratives come into their own in times of crisis, or 'periods of rupture', when identities are called into question by those who bear them or by other people, or severely testing events.[23] Those who would attempt to modify a group's identity narrative, or who were perceived by others as intending to destroy it, are thus involved in a power struggle between rival versions of a previous common identity narrative. Thus there were fierce debates amongst the numerous Jewish factions of the first century concerning major and minor aspects of shared identities within the common narrative. These divergences of opinion were regarded as most crucial in their practical outcome in everyday life. But despite this the overriding assumption was that, however different, they were all children of Abraham sharing the common Jewish narrative.[24]

Thus within the diversity of the Judaism of this period, Christ-followers were only one among the varied groups claiming to live as children of God. These various groups differed in their understanding of how Torah should be interpreted in relation to daily life but these were 'inner-Jewish' differences among Jews themselves even though these also concerned the status of gentiles attached to synagogue groups.[25] The new challenge presented by Paul's mission to the gentiles was that these Christ-followers should be accepted as gentiles and that they ought not to become proselytes. This involved major innovation, since Paul placed no obligation on the part of these newcomers to conform to the demands of Torah, but only to the Noachide regulations.[26] Such an innovation was viewed by many Jews as a threat to the very identity of their faith, a threat to their distinctive way of life.

1.2 *Ethnic Issues in the Pauline Letters*

This would appear to be the conflict situation faced by Paul when he attempted to adjust or modify the self-understanding of his Jewish contemporaries by introducing Christ-following gentiles as (gentile) children of Abraham. For Paul this radical step is justified by the dawning of a new age in Christ, despite its seeming dilution of the age-old ethnic boundary between Jew and gentile. In this revision of Israelite self-understanding, the Christ-event is added to the events that were central to their history, not simply as an additional item but rather as a decisive factor which demanded a reconfiguration of the entire narrative. The preceding centuries of conflict with distinct ethnic dimensions, however, were detrimental in the extreme to such a project, having produced a strong resistance

---

23. Cornell 2000: 44–5.
24. Whether this is commonality is best described with Sanders as 'covenantal nomism' is still much disputed, but this does not annul the point we are making here.
25. We are aware of Nanos's useful differentiation between 'intra-Jewish' and 'inter-Jewish', but in this instance feel that 'inner-Jewish' is simpler and clearer. Cf. Nanos 2002a: 7–9.
26. Here we follow Wyschogrod 2004: 90–8.

among some groups of the Jewish people to any obvious attempt to redefine the boundaries between Jew and gentile and thus endangering their hard-won distinctiveness. Although physical descent from Abraham was theoretically indispensable, the strongest opposition came against those whose life pattern seemed to threaten the established *mores* of the community. In first century Judaism, especially in the Pharisaic faction, the religious and affective element was strongly nurtured in the maintenance or attempted maintenance of a distinct pattern of life which tended to isolate them somewhat from their neighbours.[27] Thus as a distinct and somewhat separated minority, some Jewish communities developed strong convictions which severely limited the choices available to them, and in many cases eliminated much that for other groups was a viable option. Such a view of these communities is essential to avoid trivializing the convictions of groups such as those described in Romans 14–15 for whom observation of days or eating of meat was a most serious matter. On the other hand, this stance does not rule out the well-documented fact that strong self-confident Jewish communities existed in places like Alexandria with its impressive synagogue, that they were or could be exceedingly flexible and were, to that extent, successful in coexisting with gentiles though not without conflict.

Paul apparently did not share these concerns about identity, either because he believed he had found a better alternative (and therefore rejected Judaism), or perhaps because he himself did not share the pessimism of some of his fellow Jews concerning the effects and outcome of the Christ-movement in relation to ongoing Jewish identity and distinctiveness. We take the latter view and will seek in this study to demonstrate that it best accords with Paul's statements in his letters, his activity in relation to both Jews and gentiles, and his self-understanding as an Israelite. This solution might suggest that Paul was naïve in that he did not foresee the outcome of his gentile mission and the theological thinking on which it was founded. Our proposal is that what eventually emerged as a mainly gentile church was not what Paul envisaged or intended.[28] For Paul, Jews remain Jews in Christ, and he also opposed all attempts to force gentiles to judaize. The Christ community for Paul is a place where ethnic distinctions are recognized whilst not being permitted to become a means of discrimination. Of course, he did not and could not see the future in the long term, but we must distinguish between what Paul attempted and worked for, and what emerged as the combined result of the gentile mission, opposition from both Jews and gentiles and the political factors constraining these, both individually and corporately, resulting from Roman imperial rule.

---

27. In relation to the affective domain, we wish to stress that convictions are not so much an attitude we adopt or choose to hold, but rather that they hold us and bind us to behaviour that can be very costly in terms of social relations.

28. Cf. J.D.G. Dunn 'Justification by faith *in Christ* is, if you like, the Jewish-Christian refinement of Jewish election theology... I do not dispute that the end result of this development was a breach between (rabbinic) Judaism and Christianity. I *do* dispute that this was ever Paul's intention or that it was inevitable within the context of the much broader stream of pre-70 Judaism' (1990: 208).

Such a solution need not imply complete scepticism in relation to the church. Paul was not an idealist in the sense of looking for some kind of theological or practical perfectionism. Like church leaders of today he had to work in terms of the feasible, the permissible and always with the imperfection of human groups and institutions. But that means we must not simply bless what emerged and confuse the actual with the possible. As a Reformed Christian, I would like to see the church being continuously reformed and thus transformed. Therefore the vision of what might be or have been is not impractical idealism, but must always be kept in view and in tension with the actual, because, if Paul's own vision had been maintained, things could have been different. As Philip Alexander claims,

> The existence of a Jewish Christianity blurred the sharp edges of Christian self-definition. From the standpoint of the Gentile Church it was expedient that the Jewish Church should fade away. Suppose the Jewish Christians and not the Rabbis, had won the battle for the hearts and minds of Israel? The result would not necessarily have meant the end of the Jewish people and their absorption into the Gentile Church. It is just as possible that two forms of Christianity would have emerged, possibly even two religions.[29]

This possibility reminds us that from Paul's perspective, the future was still open and Israel had not decided (finally) against the Christ-movement.

Most Jews and Christians have failed to recognize the significance of Paul's proposals for the relation of gentile members of the Christ-movement to Israel and what this might entail. Christians tend to equate what actually is with *what might have happened*, and thus to credit Paul with pessimism or antipathy towards his ancestral faith. Likewise Jews are fearful of what might have happened if Paul had been more successful than he actually was in his influence with fellow Israelites. As Schiffman claims,

> Had the rabbis relaxed these standards, accepting either the semi-proselytes or the earliest Gentile Christians into the Jewish people, Christians would quickly have become the majority within the expanded community of 'Israel', Judaism as we know it would have ceased to exist even before reaching codification in the Mishnah and the other great compilations of the tannaitic tradition. Christianity would have been the sole heir of the traditions of biblical antiquity, and observance of the commandments of the Torah would have disappeared within just a few centuries. In short, it was the *halakhah* and its definition of Jewish identity which saved the Jewish people and its heritage from extinction as a result of the newly emerging Christian ideology.[30]

In either scenario, whether from a Christian or a Jewish perspective, Paul suffers from an identification between his self-enunciated goals and the outcome and evaluation of these at a later period supported by all the wisdom of hindsight. It can confidently be claimed, however, that Paul's intention was not to blur the boundaries of Israel's ethnicity, nor did he intend that gentiles become Jews. Rather, his aim was to reconfigure the relation between people who are and who remain different. But this new relation implied a transformation in the symbolic universe of these peoples in the light of the Christ-event.

29. 1992: 25.
30. 1985: 77.

1.3 Paul and the Politics of Difference

Paul's distance and difference, both from the contemporary church and from modern interpreters, must continue to be emphasized. This is especially significant amongst those who revere the apostle and who might assume too readily that Paulinism has captured the essence of the apostle's vision. Too often, in this perspective, Paul's attitude to difference has been viewed as negative, difference to be overcome, rather than difference to be negotiated, perhaps even celebrated. The almost complete scholarly consensus that Paul aims to achieve equality between Jews and gentiles in Christ has been mainly responsible for the unquestioned assumption that Paul's advocation of equality involves, even necessitates, the abrogation of difference, or the elimination of ritual distinction, or at best the indifference to difference.[31] In addition it has been argued by Sanders that Paul's policy of indifference to difference, whilst theoretically feasible, just did not work out in practice with the result that where conflict arose between Jews and gentiles in Christ those things that were offensive to gentiles had to be given up by the Jews.[32]

In her important work on *Justice and the Politics of Difference*, Iris M. Young has usefully distinguished two differing meanings of equality, the assimilationist and the emancipatory politics of difference. The latter, in contrast to the ideal of assimilation, 'sometimes requires different treatment for oppressed or disadvantaged groups'.[33] As Young emphasizes 'Difference means the irreducible particularities of entities, which makes it impossible to reduce them to commonness or bring them into unity without remainder. Such particularity derives from the contextuality of existence'.[34] In contrast, when Paul's quest for equality is represented as a quest for sameness, this thus negates the right to be different in Christ, effectively dissolving all 'others' into a single essence in which matters of cultural practice are irrelevant.[35] As Emmanuel Levinas maintains, 'Western philosophy has often been an ontology; a reduction of the other to the same by interposition of a middle and neutral term that ensures the comprehension of being'.[36]

Such a perception reflects two related factors in Paulinism. Firstly there has been a tendency to decontextualize Paul so that his relational and contextual argumentation is overlooked. Secondly, the tendency to conceptualize Paul's thinking has led to terms such as equality[37] being interpreted as an abstract

---

31. See Jae Won Lee 2005: 6; Gundry-Volf 2003: 8–36. Rather than adiaphorization, I prefer to use the term relativization in relation to Paul's understanding of how the Christ-event impinges on the understanding of difference.
32. 1983: 143–62.
33. Young 1990a: 158.
34. Young 1990b: 304.
35. Boyarin 1994: 181.
36. Levinas 1992: 43.
37. The Enlightenment roots of the term 'égalité' remind us that historically this term is part of a movement to overcome social differences for the benefit of the deprived. The problem is that if the

philosophical category which carries its own inherent and universal content that inevitably binds us to certain specific conclusions that tend to denigrate difference with the aim of transcending group difference.[38] On the contrary, however, when Paul is interpreted from the perspective of the politics of difference in the contextuality of existence, as Young advocates, and, theologically speaking, in accordance with the biblical understanding of creation, then Israel and the nations, however related, can be perceived as two separate entities and that according to divine purpose. God is thus the God of two distinct entities, both of Israel and the nations. In the light of these perspectives, difference is not to be deplored but is perceived as divinely given and thus to be respected, even cherished. Thus Paul continues to distinguish Jew and gentile even in Christ. Equality in this context is not sameness nor is it equality despite difference nor an imperfect equality temporally tolerating difference but a genuine equality in and with difference. Particularities are not an obstacle to be overcome in Christ, nor are they to be perceived as absolutely in opposition to universalism.[39] Pauline universalism is one that can coexist with particularities. The universal dimension of the gospel acknowledges its inclusive reference to both Jews and gentiles.[40] The intention of this book is to demonstrate that when this understanding of equality and difference is applied to the interpretation of Paul, a paradigm very different from historic Paulinism results.

1.4 *The Approach of this Study*

The approach I will follow in this study is one that seeks to take both social context and theology/ideology into account. There can be no doubt that Pauline interpretation has hugely benefited from the application of social-scientific and other models to the biblical texts. There can be no return to a stance which treats texts or theology as having been formulated in a historical or ideological vacuum. The influence of historical context, of the 'Sitz im Leben', cannot be ignored. Nor can the dynamic interaction of social factors be disregarded in favour of a simpler static scenario. It is our intention in this study to stress that Paul takes the concrete realities of existence into account as a basic dimension of his theologizing. He writes as it were, within context, where his communities existed, and the problems arising from and associated with this context. Viewed in this perspective, social factors, or a sociological approach, are not in opposition to a full

---

context is not properly observed, then the very presence of such a term may point towards a different intention than Paul had in mind.

38. 'The assimilationist ideal assumes that equal social status for all persons requires treating everyone according to the same principles, rules and standards', Young (1990a: 158).

39. Cf. Munck (citing Sundkler 1937) 'The opposition between particularism and universalism is the product of a modern cosmopolitan outlook, and has nothing to do with the biblical conception of the mission' (to the gentiles) (1959: 71). Cf. also Nanos 1996: 181-2.

40. We need to distinguish between 'universalizing' and the acknowledgement that the scope of the gospel is universal.

1. Introduction

understanding and elucidating of Paul's theologizing.[41] The social dimension is an indispensable factor in understanding Paul's letters.

Our intention, however, is not to allow sociology to displace theology. It is beyond debate that within Paul's letters, theological factors are equally important. There can and there may sometimes be, conflict between the results obtained from the application of socio-historical or theological approaches. Nevertheless, both are necessary to Pauline interpretation. A careful look at Paul's statements in his letters demonstrates his response, indeed reaction, to social factors. The social dynamics are the subject of his theologizing, whether it is weakness in Corinthians, or ethnicity in Romans. Yet this interaction with context does not represent the whole of Paul's theologizing. Along with this, inextricably intertwined, is the Christ-event as a radical new perspective on the actual context and the vital relationships taking place there. And the Christ-event is not the only narrative into which Paul sets the issues he has to deal with in Corinth or elsewhere. There is also the wider story of Israel and Israel's scriptures in which the interaction between this people and their God is the primary focus. Paul does not simply report or repeat the theological tradition of Israel's scriptures. Rather, he combines all the above-noted factors in a marvellous fusion of creative imagination in which his pattern of, what some have termed, 'scriptural reasoning'[42] results in contextually-related letters in which theological and social factors are dramatically fused to offer practical guidance within an implicit and/or explicit eschatological framework.

Paul's theologizing did not take place in a vacuum, nor was it an additional abstract structure of thought imposed from without. Rather Paul theologized on the basis of concrete realities such as those discussed above, i.e. identity, ethnicity etc. His theological formulations were not later, systematized, and therefore separate, reflections on his own and his communities' activities. Rather they arose from and were inextricably intertwined with the life and events within his communities in the context of the wider Graeco-Roman world. My aim in this study is not only to consider historical and social aspects of identity, ethnicity and difference in the first century but to include, in association with these, Paul's theologizing and the outcome of this in the formation of Christian identity.[43] In my opinion Paul's theologizing in the context of, and in relation to, similar issues that confront us in contemporary society is his incomparable legacy to posterity and one which needs to be understood afresh in order to prevent us from simply inheriting and repeating the mistakes of the past.

---

41. We use the term 'theologizing' to stress that this is an activity in which Paul engages, rather than 'theology' with its emphasis upon conceptualization, distance from context, and tendency towards offering a static understanding of Paul's theological thought. We will develop this approach in some detail in Chapter 10.

42. Cf. Ehrensperger 2004b.

43. In order to maintain this focus, I will deal only with those aspects of topics that relate to or impinge on, the theme of ethnicity and identity. This I sometimes found frustrating, but I felt I could not possibly attempt to deal adequately with the wide range of issues to which these chosen topics have a connection.

1.5 Terminology

We do not use the term 'Christian' in relation to Paul's converts during his lifetime. It is anachronistic to identify the Christ-movement, even in its Pauline form, with emergent Christianity. I have sometimes in the past used the term Christ-believers to describe both Jews and gentiles who were part of the new movement. I now regard the term Christ-follower to be more appropriate. Christianity has tended to over-emphasize the place of belief as such in the earliest period in order to contrast a posited Jewish tendency to stress good works. The term Christ-follower is in my view useful in that it tells what Christians did as well as what they believed about their faith in Jesus as Messiah. Thus, instead of talking of certain Jews who refused to join 'Christianity' (since this as such did not yet exist), it makes better sense to say that these refused to join the Christ-movement.

If we are to avoid anachronistic interpretation by not recognizing the distance between the first century and our own, then terminology should be consistent in relation to Jews as well as Christians. Esler's proposal to translate Ἰουδαῖος in most instances as 'Judean' has its merits. By this he distinguishes Israelites of the first century from the Jews of later times, not of course with any negative implications but as a way of differentiating and of avoiding anachronism. With him we recognize that 'Israelite' is another possible and appropriate term to describe the self-understanding of Paul the apostle. It is useful in that it tends to stress the religious affiliation of Jews/Judeans. It is not however to be regarded as *purely* a religious term signifying any group of God's people whether Judean or Greek. Also it is not to be favoured simply because it does not carry an ethnic dimension. In Paul's use it certainly does. But in the term Judean, the geographical link to Judea is prominent and reminds us that in the ancient world our modern separation between religion, land and people did not yet exist.[44] It thus ties the label more closely to its referent and avoids symbolic usage which tends to blur distinctions and to allow opportunities for displacement theologies in less obvious forms. Above all it indicates how difficult it would be for Judeans to give up being Judean, an aspect not so obvious when we speak in terms of Jews or Jewishness. However, despite being attracted by Esler's arguments and his fruitful deployment of the new terminology in his book,[45] at present, whilst taking into account the issues he raises, we will stay with the traditional terminology, (mainly translating Ἰουδαῖοι as Jews) until we can reflect further on the significance of his proposal.

The term τὰ ἔθνη like the term Ἰουδαῖοι also suffers from being read from our modern perspectives. Recently references to it have been translated as 'Gentiles', a capitalized ethnic term equivalent and opposite to 'Jews'. This suggests

---

44. Cf. Boyarin 2004 also Esler 2003a: 7–8, following W. Cantwell Smith's argument that our modern notion of religion, essentially meaning a specific system of belief embodied in a circumscribed community, is a modern concept that dates from the Enlightenment (1992 [1962]).

45. Esler 2003: 40–76.

that there existed some distinct ethnic identity such as Syrians or Bithynians, indicated by this composite term 'Gentiles' which is certainly not the case.[46] Authoritative biblical translations, especially the NRSV, reinforce this erroneous impression.[47] When Paul writes concerning τὰ ἔθνη, however, he is referring to the nations in relation to Israel, and these nations though described with one term are by no means one entity. Paul can speak just as easily of 'Greeks' or 'barbarians' and the multi-ethnic composition of cities such as Rome, Alexandria, and Antioch, was a visible demonstration of the existence of diverse nations as well as of Jews. We will therefore translate the term τὰ ἔθνη as 'gentiles' or 'gentile nations', recognizing that it refers to a diversity of nations.[48]

1.6 *Plan of the Book*

Interpretation never takes place in a vacuum. The social location of thought is not something we can afford to ignore if we are to take seriously into account our own context as well as that of the Pauline texts. This includes the variegated history of Pauline interpretation by which we are informed (and possibly formed) and in dialogue with and in reaction to which, our thinking proceeds.[49] Chapter 2 of this book will seek to set the scene from which such contemporary interpretation of Paul proceeds. This is to demonstrate the continuity and discontinuity of interpretation from the 19th century until the present, not in the sense of a detailed history, but looking rather at those seminal figures and periods when great changes, relevant to the understanding of the formation of Christian identity, were instituted and effected. Even when scholars react against their predecessors, there is negative influence and thus not real discontinuity. We begin with Ferdinand Christian Baur whose influence still continues to determine aspects of Pauline interpretation, particularly in relation to issues concerning the compatibility of Christianity and Judaism. These in turn are influential in the construction of modern Christian self-understanding and identity. Following Munck's detailed attempt to refute Baur in the 1950s, subsequent developments by Stendahl, Sanders and Dunn led to a 'New Perspective on Paul' which to a certain extent reduced the influence of the Tübingen School mainly by paying more adequate attention to Paul's Jewish heritage. The conclusion to which we are drawn in this overview of interpretation is that despite developments since Baur, and even despite the insights of the New Perspective, Baur's posited antithesis between Paul and Judaism is still visible and the opposition to the particularity of differing identities among Jewish and gentile Christ-followers has not yet been overcome in much contemporary Pauline interpretation.

46. Cf. Elliott 2005b: 7–10.
47. LaGrande 1996: 77–87.
48. The significance of this is well demonstrated by Elliott in developing his thesis that the real problem Paul faces in Romans is not Jewish ethnocentrism but Roman ethnocentrism, something that would be missed if we used the traditional terminology (2005b: 22).
49. I am very conscious of the great debt I owe to countless New Testament interpreters whose insights and labours have illuminated my understanding of Paul, not least the stimulating group of colleagues in the SBL 'Pauline Theology Group' with whom I interacted for a decade.

In Chapter 3 we will consider Paul's relation to Jerusalem and his ethical stances towards Peter and others who differed from him, arguing that the Lordship of Christ obligated Paul, Peter and others, including James, to mutual recognition and the recognition of each other's mission. In Chapter 4 we consider the problems peculiar to Paul's mission to gentiles due to the fact that he associated gentile Christ-followers with Abraham and Israel but insisted they remain gentile. Chapter 5 argues that we should not regard the conflicts of the first century gentile mission as having been determined mainly by conflict between Christ-following Jewish and Pauline communities, but rather as springing from a tripartite interaction between Jews, Christ-following gentiles and the Roman imperial powers, including local civic leaders. Chapter 6 considers Paul's foundational design for the church in which we claim that both Israelite and gentile Christ-followers are to remain in the situation (and hence identity) in which they were first called. Chapter 7 deals with Paul's attitude towards Jewish identity in Romans considering both positive and negative aspects. In Chapter 8 Paul's terminology in relation to Israel is reviewed concluding that gentile Christ-followers are not, in Paul's terminology, Israel or New Israel, and that the identity of Israel is not transferable. Chapter 9 focuses on the meaning of Christ-defined identity. Followers of Christ are not a new creation in the sense that their past is entirely annulled or negated, and that there are multiple identities in Christ.

The conclusion of our study in Chapter 10 claims that Paul's theologizing is best described as leading to a theology of transformation. The old Saul still lives in Paul but Paul can claim, 'I live and yet not I but Christ lives in me'. Thus it cannot be claimed that in Christ the past is obliterated with all its culture and identities. Rather the past is transformed in Christ and Christ-identity can pervade all cultures, transforming them but not imperialistically obliterating everything as if Christian faith were an entirely independent culture which replaces, and is discontinuous with, previously existing patterns of life.

Chapter 2

PAULINE INTERPRETATION AND CHRISTIAN IDENTITY:
ASPECTS OF THE HISTORY OF RESEARCH

2.1 *F.C. Baur and His Legacy*

The dominant portrait of Paul behind much modern interpretation of his life and letters is shaped by F.C. Baur, particularly by his innovative introduction and application of the historical-critical method to Paul's letters and Acts, beginning in 1831.[1] So much intellectual history now lies between us and Baur's initial reconstructions of early church history, that it is extremely difficult to bridge the gulf without oversimplification or anachronism. One example may illustrate the issue. Shortly after the publication of Baur's article, Charles Darwin was beginning his search in the Galapagos islands for evidence for his theory of evolution. *The Origin of Species* was not published until 1859 and helped to change the conception of history so much that it is now difficult for us to envisage how it was previously conceived. For Baur history is the self-expression of God as Absolute Spirit. Baur sought to correlate a philosophy of history and an objective study of the data, thereby enabling fact and interpretation to work together in a continuous dialectical relationship.[2] Baur's fresh approach marked a radical change in Pauline scholarship in reaction to previous dogmatic and church dominated theological approaches. His proposal to make Romans 9–11 the focus of Paul's thought in the letter rather than, as had previously been the consensus, chs 1–8, was an attempt to reinterpret the letter without being completely dominated by the Lutheran emphasis on justification by faith. In the light of Stendahl's use of the same proposal and for a similar reason nearly one and a half centuries later, Baur's genius is obvious.

His contribution to scholarship, however, has been vitiated by an ongoing debate over his (possible) indebtedness to German philosophical idealism, particularly to the philosophy of Hegel.[3] The parallels with Baur's strong contrast

---

1. Of particular note is Baur's famous article, 'Die Christuspartei in der korinthischen Gemeinde, der Gegensatz des petrinischen und paulinischen Christenthums in der ältesten Kirche, der Apostel Petrus in Rom'. Tübinger Zeitschrift für Theologie 5 (1831): 61–206. Baur's essay is available in F.C. Baur 1963: 1–146.
2. Cf. W. Baird 1992: 260–2.
3. Baird acknowledges that, in his opinion, Baur was not an uncritical devotee of Hegel and believes that Peter Hodgson has largely defused the charge that Baur's reconstruction was flawed by his arbitrary adoption of the Hegelian dialectic (1992: 269). Similarly, J.B. Tyson notes 'it is no

between the universal and the particular are significant. On the other hand, the nature of the link with Hegel is not so crucial as whether in this or other of his major emphases, Baur's exegesis and reconstructions are any longer convincing. What is appropriate in our contemporary interpretation necessarily differs greatly from that of Baur's lifetime, and simply to repeat the views of a great scholar will not prove adequate. In the last analysis, it is not the source of opinions but their validity that is the issue.[4]

Baur is important for contemporary understanding of Paul and particularly relevant to the topic of this book. This is because he contributed enormously to the tendency in the Paulinism of the last century and a half to denigrate the image of Judaism in the New Testament. For Baur, Jesus is the founder of a new religion, Christianity, which, as the absolute religion, is superior to all others.[5] Baur saw it as his task 'to define the essence of Christianity by purging it of anything that smacks of Judaism, of nationalism and particularism'.[6] Baur was critical of the particularity of Judaism that in his view distinguished its (inferior) quality from that of Paulinism.[7] For him, Judaism, like the rest of the Oriental world, suffers from a failure of recognition of the spirit and all that spirit entails.[8] Christianity, in contrast, is a more spiritual (geistigere) form of the religious consciousness.[9]

This perspective, as noted above, had the long-term effect of depicting Judaism in a negative light. It also included an innate tendency to read the New Testament primarily as a story of opposition and conflict. This in turn oversimplified into a basic binary opposition the diversity of forces that were in operation in the period of Christian origins. Thus in his famous and characteristic essay, Baur reduced the number of the conflicting groups in Corinth to two, the Pauline group (the followers of Paul and Apollos) and the judaizers (the parties of Cephas and Christ), reflecting the basic conflict between Pauline and Petrine Christianity in the church. Baur's primary New Testament canon was a much reduced affair, with only Galatians, 1 and 2 Corinthians and Romans representing the authentic

---

longer permissible to dismiss Baur's work as nothing more than the imposition of Hegelian philosophy on the history of Early Christianity', but Tyson also notes that 'the discussion of Hegelian influence continues' and he is critical of how Baur's speculative judgements in historical reconstruction affect his exegesis, 1999: 26–7. Similarly cf. Baird 1992: 246 and 259.

4. My own view is that Baur imbibed the spirit of an age which is typified by Hegel, whether or not he knew the latter's writings prior to the formulation of his own theses. Just as Darwin conceived of the theory of evolution and went in search of evidence for it, long before the publication of his famous book, so too ideas are in some sense already implicit some time prior to being expounded in print.

5. F.F. Baur 1864: 45.
6. Kelley 2002: 36–7.
7. After acknowledging Judaism's pure monotheistic conception of God, Baur goes on to add, 'But on the other hand the Old Testament conceived God as the God, not of the human race, but of a particular nation' (1878: 77).
8. Kelley 2002: 69.
9. See Baird 1992: 264–5.

2. Pauline Interpretation and Christian Identity

position of the apostle. These letters cohere in that together they represent the ongoing and developing battle between Paul and his judaizing opponents.[10]

E.P. Sanders reminds his readers of a significant article by George Foot Moore in which he demonstrated that whereas throughout the eighteenth century, whilst Jews were still under attack from Christian propaganda, the overall intent was to show the *agreement* of Jewish views with Christian theology, there was a radical change in the nineteenth century. 'With F. Weber, however, everything changed. For him Judaism was the antithesis of Christianity. Judaism was a legalistic religion in which God was remote and inaccessible.'[11]

Thus Christianity in its purest (Pauline) form is presented in stark contrast to Judaism, one of the most serious and abiding aspects of Baur's legacy,[12] (though in all fairness we must recognize that it was not really Judaism as such that Baur was interested in, but rather the 'purification' of Christianity.) In relation to our research into the origins of Christian identity, it is significant that Baur, at the commencement of modern historical research, presents Christianity both in contrast to Judaism and as a new and superior religion, brought to its true self-understanding by Paul. In the later formulation by F. Weber, this denigration was compounded by the addition of the concept of Judaism as a religion of legalism. Such a portrayal of Judaism and the resultant depiction of Christianity has assisted in our opinion to produce an on-going deficient view of Judaism in its own right as well as an inadequate understanding of the indebtedness of Christianity to Judaism.

2.2 *The Recovery of Paul in His Jewish Context*

The Jewish heritage of Paul is an essential topic of interest to us because, if Christian identity is not simply formulated in antithesis to Judaism, then there could be significant positive links between Jewish roots and Christian self-understanding. The stress upon Paul's positive understanding of Judaism is closely identified with the work of W.D. Davies. When, after graduating in Greek and Semitics, Davies began his theological studies in the mid-1930s, the dominant scholarly tendency was to view Paul as the Hellenizer of Christianity, a view which was in keeping with the Greek bias of New Testament scholars.[13] At the Memorial College Brecon in Wales, Davies began to read the Mishnah, and discovered both post-biblical Judaism and a world he found familiar with the New Testament. Associated also at this time with the tendency to view Paul as a Hellenizer, was another, to contrast the New Testament with Rabbinic literature.

---

10. Cf. Baird 1992: 264–5.
11. Sanders 1977: 33. Sanders also points out the continuation of Weber's picture of Judaism in Schürer and Bousset (as well as how inadequate and poorly founded such a construction is).
12. Thus even in 1954, J. Munck was still fighting the views of Baur and the Tübingen School. Munck points out that whilst it is not in his interest to trace the fortunes of the Tübingen School, 'it is important to be clear how many of Baur's ideas meet us in the most recent discussion of Paul and Primitive Christianity' (1954: 72–3).
13. See E.P. Sanders' Foreword to W.D. Davies 1998: ix.

However, as a result of his immersion in Rabbinic literature, Davies began to *compare* rather than to *contrast* this with the New Testament, and to look for parallels between Paul and the Rabbis.[14] This comparison was to be Davies' particular contribution to future New Testament scholarship in the post-War era. In it we see an ongoing British reaction to some aspects of the continuing legacy of Baur[15] which remained quite influential. Davies was willing to acknowledge that Palestinian Judaism was not a watertight compartment closed against all Hellenistic influences but that 'there was a Graeco-Jewish "atmosphere" even at Jerusalem itself'. Nevertheless he maintained against C.G. Montefiore that Paul as a Diaspora Jew really did know Rabbinic Judaism and that it is in these Rabbinic sources that we can find the material that explains the genesis and development of his thought rather than in Philo, Joseph and Aseneth or other Diaspora Jewish literature.[16] Rather than contrasting Paul with Pharisaic Judaism, Davies set his views in contrast to the History of Religions School which, to explain Christianity, had turned to Hellenistic religion (especially the mystery religions), Gnosticism, and Mandaism.[17]

It was this relocation of Paul firmly in his Jewish context that was to prove one of the most significant contributions of Davies. It is of particular importance in the discussion of Paul and the creation of Christian identity because Davies did not view Judaism as something entirely alien to Pauline Christianity, nor something to be discarded as completely as possible. In this respect he helped to reduce the tendency to view Paul and Judaism as being in direct antithesis, thus opening the way for a more positive view of Jewish Christ-followers and their pattern of life.[18]

Writing in the aftermath of the Second World War, Johannes Munck maintained that many of Baur's ideas were still current.[19] His main criticism was that, 'as regards method, modern Pauline research suffers from having broken with the

---

14. As Sanders notes, Davies resolutely opposed the view that Paul in Galatians attacked Pharisaic soteriology in a battle against legalistic work righteousness. Davies did not succeed in dismissing entirely such a view of Paul, but as Sanders notes, 'it is fair to say that English–speaking Pauline scholarship has been permanently improved in this regard, thanks in no small measure to Professor Davies' work' (Davies 1998: ix).

15. On the response to Baur by J.B. Lightfoot see W.G. Kümmel 1972, esp. Ch. 3 'The Correction of Baur's View of History', 168–84 (174). Cf. also J.D.G. Dunn 1990b: 369–71.

16. Cf. Sanders in Davies 1998: xii–xiii. On the difficulties surrounding the use of Rabbinic material see Sanders 1977: 59–75.

17. Sanders in Davies 1998: x, also Käsemann 1980: 254. There can be no doubt that Davies was also indebted to J. Weiss and A. Schweitzer's new emphasis on eschatology – a stance also to be later developed by J. Munck.

18. As Sanders notes, 'It is instructive to compare Davies's position with that of what I believe to be the majority of New Testament scholars, the position which we above illustrated with citations from Thackeray, Bultmann, and Schrenk: that despite parallels in detail, there is a fundamental antithesis between Paul and Judaism, especially Rabbinic Judaism... He identifies the idea of being "in Christ" as the central soteriological concept. The latter, while the opposite of being "in Israel", Davies does not see as constituting an antithesis to Judaism', Sanders 1977: 9.

19. Munck 1954, ET 1959. It represents a sustained attempt at a detailed refutation of Baur's major theses. Munck's other well-known work, *Christ and Israel* first appeared in 1956 (ET 1968).

Tübingen School's literary theory, but not with its historical theology'.[20] In his preface to the English translation of Johannes Munck's *Christ and Israel* in 1967, Krister Stendahl stated that it was 'the reading of this book that literally lifted hundreds of verses in the Pauline epistles out of a glorious haze of homiletical rhetoric and theological over-interpretation. It gave to the Pauline writings and to Paul the apostle a historical reality which – I hope – has remained with me ever since.'[21]

It is no surprise then that Stendahl also notes that this, Munck's *magnum opus* which has the character of a thesis with a distinctive thrust, 'has for some reason come to play less of a role in the contemporary discussion of Pauline problems than it deserves'.[22] It is in fact not at all surprising that in 1956, the consensus of Pauline scholarship was unable to give due recognition to Munck's innovative work, it simply did not fit easily into the prevailing patterns of interpretation. Munck's greatest gift as a biblical scholar was 'the ability to read an ancient text with fresh eyes',[23] and it was partly because he was so different that his fresh insights were somewhat lost on many of his readers.

Munck's understanding of Paul had, as Stendahl notes, two foci. The first concerns Paul's status and his self-understanding as the apostle to the gentiles, an elevated status capable of comparison with Moses and the great prophets of old. The second relates to Paul's mission and work – his special revelation – the mystery and the gospel which he had received and which constituted a reversal of the expected timetable for the salvation of Jews and gentiles.

Thus for Munck, Paul is somewhat of an activist – his eschatologically oriented mission is the focus of his thought and not some dogmatic or timeless reflection on philosophically oriented universal truths. We understand Munck best when we recognize his work as a reaction to F.C. Baur and the Tübingen School, and above all the Hegelianism that resonates with it. Munck notes: 'it is important to be clear how many of Baur's ideas still meet us in the most recent discussion of Paul and primitive Christianity'.[24] Again for Munck, Paul has a special role in relation to the gentiles. His churches are basically gentile in composition, and although all of Paul's time and energies are devoted to gentiles, it does not mean that he has no interest in Jerusalem or the Jewish mission.

By way of undoing the entrenched image of Paul and his theology in the legacy of the Tübingen School, Munck proposes certain principles which he will follow: 1. Paul's letters are to be interpreted as such (statements from Acts or elsewhere may be used only if they agree with or do not clearly contradict what we find in the letters, but such extraneous material must not determine the exposition of the letters). 2. Paul's individual letters, and the situation that forms the background

---

20. Munck 1959: 77. Since Stendahl says in his Preface that it was more than twelve years earlier that he had first read the German version of Munck's book, it probably means he had read it already in 1955, i.e. prior to publication in the following year.
21. Munck 1967: vii.
22. Munck 1967: vii.
23. So Stendahl in his preface to Munck 1969: viii.
24. Munck.1959: 73.

of each individual letter, must be viewed on their own merits in each case. Indeed 'the material in the letters and behind these supposed situations may be unified only if such a procedure does not violate the individual nature of a particular letter and the situation that lies behind it'.[25] 3. A historical situation, in this case a situation that is the background of a particular Pauline letter, despite the fact that it may not be the expression of a clearly systematized theological position (and as such not suitable for any systematic investigation), is nevertheless historical and its historical character must not be disregarded.

By following these principles, Munck hoped to release Paul's letters from the traditional exposition going back to the Tübingen School, and thus not only to get a more coherent picture of Paul, but also to discover more of the diversity of Early Christianity. Acts, also, freed from the load of tradition will offer a much clearer picture of primitive Christianity; its presentation of Jewish Christianity will then not open between Paul and Jerusalem 'the deep chasms that the Tübingen School took for granted'.[26] By his stress on the particularity of each letter and its context, Munck successfully undermined what Dunn describes as 'Baur's grandiose reconstruction of Christian development across the first two centuries'.[27] There was no 'judaizing' party in Jerusalem. Paul's letters were addressed to differing situations with differing opponents (rather than only Jewish Christians).[28] Above all, the compulsion to judaize did not come from Jewish Christianity which was concerned only with its mission within Israel.[29] This latter concern was part of the purpose of Munck's book, *Christ and Israel.* Munck stressed the central role of apocalyptic in Paul's self-understanding. Paul's mission is not a counter-mission to Peter and Jerusalem; rather Paul perceives himself as 'apostle to the nations', playing a decisive role within the divine purpose, as symbolized in the collection for Jerusalem. The apostle evangelizes an area, thus viewing his converts not simply as individuals, but as representatives of larger groups. His concern is with Israel and the nations, with peoples rather than only with individuals. In keeping with the dominant emphases in his portrait of Paul, Munck challenged the traditional view of Romans as a dogmatic treatise, preferring to describe it as 'a missionary's contribution to a discussion'.[30]

25. Munck:1959: 85.
26. 'Thus despite all the diversity between the earliest disciples and Paul, there does exist a connection that brings them close to each other.' Munck 1959: 85.
27. Dunn 1990b: 370–1. Dunn also notes that breakdown in turn discouraged the use of the term 'judaizer' outside the context of Paul's mission and writings, with Ignatius as the only significant exception.
28. Thus there were no 'judaizers' in Galatians, but rather gentiles who were keen to adopt the practices of the law (thus retaining the proper meaning of the term, 'judaizer'). The opponents in Phil. 3.2 were not judaizers, but Jews. (It is worth noting that this latter emphasis upon Jews rather than Jewish Christians interfering in Pauline communities, is now resurfacing in, e.g. M.D. Nanos 2003.)
29. Dunn.1990b: 370.
30. Munck here drew upon T.W. Manson's essay (1948) which he praised because in his view it had invalidated a 'widespread assumption that it (Romans) is a theological presentation unaffected by time and history' (1959: 200). The effect of regarding Romans as a missionary document was to

Although he did not particularly stress this in his own perception of Paul, when Munck is set in historical context, what is most significant in his own contribution to Pauline research, is that he did in fact portray an eschatological understanding of Paul which harmonized much better with an understanding of the apostle in the light of his Jewish heritage.[31]

It is interesting to note, however, that both he and Baur were in broad agreement on the significance of Romans 9–11. Yet this original insight of Baur concerning the centrality of chs 9–11 within the letter had not really been appreciated, partly due to Baur's mistaken view that Jewish Christians were dominant in Rome.[32] In this respect Munck, in a new era and with fresh perspectives, brought once again to scholarly attention an aspect of Paul long ignored.[33] As Terence Donaldson notes,

> ...by establishing the centrality of Romans 9–11 for both the epistle and its apostle, he has closed off the entrance to one common approach to Paul's gentile mission: no longer is it possible to assume that Paul went to the gentiles because he believed that in Christ 'Jew' and 'Israel' had been emptied of their ethnic denotation. It is as a Jew, and for the sake of Israel, that Paul engages in his activity as apostle to the gentiles.[34]

2.3 Paul Among Jews and Gentiles

Munck's insights were developed and carried forward by fellow Scandinavian, Krister Stendahl, who as we already noted was familiar with Munck's work and greatly influenced by it.[35] Stendahl questioned whether the original framework of Paul's thought was not the missionary concern of Jews and gentiles rather than a

---

highlight the significance of chs 9–11 (and thus allocating less significance to the dogmatic aspects), hence Munck's monograph on these chapters. For Munck these chapters represent Paul's reconstruction of the order of events in Heilsgeschichte in the light of Jewish failure to recognize Jesus as Messiah, and in face of his own successful gentile mission. Munck 1967: 123–5.

31. Cf. Sanders' comment, 'Although Munck did not explicitly deal with the question of Paul's relation to Judaism, his supposition that Paul's whole activity was dominated by his eschatological outlook helped to drive home the point that Paul is to be understood on the basis of his Jewish background – and Palestinian Jewish at that' (1977: 8). Donaldson claims that 'Munck's work as a whole needs scrutiny at some points. His reinterpretation is distorted considerably by an overreaction to Tübingen, and marred by an ungenerous treatment of Judaism and its attitude towards the gentiles' (1997: 20).

32. See Käsemann 1980: 254.

33. In Käsemann's view, even though Baur had shown the weakness of the Reformation's failure to integrate 9–11 with the message of justification, and pioneered a historical understanding (rather than a theological focusing on predestination), 'It was here that the future journey should have been determined. 'Openness to the message of these chapters could no longer follow the tracks of the older dogmatics but nevertheless, 'twice in the nineteenth century, the chapters achieved importance in theological history without any clear decision being reached about them or at least their importance in the interpretation of Paul as a whole being recognized'. Käsemann 1980: 253–5.

34. Donaldson 1997: 20.

35. Stendahl's major themes first emerged in two series of lectures delivered at Austin Presbyterian Seminary and Colgate Rochester Divinity School in 1963 and 1964 respectively. As Stendahl states, 'When I gave these lectures, I was heavily under the spell of Johannes Munck's studies of Paul' (1976: v–vi). But see also p. 87.

dogmatic perspective such as justification by faith, and whether Romans 9–11 rather than 1–8 was the climax of the letter's argument.

In relation to this Stendahl's new insights are often associated with the increasing interest in Jewish-Christian dialogue in the latter half of the 1970s. However, this is not correct. Stendahl's concern with Romans goes back to the mid-1950s inspired, as we have noted, by Munck's work, and it is not justified to claim it originated simply as a concern for Jewish-Christian dialogue (any more than that he ever advocated the two covenants' theory as a solution). When we compare Stendahl's insights with those of Munck (whose views no one would suggest were motivated by Jewish-Christian dialogue, then only in its infancy), it is clear that Stendahl's image of Paul was in continuity with his own Scandinavian background and contributed to his interest in Jewish-Christian understanding rather than originating as a result of it. Stendahl's own agenda was to resist and redress an overly dogmatic and theological image of the apostle. This characteristic emphasis emerged in a famous essay, 'Paul and the Introspective Conscience of the West', first delivered to the American Psychological Association in 1961. Stendahl argued that we should not mistakenly read Paul in the light of Luther's agonized search for relief from a troubled conscience.[36] This certainly was a felt need in the sixteenth century, but only emerged as a post-Augustinian phenomenon, and was certainly not evident in the first century. Stendahl called for a clear distinction to be drawn between Paul's letters as first written and their subsequent theological interpretation. The letters were originally occasional communications to local communities but once they were acknowledged as Scripture they quickly suffered homogenization – the human predicament became the generalized context for the church's interpretation of Paul's thought.[37] Thus their particularity was lost and their occasional nature diminished when they were regarded as timeless theology, related specifically to general and universal human failings. Paul's own concerns were much broader than individual salvation. As Stendahl maintains '…Paul's doctrine of justification by faith has its theological context in his reflection on the relation between Jews and gentiles, and not within the problem of how man is to be saved, or how man's deeds are to be accounted, or how the free will of individuals is to be asserted or checked'.[38] Thus the doctrine of justification was a means rather than an end in that for Paul, it served the function of 'how to defend the place of gentiles in the Kingdom…the task with which he was charged in his call'.[39] Stendahl's view is that even justification, important though we have seen it to be, must be subsumed in the wider context of Paul's mission to the gentiles, part of God's total plan for his creation.[40]

36. Stendahl 1976: 7–17.
37. Stendahl 1976: 5–6.
38. Stendahl 1976: 26.
39. Stendahl.1976: 27. As Markus Barth emphasized, the function of a doctrine or an axiom may differ in different contexts, and does not have an inherent fixed or unchanging meaning (1968: 78f.).
40. Stendahl 1976: 40. On this see Käsemann's reference to the Reformation's failure 'to integrate (Romans) chs. 9–11 into their message of justification' (1980: 253).

An important emphasis of Stendahl is that Paul is not dealing with Jews or the Jew in the abstract – when Paul speaks of the Jews, he speaks about real Jews and not about the fantasy Jews who stand as the symbol or as the prime example of a timeless legalism.[41] Stendahl is particularly concerned with the uniqueness of Paul's theology, of each of Paul's letters, and of the uniqueness of the theologies we find in the New Testament. The richness of revelation cannot be maintained when the apologetic needs for harmonization are allowed to swallow up the uniqueness of the distinct messages. He seeks to recapture Paul in his full uniqueness. For him there is no one universal 'Biblical' or even 'New Testament' language; 'the clarity, integrity, and power of the message is available to us only in the uniqueness of each of these distinct theologies'. He concludes that even Paul himself 'would be willing to be only one of many, unique, incapable of being universal without the help of others'.[42] One senses that in this aspect of Stendahl there is a strong implicit response to Baur's quest for universalization.

Like Munck, Stendahl was more interested in Paul's missionary activity rather than merely in religious ideas or dogmatic theology; Paul regarded himself as having a significant role in God's plan for the fulfilment of history in winning communities of gentiles.

The significance of Stendahl's advocated approach to Paul is that he became a link and a vehicle whereby the advances of Munck were developed and the impetus carried forward.[43] They both realized that there was something inadequate in the dominant Lutheran approach to Paul, and as Scandinavians they were very well placed to encounter this at first hand, though more ready to admit the need for change than some of their German counterparts in the 'Tübingen Schule'.

2.4 Ernst Käsemann and the Righteousness of God in Paul

The target of some of Stendahl's criticisms of Pauline interpretation was of course certain aspects of German 'Lutheran' interpretation of Paul. Ernst Käsemann in his various writings had stressed the centrality of justification in Pauline theology.[44] In a series of essays dating from 1954, Käsemann sought to modify the existentialist approach of Rudolf Bultmann, his esteemed teacher. He was of the opinion that this approach had allowed, even caused, justification to deteriorate into a theory concerning the rescue of the individual.[45] In this anti-individualist

---

41. Stendahl 1976: 36–7
42. Stendahl 1976: 72–5.
43. In this evaluation we do not overlook the fact that many of Stendahl's fascinating theses were mere outlines, the central contents of which were not developed (on this see Donaldson. 1997: 17–18). I think this is one reason why the relevance of Stendahl's views has not always been recognized.
44. Most of Käsemann's more important writings have been translated into English: see the collection of essays 1969a, and 1971a. His *Commentary on Romans* was completed in 1973 (Tübingen: Mohr Siebeck, ET 1980).
45. For Käsemann, apocalyptic both in Jesus and Paul became the instrument by which to challenge the existentialist approach. See esp. the essays, 'The Righteousness of God in Paul', and 'On the Subject of Primitive Christian Apocalyptic' in 1969a: 168–82 and 108–37 respectively.

stance he was tending in the same direction as Stendahl. According to Käsemann, Bultmann had reduced Paul's theology exclusively to anthropology, whereas anthropology is only a part of it, being subordinate to the doctrine of God, Christology and cosmology. Salvation cannot possibly be limited to a new self-understanding, nor refer primarily to the individual. On the contrary, the lordship of Christ is expressed not merely in terms of personality or self-consciousness, but of one's body and in terms of the 'extra nos', the entire creation is involved as Romans 8–11 indicate. In opposition to what he perceived as the explicit weaknesses of the existentialist approach, Käsemann stressed Paul's apocalyptic theology under the central theme of the righteousness of God. God's righteousness, δικαιοσύνη θεοῦ, is the rightful power with which he causes his cause to triumph in a world which has fallen away from him and which yet, is his inviolable possession. It is essentially, 'God's sovereignty over the world revealing itself eschatologically in Jesus'.[46]

Käsemann's emphasis upon divine righteousness was set in the traditional Lutheran framework of antithesis between gospel and law which tended to distance the church from Israel. In emphasizing the faithfulness of God, it might have been possible to include faithfulness to Israel within that rubric. However, Käsemann stressed instead God's faithfulness as Creator to count whom he wills as his seed, thereby loosing the divine election from the physical seed of Abraham. Käsemann can speak of 'God's hidden faithfulness' in Israel's history, but only in dialectical terms as e.g. when commenting on Rom. 9.6–13 in relation to Rom. 11.11–24. 'Previously the emphasis was on the selection which breaks the earthly continuity again and again. Now, conversely, the faithfulness which makes earthly continuity possible is underscored.'[47] The salvation-creating power of God, one of the most valuable emphases in Käsemann's understanding of Paul, was thus rendered less comprehensive than it might have been had he fully recognized the extent to which in Romans 9–11 the discussion centres around divine faithfulness to Israel rather than to the creation as a whole.[48] Despite this weakness, Käsemann's critique of the existentialist approach was timely and convincing, putting more emphasis on the 'extra nos' and the corporate aspects of salvation. As he admitted, 'I find myself totally unable to assent to the view that Paul's theology and his philosophy of history are orientated towards the individual.'[49]

An outcome of this understanding was that Israel and the Law were completely relegated to the old aeon. Käsemann did not manage to escape from viewing Paul's theology from being directed to man in general, nor did he fully

---

46. Käsemann 1969c: 180. There is according to Käsemann, an indissoluble connection between power and gift in Paul – the gift cannot be separated from the giver, and thus the gifts of God can only be found and enjoyed in association with the Lordship of Christ.

47. Käsemann 1980: 308.

48. On this see Karl Kertelge's criticism of Käsemann and some of his students' approach (including Peter Stuhlmacher and Christian Müller), Kertelge (1967). For Kertelge, God's creative action is an emphasis always present in Paul, but never at the centre (1967: 308).

49. Käsemann 1969c: 176. Cf. also 1971c: 60–78.

2. Pauline Interpretation and Christian Identity

recognize how abhorrent it was to some New Testament scholars for the Jews to be made an abstraction, 'the Jew in every man'.[50]

The explanation for this may be found in Käsemann's view that, 'Through thick and thin, Paul holds to the view that God activates his righteousness not in a renewed but in a totally new Covenant'. Paul can thus 'legitimately transfer the motif of the people of God on to the Christians as the eschatological Israel'.[51] It is no surprise that eventually there arose a public debate between him and Stendahl on the subject of the nature of Paul's theology.[52] In fairness to Käsemann, it must be recognized that he was seeking to maintain and to sustain the view of righteousness by faith as central to a proper understanding of Paul, which he saw as vital to the life of faith in the German churches and which alone would serve to counteract those tendencies in European culture that had allowed or even encouraged the Nazi era in Germany, which Käsemann with Karl Barth and a few other theologians opposed with complete dedication.

It is interesting at this point to note not just the differences but also some of the similarities between Käsemann's and Stendahl's view of Paul. Both recognized that Paul was not primarily focusing on individual salvation.[53] Both stressed the significance of divine righteousness. Both exhibited an appreciation of the significance of Paul's Jewish background and related eschatology.[54] Where they differed was on the relation between, and the significance of, the doctrine of justification and salvation history. Käsemann insisted that God's righteousness is the centre of salvation history, the latter being the worldwide dimension of the former.[55] Stendahl by contrast saw justification only in relation to the two peoples, Jews and gentiles. But Paul's primary focus on Jews and Gentiles was lost in the history of interpretation. Justification, instead of serving the very specific and limited function of showing how the gentile mission fits into God's total plan[56] 'no longer "justified" the status of gentile Christians as honorary Jews, but became the timeless answer to the plights and pains of the introspective conscience of the West'.[57] Stendahl opposed the homogenizing of Paul's letters and theology, and set his face against an overly dogmatic and theological

---

50. Käsemann 1969b: 183–87 (184). Note also Käsemann's somewhat Barthian comment, 'religion always provides man with his most thorough-going possibility of confusing an illusion with God. Paul sees this possibility realized in the devout Jew'.

51. 1969c: 180.

52. See Käsemann's response to Stendahl's 1963 essay, 'The Apostle Paul and the Introspective Conscience of the West', in the essay 'Justification and Salvation History in the Epistle to the Romans' (1971c: 60–78).

53. Cf. Käsemann 1971c: 74. Cf.also Sanders.1977: 435–38.

54. Cf. Käsemann's comment, 'the religio-historical alternative has steadily lost its original fascination as the Jewish heritage of the apostle has increasingly shown itself to be the native ground, and eschatology the horizon of Paul's theology' (1980: 254).

55. Käsemann 1980: 255–56.

56. This insight goes back to W. Wrede as well as A. Schweitzer, Cf. Käsemann 1980: 253.

57. 1976: 4–5. Stendahl's critique also contains the assertion that Paul 'sees that God has mysterious and special plans for the salvation of Israel'. In contrast to this, although Käsemann claims that Paul concedes to Israel the rights of the first-born, 'the problem of Israel' seems to have only 'exemplary significance for Paul' (1969b: 186–7).

image of the apostle. He rejected the view that the human predicament should be the generalized context for the church's interpretation of Paul's thought.

But Käsemann's concern was to oppose an over-realized eschatology – apocalyptic was the means to accomplish this. The righteousness of God has itself, a continuity in operation, but not a continuity perceptible in human history.

> The idea of the people of God could now only be used figuratively and clearly no longer as an argument for a continuity which could be historically demonstrated but solely for a continuity of grace which could only be believed. For those who received the promise no longer coincided exactly with those who received the fulfilment.[58]

An overview of the tensions in the understanding of Paul between these two scholars suggests that their differing views represent two distinct attitudes towards Paulinism. Käsemann was content to modify Bultmann's existentialist approach but Stendahl wanted a fresh start. He was in fact seeking a new perspective, whereas Käsemann because of his concern for justification by faith was seeking to defend what for many was the Pauline consensus.

2.5 Sanders' and Dunn's New Perspective

Research into Paul's Jewish heritage, so strongly pursued by W.D. Davies, was powerfully developed and the quest reinvigorated by his former student, E.P. Sanders.

We note already in Stendahl a critique of Lutheran Paulinism. Sanders, in his conviction that for the past century the majority of New Testament scholars have interpreted Paul in antithesis to Judaism, continued this critique. He developed it in a devastating criticism of Bultmann and Käsemann (among others), and in seeking to cause a revision of the image of Palestinian Judaism.[59] Even if Sanders' image of First Century Judaism is not entirely accurate at every point, his other complaints still stand. Luther, having identified Paul's subjective struggles with his own, similarly perceived his own unreformed opponents as disputing the very same issues as those who opposed Paul. Thus the Judaism Paul opposed was reconstructed, 'read through the grid of the early sixteenth century Catholic system of merit'.[60] and became caricatured as a legalistic religion with good works as the way to achieve salvation. My point here is that even if Sanders' depiction of Palestinian Judaism is flawed – and that has yet to be convincingly demonstrated to me – nevertheless his description of Luther's reading his own issues into First Century Judaism still stands. As Sanders himself maintains, 'To a remarkable and indeed alarming degree, throughout this century the standard depiction of the Judaism which Paul rejected has been the reflex of the Lutheran hermeneutic.'[61]

58. Käsemann 1969d: 108–37 (129).
59. Sanders.1983: 154–7, 1977: 1–29.Cf. his comment on H. St. John Thackeray, 'The two elements which constitute Thackeray's view – *on the whole* Paul represents the *antithesis* of Judaism, while being *dependent* on it with regard to *individual motifs* – also constitute the view of many other scholars' (1977: 3).
60. Dunn 1990c: 185.
61. Dunn 1990c: 185.

2. Pauline Interpretation and Christian Identity

What is wrong with this depiction is that scripture is being viewed via Luther and not Luther via scripture. The pattern of interpreting Paul in antithesis to Judaism is an unfortunate legacy of this hermeneutic which must still be challenged, whatever our view of First Century Judaism.

Sanders' achievement was that he identified the subjectivity of the Reformation critique of First Century Judaism, demonstrating thereby that antiquity is a construct of our contemporary perspective and not simply a given. He succeeded on two other fronts simultaneously. He avoided the innate tendency in Pauline studies towards anti-Judaism, and secondly he maintained a Christological focus. For Paul, Sanders insisted, participation in Christ was central, not justification by faith. Moreover, Paul's argument proceeded not from need to solution as might have been expected. Paul did not find certain things lacking in Judaism, he was later to discover present in Christianity. Paul's critique of Judaism was simply a post-conversion perspective the essence of which was that it was not Christianity – Paul's argument was retrospective, proceeding from solution back to problem requiring solution. Paul does know of two righteousnesses, but these are not the righteousness through Christ and one's own meritorious righteousness (Sanders takes this to refer to Jews seeking a righteousness for Jews only and not open to gentiles also). The difference between them is not the distinction between merit and grace, but between two dispensations – it is the new dispensation, a concrete fact of *Heilsgeschichte* which makes the other righteousness wrong, not the abstract superiority of grace to merit.[62] Paul was engaged in a thoroughly Jewish task – bringing the gentiles into the eschatological people of God – the failure of some Jews to accept this was, as Räisänen asserted, a christological error rather than an anthropological one.[63]

It is apparent, following Sanders' reading, that a later inner Christian debate about grace and works was retrojected into earliest Christianity causing our understanding of Christian origins in relation to Judaism to become somewhat skewed. In some sense this is really more a debate about grace within Christianity. It is illuminating to note that it was Augustine's anti-Pelagian writings that Luther found most useful. For Luther, Augustine is his preferred authority, his main ally in his fight against the Pelagian tendencies of scholasticism.[64] But arising from this, the Jews were seen by Luther as representing a type of Pelagianism and as such were enemies of the gospel as much as the unreformed church. We can see here how, in a new historical development and context, a reformer's attitude to Judaism eventually came to be coloured by an inner Christian debate on grace and works originating with Pelagius and Augustine.

Despite being impressed by Sanders' mould-breaking reconstruction of the first century context of Paul and Judaism, James Dunn felt that Sanders had missed an opportunity which his new insights could have provided.

> The most surprising feature of Sanders' writing, however, is that he himself has failed to take the opportunity his own mould-breaking work offered. Instead of trying to

---

62. Sanders 1983: 140.
63. Sanders 1983: 141 n. 6. Cf. Räisänen 'Legalism and Salvation by the Law' (1980: 71).
64. See Campbell 2000: 103–14; also W. Pauck 1961: 216–18. Cf. also Campbell 2006.

explore how far Paul's theology could be explicated in relation to Judaism's 'covenantal nomism', he remained more impressed by the *difference* between Paul's pattern of religious thought and that of First Century Judaism. He quickly, too quickly in my view, concluded that Paul's religion could be understood only as a basically different system from that of his fellow Jews.[65]

For Dunn this explanation is unconvincing – this presentation of Paul is only a little better than the one rejected. In Dunn's opinion, Sanders still portrays Paul in antithesis with his Jewish heritage. There remains something very odd in Paul's attitude to his ancestral faith. 'The Lutheran Paul has been replaced by an idiosyncratic Paul who in arbitrary and irrational manner turns his face against the glory and greatness of Judaism's covenant theology and abandons Judaism simply because it is not Christianity.'[66] Sanders later elaborated these views of what Paul found defective in Judaism in his book *Paul, the Law and the Jewish People* published six years later in 1983. Here he argues that Paul attacks covenantal nomism, the view that accepting and living by the law is a sign and condition of favoured status. What is wrong with the law, and thus with Judaism, is that it does not provide for God's ultimate purpose, that of saving the entire world through faith in Christ. But Dunn is still not convinced and accuses Sanders of posing an antithesis between faith in Christ and Paul's Jewish heritage thus creating an abrupt discontinuity between the new movement and the religion of Israel.[67]

Dunn rightly noted that Sanders had failed to give any good reason, apart from conversion, why Paul should have departed from his ancestral traditions. His defection was arbitrary. In contrast to Sanders, Dunn emphasizes the covenant language which stems from Israel's consciousness of election. Against Sanders, Dunn maintains that to be justified in Paul cannot be treated simply as an entry or initiation formula. God's justification is his acknowledgement that one is in the covenant whether this is an initial, repeated or final acknowledgement (or vindication) by God.[68] What is most significant here is Dunn's assertion that justification by faith is not a distinctively Christian teaching,[69] a factor of some significance since in the past and even today, it did and still does function as an anti-Jewish doctrine. For Dunn the phrase 'works of law' cannot refer to 'covenant works', that is, works related to or done in obedience to the law of the covenant. Instead Paul is referring to particular observances of the law like circumcision, food laws and special days and feasts, which were regarded both by Jews and their neighbours as 'badges of covenant membership', distinctively Jewish identity markers.[70]

65. Dunn 1990c: 186.
66. Dunn 1990c: 187. Dunn notes that Sanders still speaks of Paul breaking with the law, he still has Paul making an arbitrary jump from one system to another.
67. Dunn 1990c: 188.
68. Dunn 1990c: 189–91.
69. 'Paul's appeal here is not to *Christians* who happen also to be *Jews*, but to Jews whose "Christian" faith is but an extension of their Jewish faith in a graciously electing and sustaining God.' Dunn 1990c: 191.
70. Dunn.1990c: 191–3.

2. Pauline Interpretation and Christian Identity

Paul attacks this Jewish self-understanding despite the fact that Jewish Christians may have felt their belief in Christ as Messiah did not require them to abandon their Jewishness. For Paul the only restriction to covenantal nomism is faith in Christ. But Paul pushed what began as a qualification on covenantal nomism into an outright antithesis. For him faith in Jesus Messiah is not simply a *narrower* definition of the elect of God, but an *alternative* definition. 'From being one identity marker for the Jewish Christian alongside the other identity markers (circumcision, food laws, sabbath) faith in Jesus as Messiah becomes the primary identity marker which renders the other superfluous.'[71] In the time of fulfilment 'the covenant should no longer be conceived in nationalistic or racial terms. No longer is it an exclusively Jewish qua Jewish privilege. The covenant is not thereby abandoned. Rather it is broadened out as God originally intended'[72] and now the more fundamental identity marker (Abraham's faith) reasserts its primacy over narrowly nationalistic identity markers.[73]

Dunn's critique of Judaism is less radical than that of Sanders in that he does not regard Paul as opposing the twin pillars of Judaism, covenant and election. His position is an advance on Sanders in some respects but in others it is not.[74] Although Dunn's view is that justification is not a distinctively Christian doctrine but in common with Judaism, he sees Paul as eventually pushing faith in Jesus Messiah from being a narrower definition of the elect of God to an alternative definition. *He has in fact reintroduced an antithesis with Judaism*,[75] thereby making gentile Christianity the norm for the whole of Christianity. This is quite serious since both Sanders and Dunn recognize that keeping the law as a Jew in Christ is in and by itself not necessarily a contradiction.

When Dunn claims that Paul pushed faith in Christ to become an alternative definition of the elect of God, what in effect he does is to deny even the legitimacy of any specific Jewish-Christian identity. It follows that there can be no real diversity in Christ.

2.6 *Opposition to the 'New Perspective'*

The 'New Perspective' seemed to be on the way towards ascendancy in Pauline scholarship. Recently, however, criticisms of this approach have increased and I will briefly note only a few of them, since the debate is not central to our study.

Sanders' own depiction of Palestinian Judaism as covenantal nomism is disputed in view of the diversities of first-century Judaism.[76] I am of the opinion that

---

71. Dunn.1990c: 196.
72. Dunn 1990c: 197.
73. Cf. Dunn 1990c: 196.
74. Dunn's 'emphasis on Jewish ethnic pride reverts to the outmoded, unhistorical dichotomy between Jewish particularism and Christian universalism'. Gager 2000: 49.
75. We will develop this criticism in Chapter 3.4.
76. Cf. M.D. Hooker 1982b: 102–14. Hooker expresses surprise that the 'pattern of religion' which emerges from Sanders' study of Judaism bears a striking similarity to what is commonly believed to be the religion of Paul. Cf. also N.A. Dahl's criticisms of Sanders in his review of *Paul and Palestinian Judaism* 1978: 153–8.

Sanders' description can still be justified.[77] Recognition of commonality across these diversities demonstrates the general perception that there are demands on those inside the covenant that differ from those on others outside. Also, diversity in Jewish groups was not the problem that it still appears to be within Christianity where there tends to be too much emphasis upon doctrinal differences. Judaism had learned to live with divergent opinions.

Again some scholars hold that certain Qumran texts seem similar to Paul's statements about 'works of law' as perceived in the old perspective. But Paul's exegesis of crucial texts (such as Hab. 2.4b) appears to be radically different from Qumran. Even in the Qumran text that seems closest to Paul (4QMMT) the concern is not with human effort but accepting a particular form of halakhah.[78] Despite similarities, only one half of Paul's binary pair is present. Righteousness linked with works and doing is present, but not the binary opposite to God's grace and human faith.[79] Evidence of the type of religiosity Paul opposes is not present. Isolated texts in themselves are no solid basis for argument since they are used in differing rhetorical situations.[80]

Yet other scholars are still not convinced that first-century Judaism was not a religion of justification by works as traditionally held.[81] Some hold that the depiction of ancient Judaism offered by Sanders is itself skewed.[82] Paul did, in their view, criticize the use of the law as a means of salvation whether by Jews or gentiles. There is a risk however, that inner-Christian debates and controversies might seem necessarily also to be present in first-century Jewish groups. As Sanders notes, in a discussion of the words translated as 'own'(in respect of righteousness) in Phil. 3.9 and Rom. 10.3, 'I do not for a moment doubt that, had the problem (of self-righteousness or accepting righteousness as a gift)...been posed to Paul, he would have come out strongly against merit-seeking self-righteousness and in favour of accepting righteousness as a gift'.[83] Sanders' important point is that in actual fact this issue was not, or not yet, a problem for Paul in the way that it was later to emerge in Christianity. This later history is very influential in how Jewish Christ-followers have been, and to some extent still are, perceived in New Testament scholarship; the fact that Christ-followers

---

77. Cf. Avemarie 1999: 108–26. Avemarie also recognizes both grace and works and tension between them as present in this literature, but holds that within this literature it is possible to speak as Sanders does, of a 'covenantal nomism' (Bundesnomismus) (1996: 584 n. 40).

78. Cf. Lim 2000: 135–42. Fitzmyer 2000: 249–52.

79. As Brooke has recently emphasized '...those using the scrolls to illuminate the writings of the New Testament should be as much concerned with the differences as with the similarities'. (2005: xviii). On this cf. also Brooke 2005: 158–76.

80. Contra, C.H. Talbert's point that in 4QMMT 111–18 one text clearly uses the expression 'works of the law' and such expression pays off at the end of time, and Talbert's assertion that 'at best this is legalistic covenantal nomism' (2001: 1–22 also 9 n. 30).

81. E.g. S.J. Gathercole 2004.For a response to some of the issues raised by Gathercole and a survey of recent literature see the useful overview by D. Garlington 2005: 17–38. Cf. also M. Seifrid 2000: 4–18.

82. E.g. T. Eskola 1997: 390–412, R.H. Gundry 1985: 1–38, and C.H. Talbert 1995: 17–28.

83. Sanders 1983: 140–1.

may have continued to keep the law appears to jeopardize salvation by faith. Again, possibly the fear of adopting a two-ways-of-salvation, two-covenant theory, has probably caused some modern interpreters to shy away from allowing any real and lasting validity to a Jewish-Christian way of life. The opposition to Sanders and the 'New Perspective' discussed above is not without parallels to the scholarly response to the question of how Paul reacted to Jewish Christ-followers who continued to keep Torah. That such Christ-followers existed is not disputed but Paul's reaction to them is disputed. The issue appears to be – if Paul recognized the legitimacy and validity of a Jewish expression of faith in Christ, and thus of real diversity in Christ, then the perceived opposition between Torah and Gospel is challenged, and for that reason this view must be opposed. Other factors may also be involved. Christians hold that the atonement of Christ should have universal significance and that the Scriptures as Scriptures must have universal application. The acknowledgement of any kind of Jewish-Christian identity, and thus of real diversity in Christ somehow seems to threaten this universality. Alternatively if Paul did recognize the validity of a Jewish way of life in Christ, then this acknowledges diversity in early Christianity and possibly points the way to a proper gentile Christian theology of Jewish roots in Christianity and a corresponding understanding of diversity within Christian identity.

2.7 Conclusion

Our overview of interpretation in this chapter demonstrates that from the time of F.C. Baur, a negative image of Judaism and a corresponding antithesis with emergent Christianity has mainly constituted the framework of modern critical Pauline interpretation. A great achievement of recent Pauline scholarship is the recognition and demonstration of how Jewish issues and Judaism have, throughout the centuries, been used as a foil in inner-Christian debates. Often there has been little real interest in Judaism as such but only in its perceived links with Christianity. It would appear that nascent Christianity needed to negate Judaism in order to confirm its own identity. Insecurity in this identity meant that Jewish stereotyping and negative self-definition became part and parcel of Christian tradition. Whether it was due to immaturity or insecurity or both, Christian history demonstrates an inability until recently to formulate its own identity positively without negation of Judaism. It seems that the only relation it can envisage is a negative one; nor will it relinquish this because it still requires a negation of Judaism for self-assurance. It cannot let go in a positive sense because it is still in the process of finding a positive self-definition that can include its Jewish roots whilst recognizing both some commonality and continuity with Judaism.

What has also become evident is that, as a result of inner-Christian theological controversies, the concrete issues Paul faced were transformed. For Paul the issue was the relation of differing peoples to the one God of Israel but over time this was quickly conceptualized to become the struggle between grace and works in the life of the individual. This was further intensified by the philosophical tendencies of the Enlightenment. The effect of moving away from Paul's concern with differing groups of people and their relationship, to an inner-Christian debate about abstract concepts such as grace and works was to decontextualize Paul's statements. Since the Reformation this tendency has, in fact, increased[84] so that the historical antecedents of these abstract concepts become foils and fodder for inner-Christian disputes, sometimes far removed from the world of Paul. This in my opinion is one of the issues behind debates about Sanders and the 'New Perspective'. There are in fact two theologies of Paul in conflict. One derives from post-Augustinian Christian theological terms and disputes which are considered normative even for Paul. The other seeks to avoid the overt theological conceptualization, to concentrate on the concrete realities of Israel and the nations in relation to God, and to limit discussion to the meaning and terminology of the contextualized letters of Paul.[85]

Over the centuries of Christian theologizing and debate with and about Judaism the core issue of the relationship of Judaism to Christian identity was never properly engaged with. The tendency was to ghettoize Jews geographically and to demonize them theologically but never to really associate with them positively in defining one's own religion. In the early centuries it was easier to build fences than use the still-existing bridges with Judaism. The fluidity of early Jewish-Christian relations over several centuries partially explains an insecurity of Christians versus Jews. Chrysostom is a shining example. We need to understand his fears in order to understand (though not to defend) his theology in respect of Jews. However the real issue of the place of Judaism in Christian identity has even in contemporary scholarship not yet been properly addressed. The strong wave of opposition to the New Perspective and the unhealthy delight of some scholars in the hope that Sanders can now be proved mistaken is an indication that many are still struggling with Jewish roots which they seem not yet able to recognize positively rather than simply to negate.

Current Christian insecurity is doubtless related to contemporary interfaith issues resulting from impingement of other world-faiths. But Christianity is unlikely to resolve these issues adequately until it resolves its relation to Judaism. In a strange way the interaction with other faiths has helped contemporary Christians to understand better the insecurity of earliest Christianity and its defensiveness against Judaism as well as its own failure to develop positively and maturely its own identity.

---

84. On this see Sanders' excellent summary based on G.F. Moore's important article, 'Christian Writers on Judaism' (1921: 197–254). W.D. Davies' criticism that for Sanders 'the Lordship of Christ in Paul supercedes that of Messiahship' (Davies 1998: xlvii) suggests that Sanders is close to Bousset, who assumed that the assumption of 'Lord' to Jesus was proof of a Hellenizing abandonment of the Jewish frame of reference in favour of a universal religion. Cf. Donaldson 1997: 198.

85. On this see Chapter 10.2 where this theme will be further developed.

Chapter 3

PAUL'S THEOLOGIZING CONCERNING THE 'OTHER'

This chapter deals with socio/historical and theological questions concerning Paul's relations with other apostles and leaders. In it we will seek to develop the significance that a distinction between these approaches involves for the resultant image of Paul and the understanding of the early Christ-movement. It also attempts to consider whether what happened historically after the death of Paul is the only legitimate development and theologically the best development.

3.1 *Paul, the Recipient and Sole Interpreter of a Divine Revelation?*

Paul has frequently been presented as a great colossus who stood independent and alone in the early church, opposing Peter and the 'Urgemeinde' in Jerusalem.[1] This image rests mainly on Paul's apologetic self-depiction in Galatians chs 1–2. Here Paul presents himself as heir to the prophetic tradition in which the prophet is directly commissioned by God to declare the content of the revelation. His focused argument is fairly selective as to what he includes and how he reports it. Paul's primary intention in Galatians is to protect his apostolic status by arguing that he is not dependent on Jerusalem leaders for his call and commissioning to the gentiles, even though he also wants to claim recognition by them. The thesis maintained is that his revelation is divinely not humanly given, needing no interpretation or explanation from any human mediator.[2] In short it was not mediated via Peter, James or others in Jerusalem. It could and frequently has been argued that this makes Paul both the recipient of divine revelation and the sole interpreter of its significance. As James Dunn maintains,

> It was not necessary for him to consult with any man about the meaning of his revelation and commissioning; the meaning came in the revelation itself, it came to him independently without human agency...he did not need to go up to Jerusalem to those who were apostles before him.[3]

But in my opinion this is to claim more than Paul really intended. Theologically understood, it is legitimate, even essential, to insist that the revelation came direct from God. Evidence from a social-scientific approach would, however,

---

1. See e.g. Goulder 1994. Cf. also Goulder's more recent book 2001 and the review of Goulder by D.A. Campbell (2002).
2. Cf. Polaski, 1999: 95.
3. Dunn 1982: 462–3.

suggest that the earliest Christ-followers did mediate in differing ways the new activity of God in the advent of Christ. At a minimum, we need only to consider the influence on Paul of those Christ-followers whom he persecuted. The very fact that Paul persecuted the early Christ-followers means that he was already conversant with their confession.[4] The confession of one who was crucified as Messiah must have been intolerable to him. In addition to this, according to the account in Acts, Paul was assisted in his interpretation of the revelation by the Christ-followers in Damascus.

There is also evidence that conversion happens through social interaction even if it seems to result from a sudden, new perspective on life. Rodney Stark has shown that a new perspective grows as a result of interaction with members of the new group that the convert joined and not the reverse.[5] If we apply this insight to Paul, whether we term his experience a call or conversion,[6] it would lead us to conclude that Paul must have had some social interaction with Christ-followers prior to his Damascus road experience. In short, 'we can assume that the great transformation Paul experienced did not take place in a social vacuum'.[7]

This is not meant to diminish the authority of the revelation, but only to describe the mode of its reception and explication. Nor does this view overlook the fact that Paul, as a devout Jew nurtured in the traditions of his ancestors, did not already possess a framework of interpretation for understanding new religious experiences.[8] But even this advantage on its own without human mediation of some kind would not have enabled Paul to arrive at a full understanding of what God was calling him to undertake. To argue otherwise is to make revelation almost a magical process and to claim for Paul a magical power. Naked experience is not self-authenticating – it requires a framework of understanding to make its content intelligible. Even to denote an experience as religious requires some frame of reference beyond the experience itself.[9]

Markus Bockmuehl considers a variety of options concerning the source of Paul's interpretation, from oracular revelation, speculative imagination to a straightforward exegesis seen in the light of the Gospel events. Significantly he concludes that

---

4. Cf. Peerbolte (2003: 160); Peerbolte argues that Paul did not kill Christ-followers but rather tried to silence their views (142–3).

5. Stark (1996: 13–21). Stark maintains that 'conversion to new, deviant religious groups occurs when, other things being equal, people have or develop stronger attachments to members of the group than they have to non-members' (18).

6. Segal (1990: 285–6) refers to Paul's changed life as a conversion on the logic that this is an *etic* term, an outside term used to describe an event that from the inside perspective would be labelled a call.

7. Cf. Peerbolte 2003: 161–2.

8. See my chapter on 'The Contribution of Traditions' in Hay 1993: 234–54.

9. Bockmuehl (1990: 9–10) stresses that in the OT revelation is never for the private benefit of the individual, and does not consist purely of a vision, but always includes a message from God for the community.

> Paul gives no palpable indication of basing the authority of doctrine on a private vision… He exercises his stewardship of the divine mysteries by couching new disclosures in fully traditional language and Biblical reasoning. It seems that we are dealing therefore with 'revelation by exegesis:a dynamic of scripture, [exegetical] tradition, and religious experience (which may or may not include a vision).[10]

Even if, contrary to Bockmuehl, we were to limit Paul's interpretation to his own individual interaction with scripture, this would not permit a claim that he was entirely without human agency, or that his revelation was, as it were, self-explanatory. This conclusion is demanded not merely by our knowledge of the biblical modes of revelation, and the history of the expansion of Christianity itself, but also because to conclude otherwise is to present Paul as a vehicle of revelation without parallel and beyond criticism. The fact that Paul, in the very passage in Galatians used by many to establish his own complete independence of all human agency, acknowledges that he visited Jerusalem and spoke to Peter and others, is proof that Paul himself realized the need for mutual recognition. The Galatian passage could also be construed as Paul's argument that he was a participant in a movement where even those who differed from him, even those whom he had never met, still acknowledged the grace of God in him, rather than a claim to be an entirely independent and, hence, a solitary colossus.

Not enough attention has been paid to the resultant image of Paul that such a perception creates. Did his theology of one body in Christ include Peter? If competition for converts between two missions did occur, would this not imply that the Church was built on opposition and conflict rather than on mutual recognition despite differences? It would be amazing if such a divided community were to survive, let alone expand rapidly.[11]

3.2 *Solidarity and Mutuality within the Pauline Communities*

In reading the letters of Paul, we are necessarily reading from an inner-community perspective. His letters were not directly addressing Jews who did not identify Jesus as Paul understood him. Moreover the letters were not addressed to other leaders of the Christ-movement nor the adherents of their missions. These leaders may be directly or indirectly in view within Paul's letters but the letters as such do not address them. Only occasionally do Peter, James or Apollos come on to the scene, but they make their appearance here for the sake of their usefulness in the context of Paul and his communities. Paul nowhere attempts a comprehensive overview of the politics and relationships of the entire Christ-following groups or their leaders, these figure in his writings only sporadically and incidentally as their work or influence impinge on his. This in itself should alert us to the danger of adopting a myopic stance that entirely disregards their existence as if they had no real links with the Pauline mission, except in times of dispute or conflict.

---

10. Bockmuehl 1990: 174–5.
11. Cf. Stark 1996 esp. Ch. 3 'The Mission to the Jews: Why It probably Succeeded' (49–71). We will return to this issue in more detail later in this chapter. Cf. also Wagner 2002: 4 n. 11.

When we investigate Paul's letters, what we find, amidst the conflicts that often characterized life within his communities, is a theology of mutuality in Christ. This mutual acknowledgement of fellow participants in the gospel originates in fact from a charismatic basis. The earliest Christ-following communities acknowledged and affirmed the gifts of God in their members even though sometimes they disagreed and needed to have strong leadership and discipline in the effort to solve the issues between them, and to maintain harmony.[12] The way of life advocated within Paul's communities is well documented in the letters. Individually believers are members of one another (Rom. 12.5). They are to love one another (Rom. 12.10; 13.8), they are to live in harmony with one another (Rom. 15.5), welcome one another as Christ has welcomed them (Rom. 15.7), and greet one another with a holy kiss (Rom. 16.16; 2 Cor. 13.12). Elsewhere we find they are to have the same care for one another (1 Cor. 16.25), through love they are to be servants to one another (Gal. 5.13) and to bear one another's burdens (Gal. 6.2). They are to abound in love to one another (1 Thess. 3.12), they are taught by God to love one another (1 Thess. 4.9), they are to comfort one another (1 Thess. 4.18), and encourage one another (1 Thess. 5.11), always seeking to do good to one another (1 Thess. 5.15). Believers form a close family of brothers and sisters in Christ who are obligated to care for each other as themselves. It was such commitment to solidarity and mutual caring that enabled the Pauline communities not only to survive but to grow despite a hostile environment. Within these communities they belong to Christ and through him to each other. Robert Banks correctly affirms that the focal point of the Pauline communities was a set of relationships christologically and communally perceived.[13]

A dominant image frequently used by Paul in his efforts to create harmony and solidarity within his communities is that of the family. By calling his converts siblings in Christ, Paul aimed at giving them a strong sense of collective identity and belonging such as, in theory at least, existed within the normal human family.[14] Doubtless, Paul's own experience and understanding of family life in Judaism provided him with the raw material for such a theological conception. But this by itself does not entirely explain the dominance of the concept in Paul's address to his communities. The sibling metaphor is Paul's most frequent way of speaking of his fellow Christ-followers, and almost his only way of addressing them directly. As such it represents a major building block in his ecclesiology (by which we must mean his understanding of all those in Christ, and not simply the members of his own communities to whom his words apply in the first instance). It is significant, however, that despite taking over the sibling metaphor and using it as a resource for his own theologizing, Paul does not set up the family of those in Christ in opposition as a new family to make good the defects of the old, or even directly to replace it. Rather Paul views siblingship in Christ in a positive analogy with the old family and its

---

12. As Weber (1968: 242) has argued, 'It is recognition on the part of those subject to authority which is decisive for the validity of charisma'.
13. Banks 1994: 108.
14. Cf. Aasgaard 2004: 306–7.

sibling relations. Thus he simply adopts and adapts the notions generally associated with social siblingship and living in a family to that of 'Christian' relations. Again, though Paul frequently uses family metaphors, he never integrates them into a consistent whole in which there is a fixed pattern such that God is Father, and Christ and Christ-followers are his children and each other's siblings.[15]

Paul not only advocated this communal way of life for his converts but significantly he himself was committed to it, being obligated to them as they were to each other. This is because the gospel Paul preached is not only something which was committed to him, but also something to which he (and his converts alike) is committed.[16] Though he is free from all men he has voluntarily enslaved himself to everyone (1 Cor. 9.19). He appeals to the Galatians to 'become as I am, for I also have become as you are' (4.12). Solidarity and mutual identification are Paul's example and ideal for his communities.

In his relationship to his communities Paul exercised significant power and authority. But he does not seek to dominate or control – 'we do not lord it over your faith: we work with you for your joy' (2 Cor. 1.24). This aspect of Paul's strategy is particularly exemplified in his frequent use of παρακαλεῖν.[17] He prefers to appeal even when he could command 'though I am bold enough in Christ to command you to do what is required, yet for love's sake I appeal to you' (Phlm 1.8). This preference for voluntariness is based on the example of Christ who 'did not please himself' (Rom. 15.1). Paul does not refer simply to Christ's teaching (which in theory at least could be used to justify differing opinions) but rather to his life and example as the normative pattern for life in Christ. Indeed for Paul, Christ's example in laying down his life is the most significant aspect of the gospel. Thus Paul seeks to imitate the weakness and self-giving of Christ, because when he is weak, by God's grace he becomes strong. Correspondingly as he imitates Christ so Paul calls his congregations to imitate him (1 Cor. 11.1). So if Paul imitates and teaches a Christ crucified in weakness,[18] this aspect of his life should be reflected in some measure at least in his theologizing concerning the other who differed from or disagreed with him. Even more significantly, such a theologizing concerning the other must have not only impacted upon but actually determined to a great extent his relations with Peter, James and the other Jerusalem leaders. In fact his theologizing concerning the other who differed from or disagreed with him both within and beyond the Christ-movement cannot but have been influenced by his perception of Christ's weakness as his power.[19] The alternative is that Paul was a blatant hypocrite or completely self-deceived. This is possible but unlikely.

15. Cf. Aasgaard 2004: 309–11.
16. Cf. Schütz, 1975: 159–86.
17. This is used some 23 times in the generally accepted letters of Paul, see Banks, 1994: 176.
18. On this see Schütz 1975: 200–3, also Bartchy (2005: 49–60) and Gorman (2001: 268–303) contra Castelli (1991: 22;119) and Polaski (1999: 123–4) who are critical of Paul's use of authority in making himself an example.
19. Wagner, having noted that Paul has made a distinction within 'Israel' between 'the remnant'

The likelihood of this ethic embracing all believers is greatly enhanced if we note also that Paul recognized and supported diversity within early Christian communities.[20] In Romans 14–15 he offers a charter for the right of sub-groups to differ from one another. Instead of regarding the 'weak' as imperfect or immature believers, who are tolerated temporarily, their right to be and to continue to be different is acknowledged. Βαστάζειν should not be taken in the weaker sense of tolerating or putting up with but rather the obligation is that the strong must support, bear up – even carry, the weaker ones. The force of this is strengthened when we note that in Rom. 11.18 the gentiles are reminded not to boast over the branches since they are not the stem but are borne (βαστάζειν) on the stem of Abraham. We note here that Paul genuinely recognizes and supports diversity in ways of life amongst those in Christ – 'let everyone be fully convinced in his/her own mind' – it is enough that what one practises s/he does 'in honour of the Lord' (14.5–6). Paul's openness to diversity is all the more significant when it is recognized that the churches in Rome were not founded by him, although he claims they lie within the area of his mission to the gentile nations (Rom. 1.5–7). It is important to note that it is in the context of a foundation he did not lay, that Paul both acknowledges the legitimacy of differing ways of life in Christ and moreover envisages these as ongoing and permanent features of the Christ-movement at Rome. As in other places in his correspondence, Paul has no problem in recognizing or referring to the 'churches' of those in Christ for whom he had not been the means of their first hearing the Gospel as e.g. the 'churches' in Judea whom he offers as a model for those facing persecution (1 Thess. 2.14).

3.3 *Paul's Relationship with Other Leaders and their Missions*

My contention in this chapter is that the life Paul advocated, in the ethos of which he participated, was not limited to believers *within* his communities but necessarily extended also to all Christ-followers whether or not they were part of the Pauline communities. Since Paul had elected to make himself a slave of all for the sake of the gospel, this means that his ethic also encompassed Peter and James and the Jerusalem believers in Christ.

Paul has no difficulty in recognizing the authority of other leaders[21] when it was rightly exercised both in terms of not exceeding that authority or its agreed sphere of operation.[22] As Schütz perceptibly observes, although Paul in his

---

and 'the rest' in Rom. 11.7, claims that Paul does not disinherit either group by employing the term to refer exclusively to one party or the other and goes on to add 'Like Paul, the Qumran covenanters did not consider themselves the sum total of eschatological Israel' (2002: 237 n. 65).

20. See Campbell 1995: 259–86. See also Tomson 1996: 268–70, and most recently Esler 2001.

21. We choose to use the broad term 'leaders' in order to be able to speak generally of Paul's relations with a group of people who may have varied greatly. Our concern is not to debate apostolic status or influence as such, but to limit the discussion to Paul's theologically undergirded understanding of his relation to fellow leaders in Christ.

22. As Nanos argues, 'I consider it crucial to isolate the data bearing directly on the identity of the influencers in the Galatian situation from the narrative discourses relating prior situations in

conflict with Peter at Antioch could have responded by denying Peter's apostolic authority, there is no evidence that he does.²³ But we are not thinking here of an inherent authority or some kind of authority which is beyond question or discussion. It is rather an authority that co-exists with mutual recognition,²⁴ and which may also be territorially defined, as 2 Cor. 10.13–16 makes clear.

The dispute with Peter at Antioch often seems to provide an image of Paul in perpetual conflict with Jerusalem as if his apostleship and mission were not recognized by the Jerusalem leaders.²⁵ But if we take Paul's own statements in Galatians 1–2 at face value, it is clear that what he is reporting is not just a recognition of his gentile mission but rather a mutual recognition of two missions, led by Peter and Paul respectively. Paul's words are revealing in his description of what took place. It is clear that both Jerusalem and Paul recognized that God was at work in the differing missions that were already in operation. They were in agreement in their recognition of diversity in the distribution of divine grace (Gal. 2.8). According to Paul, the entire group who met together acknowledged that both he and Peter 'had been entrusted' with leadership in this work. Here again we have a recognition of diversity, this time not just in ways of life but in mission also. The basis of this double recognition is a theology of charisma in which God gives differing gifts to differing people. But although different, all God's gifts serve one common end, the upbuilding and unity of the people of God. Whether he assented to, or as I believe, was personally committed to such a theology of diversity in ways of life and mission,²⁶ Paul in all consistency, could not have continuously opposed Peter and his mission if, as I take to be the case, Paul was insisting on both his and Peter's (as well as the others') mutual subordination to the Gospel.²⁷ Common to both Acts 15 and Galatians 2 is the recognition that Peter and Paul were not competing to win the same groups of people.²⁸ It is two parallel missions that are acknowledged rather than authority

---

Jerusalem and Antioch', allowing him to exegete the Antioch narrative on its own terms and to conclude that 'he [Paul] is *not* concerned to oppose his apostleship, mission, or message to that of the Jerusalem apostles'. Nanos 2003: 402.

23. Schütz asserts, '...He went to Jerusalem from Antioch as a proponent of the unity of the Church and in the name of that ideal. It is doubtful that he left Antioch any less convinced of this necessity'. Schütz 1975: 249–50. I disagree with Schütz's claim that Paul understands his authority and the church's unity to rank as priorities lower than that of the gospel and its truth. Cf. Polaski 1999: 99–100 n. 95.

24. As Schütz notes, decisive against the view that the 'letters of recommendation' in 2 Cor. 3.1ff. are official, binding, authoritative documents is the fact that Paul's opponents not only *bring* letters of recommendation *to* Corinth, but also *solicit* them *from* Corinth. Schütz (1975: 171).

25. For a survey of the prevailing alternatives, see the essays in Nanos (2002e) by Dunn ('The Incident at Antioch [Gal 2:11–18]', 199–234), Esler ('Making and Breaking an Agreement Mediterranean Style: A New Reading of Galatians 2:1–14', 261–81), and Nanos 2002c. For a critique of the ideological implications of the interpretation of the Antioch Incident for Paulinism, see Nanos (2005: 292–300).

26. 'He joins the leaders in Jerusalem acknowledging that they are mutually bound by the gospel of Christ'. Polaski 1999: 90.

27. Cf. Lyons 1985: 90.

28. As Schütz recognizes in relation to Galatians 2, 'Despite the unmistakable fashion in which

being given to Paul to compete in the same mission to the same people.[29] The significance of Peter in the Christ-movement at this time is denoted by his acknowledged leadership of the mission to the 'circumcision' (Gal. 2.11–14). But the Antioch incident appears to reveal differences within the mission to the 'circumcision' i.e. between James and Peter, and not just differentiation between Paul and the rest. John Painter argues that though Acts names no single leader 'where leadership is clearly described James is so described', in Acts also Peter is portrayed in mission to the community outside rather than in leadership of the believing community in Jerusalem.[30] The chiastic parallelism in Gal. 2.2–8 between the missions of Peter and Paul lies in their both having being sent, whereas James remains the leader in the 'church' at Jerusalem.[31] In contrast to previous tendencies to see only a tension between two missions, Painter speaks of two missions with as many as six factions in total, some of which overlapped whilst others were more or less totally opposed.[32]

The issues in the Antioch dispute are clearer if certain aspects are recognized. James is concerned not with the gentiles but with the behaviour of the Jewish Christ-followers. Therefore there can be no question of judaizing on his part. His concerns are legitimately those of the mission to the circumcision. So Paul's dispute is not with James and therefore not with the 'church' in Jerusalem. Nor is the issue about the Apostolic Decree. The reason for James's intervention is therefore more likely to be political rather than theological. Probably the danger of the 'church' in Jerusalem facing severe persecution was a real possibility which would have been heightened by rumours of unrestricted fellowship with gentiles, and James's envoys come to seek solidarity between the Christ communities of Antioch and Jerusalem. It is not stated that James proposed separate Jewish and gentile Christ communities but rather that Peter first accepts and then later rejects table fellowship (though this does not mean that the Jewish Christ-followers had previously simply abandoned Jewish observance in favour of a law-free gentile pattern).[33] Even so, despite his rebuke of Peter, Paul still stresses common ground far more than differences as indicated by his inclusive 'we know' and the distinction drawn between them and 'gentile sinners'. The dispute therefore is not primarily theological but concerns halakhic differences between those in Christ.[34]

---

he introduces his own person into the centre of the discussion, Paul does not wish to reduce the matter of apostolic authority or the norm of the gospel, to personal competition or argument' (1975: 60).

29. It is not my intention in this chapter to deal with the problems of relating Galatians 2 to Acts 15. My interests lie elsewhere but I take this assertion as being a minimal statement of the agreement between them.

30. Painter 2005: 155–8.

31. Schmithals (1960) argues that Paul did not wish to call James an apostle and refers to him only as 'James, the brother of the Lord' (Gal. 1.19), 65. Painter (2005: 167) considers this 'an extraordinary reading'.

32. Cf.Painter 2005: 180–7.

33. This would be unlikely if Antioch were perceived within the scriptural *Eretz Israel*. Cf. Bockmuehl 2000: 75–9.

34. Cf. Bockmuehl 2000: 80.

What cannot be denied is that whatever agreement was achieved at the Jerusalem conference, this included an ethnic dimension, and therefore implicitly to some extent, a territorial or geographic dimension also, as is clearly denoted by the descriptions 'circumcision' and 'uncircumcision'. An interesting possibility is that in Paul's own self-understanding as apostle to the gentile nations, and in conformity with an agreement universally acknowledged, and affirmed also at the summit meeting in Jerusalem, his mission like that of the others involved a limitation to those areas where the name of Christ has not yet been mentioned (Rom.15.19).[35] This was meant to avoid both confusion and competition, but would also signify a respect or at least a recognition of the prior activity of other leaders, a policy of non-interference.[36] Bockmuehl claims that Paul 'never regarded areas of Palestine or Cilicia to be specifically his mission field for taking his gospel to the gentiles'.[37] He also suggests that the restoration of the twelve tribes of Israel which was expected to be part of the eschatological work of Elijah or the Messiah was reflected in the ministry of Jesus and may well have played a role in the presuppositions underlying the Antioch dispute. If Damascus and Antioch were perceived to be within the scriptural *Eretz Israel* or immediately contiguous with it and the Jerusalem agreement is addressed in the first instance to the believers 'in Antioch, Syria, and Cilicia', then it is conceivable why James intervenes here and not in Alexandria, Corinth or Rome. Issues of purity would matter more literally here than in the Diaspora where enforcement was more difficult. Such a view not only renders the Antioch dispute more intelligible, but again shifts the emphasis from theological difference to differences concerning halakhah (with resultant divergences despite the shared convictions of Paul, Peter and James).[38] Implied beyond doubt is that Paul himself fully recognized the mission to the circumcision in parallel to his own apostolic commission, and that he acted not purely out of his own principles but in association with patterns agreed with the other apostles.[39] The presupposition that differing missions were primarily based on differing theologies has hindered the attempt to understand the diversity of the early Christ-movement, and reflects the tendency in later Christianity to regard doctrine rather than practice as determinative of boundaries.

From this understanding of the Antioch incident, it emerges that Paul recognized the right of Jewish Christ-followers to express their faith in Jewish ways of life. The problem with Paulinism within the last century or so is the failure to recognize, as Paul recognized, the integrity and faithfulness to the gospel of Jewish Christ-followers. We now know more clearly than previously that various Jewish forms of Christianity not only survived but continued to flourish in various regions of the empire for several centuries. However, because Jewish

35. Cf. Wilckens (1982: 120) on Rom. 15.19.
36. That this policy was important for Paul is clearly denoted by his cautious, almost apologetic approach to the Christ-followers in Rome.
37. Bockmuehl 2000: 79.
38. See Bockmuehl 2000: 78–9.
39. Contra Taylor's claim that 'Paul took his stand on principle in a matter on which James, Peter and Barnabas exercised pragmatism rather than dogma', Taylor (1992: 135).

forms of 'Christianity' have been regarded as theologically imperfect or immature, their history has been sidelined and their insights ignored. This is because Paulinism has tended to see diversity as having been overcome by the gospel rather than affirmed so that the gentile form of Christianity is universalized to become the norm and all other expressions of Christian faith are regarded as aberrant. Behind this lies an Enlightenment perception of universalism in which oneness is viewed as equivalent to sameness thereby establishing one understanding and way of life as normative and thus rendering all alternative patterns of life invalid.[40] In contrast to the varieties of Judaism of the first century, such a conception elevates a conceptualized theology as a binding norm over against the flexibility and diversity of practice.

3.4 The Antioch Incident: The Catalyst of the Perception of Incompatibility Between Faith in Christ and Life as a Jew?

It is beyond dispute that, at a later date in history, Jewish patterns of life were perceived to be incompatible with the gospel. It is also undisputed that in the very early days of the 'church' compatibility was not an issue.[41] *The crucial question concerns when Jewish identity was first perceived to be in opposition to the gospel.* This is a theological question – not the same as the historical question of the partings of the ways – now seen to be so imprecise a designation as to be more confusing than illuminating. Our assertion is that in Paul Jewish identity *per se* is not seen to be in opposition to Christ.[42] Whenever it was first perceived as such, no *explicit* foundation for this is to be found in the apostle's letters or life.[43] And even if there were those in the earliest days who already asserted incompatibility, this was not done with Paul's agreement or at his instigation. Others, however, at a later date, perhaps even some in the Pauline school, may have contributed to a tendency to alienate Paul's gospel from Judaism.

One factor that may have encouraged anti-Jewish readings of Paul's letters is that when they were first read apart from their original context their particularity was forgotten and a generalized reading replaced it.[44] Thus statements that were not originally anti-Jewish could be read as such in the new context. Moreover, when Paul was writing his letters there is no doubt that he wrote when all the Christ communities were still part of Judaism. Quarrels and disputes were then inner-house conflicts, not inter-religious disputes, in fact intra-Jewish[45] in nature.

---

40. A critique of this aspect of Paulinism has been well developed by Ehrensperger (2004: 11–23).

41. Dunn speaks of a more or less unbroken spectrum in the first century across a wide front from conservative judaizers at one end to radical gentile Christians at the other. Dunn (1991: 5).

42. On this see the work of Tomson (1990).

43. This is not to overlook or minimize the fact that Paul's letters were frequently misunderstood, or that his actions may have results he did not intend, cf. Donaldson (1997: 305–6).

44. On this see Dahl 1963: 260–71.

45. Cf. Nanos' use of this term in Nanos (2000: 146–59).

3. Paul's Theologizing Concerning the 'Other'

There could not then have been any blanket condemnation of Judaism as such but only of aspects of it.

This difference of perspective is crucial in the interpretation of Paul. Since Christianity had not yet emerged as an identifiable new movement distinct from Judaism, there could be no possibility of contrasting the two entities in the manner implicit in much modern interpretation. The Christ-movement was still operating under the umbrella of Judaism. Though Paul's claim that Jesus was the Messiah and that gentiles could therefore be accepted on equal terms with Jews was by no means generally accepted by Jews, the dispute concerning this involved only certain aspects, however crucial, of Jewish self-understanding.[46] Moreover, the debates arising from this claim were not debates about the superiority of 'Christianity' over Judaism. There was no sense of a competition between two religions such as existed several centuries later and until now. There was then in Paul's time as yet no conception of a new religion springing up in opposition to Judaism. The term 'Christian' had not yet been coined and Paul might have rejected it if it had.[47]

Where contemporary interpreters' interests differ from those of Paul and his contemporaries is that in any modern discussion of Judaism, Christian interpreters may not simply be maintaining that Jesus was the Messiah. Nor are they with Paul merely arguing that Christ-faith is true in that it is consistent with e.g. the faith of the Old Testament patriarchs and prophets. They are also frequently engaged in debating the issue whether Christianity is true in the sense that it alone is *the* true Judaism and that it should thus legitimately displace all other 'untrue' or 'imperfect' forms of Judaism. Whether consciously or unconsciously, some Christian interpreters are in fact engaged in a process of comparison of one religion with another competing religion. The result of this is that the ensuing interpretation of those texts in Paul's letters, particularly where he engages with his ancestral faith, is based not simply upon the issues which concerned Paul and his communities but includes in addition an ongoing agenda of whether Christianity is the true Judaism or its true heir and whether Christians are the true Jews.[48] Thus such interpretation involves a concern for Christian self-understanding and identity that must necessarily differentiate the modern post-Enlightenment agenda from that of Paul.[49]

If Paul's distance from us is not clearly and conceptually recognized, then motives for Paul's actions or advice may be introduced which originate from a knowledge of a later separation between Christianity and Judaism to which Paul

---

46. Cf. Nickelsburg 2002: 115–17.
47. Cf. Sanders 1983: 175; also Eisenbaum 2005: 236–7.
48. Evident in the stance of Wright, e.g. 2000:160–83. On this see Harink 2003: 151–207.
49. This is not to deny that the study of religions in their uniqueness and commonality is not a valid intellectual activity, but only if undertaken in an impartial and scholarly manner, rather than implicitly. Cf. the critique of Nanos of J.L. Martyn's commentary on Galatians. Nanos (2005: 255–67). Cf. also Sanders (1973: 455–78 similar to the Introduction to Sanders 1977). Sanders stresses the need to compare religions as a whole with one another, and not merely their individual elements or motifs.

could not possibly have had access. Thus, as we will argue later, it is not legitimate to claim that Paul sought to develop a sense of solidarity in his communities in preparation for an inevitable and impending break with Judaism. One instance where modern discussion of Paul differs from that of the first century is in the use of terms and the mind-set that accompanies this.

In discussions of Paul in relation to Judaism, there is a tendency to use 'true' in the sense of 'true or false' rather than of 'true or inconsistent', thus tending towards oppositional terminology in which one can only be right or wrong.[50] George Nickelsburg aptly describes this as 'a mindset that identifies right and wrong *doctrine* as the touchstone of true religion'.[51] This demonstrates and also facilitates an exclusive claim by Christianity to the heritage of Israel, and a persistent emphasis on antithesis rather than commonality between the two. The problem with the oppositional thinking that pervades much modern Pauline interpretation is that it can become a hindrance towards a more adequate understanding of relations between differing factions within Judaism in the first century, especially where it is insisted that what appears to us to be entirely incompatible, must necessarily have been viewed antithetically by Paul. This is not to deny the need in the modern period where, when faced with two or more existing religions, an exclusive commitment to one or the other is obligatory. But this was not the situation that Paul faced, when the Christ-movement was only a minority movement still adhering to its Jewish roots and where his hope was still that this new movement would eventually permeate the whole of Judaism.

As we have already acknowledged, that conflict was common in Early 'Christianity' need not be disputed; but despite the tendencies of oppositional thinking noted above, such conflicts should not be ideologically and simplistically limited to only two main groups. The entire Judeo-Christian entity was marked by great diversity at this period and conflicts were normal. However, the nature of such conflicts is a vital issue. Conflicts can be conducive to growth and development in social movements. But extreme opposition and division are not only detrimental but, for a small movement in an alien and hostile environment, these could well prove fatal. If the Christ-movement had been as divided within itself, and as alienated from Judaism as has sometimes been proposed, in my view it could and should never have succeeded as it did. As Rodney Stark has argued, the phenomenal numerical growth of the early Christ-movement is explicable only if it continued to attract a steady stream of Diaspora Jews.[52] If, on the other hand, there was inherent opposition between Paul and other apostles and Jewish identity was widely negated within the movement, such progress is inexplicable.

50. For a useful discussion of the tendency toward oppositional thinking in Pauline scholarship, see Ehrensperger (2004: 53–5).
51. Nickelsburg 2003: 30–1. Nickelsburg traces the development of this mindset back to the first disputes with Jews concerning the divine nature of Christ and then via the Marcionite and Gnostic controversies to other inner-Christian debates about orthodoxy 'ironically spawning the kind of debate and conflict that its theologians would later attribute to the rabbis and the kind of self-righteousness that they would claim was a hallmark of the Pharisees' (2003: 30).
52. Stark 1996: 49–71. I think, however, that Stark's estimate of Christ-followers around 50 CE as perhaps as low as 1,400, is somewhat conservative (1996: 67). Cf. also Zetterholm 2002: 216–18.

In contrast to and in spite of such conflict we have noted alternative evidence of agreements in mission strategy and policy. Within the Pauline movement there seems to be good evidence of a dividing up of geographical areas to facilitate mission, rather than because of theological disagreement (2 Cor. 10.13–16).[53] Moreover, where conflicts did occur and are clearly documented, in keeping with the diversity typical of the 'Judeo-Christian entity' at this time, they were not limited to only two parties but were as diverse as the movements within the Judeo-Christian entity of which they were a part.[54]

As noted earlier, the crucial question for interpreters is whether the perceived incompatibility with Judaism later evidenced in Christian communities originated in Paul's letters and lifetime or whether it is a subsequent development. Since the advent of the New Perspective, a transformed view of Paul's relations with Judaism might be expected, including relations with Peter and Jerusalem, and requiring also a serious revision in our image of Paul. Yet even in the New Perspective on Paul incompatibility with Judaism is attributed to the later Paul, that is, according to James D.G. Dunn, the Paul after the Antioch incident.[55] In some ways Dunn's understanding of the outcome of the Antioch incident makes good sense theologically:

> '...so far as the Jewish Christian was concerned, belief in Jesus as Messiah did not require him to abandon his Jewishness...but Paul followed a different logic... Paul pushes what began as a qualification on covenantal nomism into an outright antithesis'. Thus '...from being one identity marker for the Jewish Christian alongside other identity markers, circumcision, food laws, sabbath, faith in Jesus Christ becomes the *primary* identity marker which renders the others superfluous'.[56]

The question that must be put, however, is whether this is a later *theological* insight read back into an earlier dispute so that, according to this scenario, theology produces and precedes identity formation? Since we have examples of Jewish Christ-followers requiring several centuries to reach the insight that accepted identity markers are no longer valid for Christ-followers, is this a case once again of theology preceding experience and history rather than succeeding it which we take to be the normal pattern?

On this understanding once the Antioch incident has taken place, we really do have a history of two opposing and competing missions in head on conflict with each other, ideologically in dispute, each regarding the other as preaching a contrary gospel. On reflection and despite some agreement with Dunn's perspective, I am forced to the conclusion that such a scenario makes it most improbable that the Christ-movement could ever have survived or succeeded as it did. I conclude therefore on this point that it is not likely, contrary to Dunn's scenario, that at

---

53. Cf. Jewett's hypothesis that Epaphras was the person who missionized the Lycus valley and was also probably the author of the letter to the Laodiceans (Col. 4.16) (1981: 5–8).
54. Boyarin stresses the inter-relatedness and interaction of the diverse Jewish and 'Christian' groups in the first few centuries (1999: 6–19; 125–6).
55. Dunn's Rylands' lecture, 'The New Perspective on Paul' (BJRL 65, 1983: 95–122) is reprinted in Dunn (1990c: 183–206; 196–8). See also Dunn (1991).
56. Dunn 1990c: 196.

Antioch Paul recognized and acted upon the incompatibility of faith in Christ and the Jewish way of life.⁵⁷ I am not convinced that the Antioch incident '...shaped the future of Paul's missionary work' or that 'it sparked off a crucial insight which became one of the central emphases in Paul's subsequent teaching, and consequently (it) determined the whole character and future of the young movement which we now call Christianity'.⁵⁸ If the dispute were interpreted as a difference that is primarily halakhic rather than theological, an entirely different and contrasting understanding would result. This is not to overlook the fact that Dunn himself is aware in his book, *The Partings of the Ways*, that these partings were later, diverse and that association between Jewish and mainline Christians continued in some areas for several centuries.⁵⁹ But my concern is to draw out the *implications* of his reading of the Antioch incident.

3.5 *A Non-Sectarian Reading of Paul*

The problem is that if Dunn's proposals are accepted, this in fact negates the agreement reported by Paul himself in Galatians 1–2. It would seem that Paul only needed the other apostles' recognition of his mission, and, once it was so recognized, he felt free to break away from them and to establish an independent mission, now to be regarded as the only fully valid and proper expression of faith in Christ. *This makes Paul, to my mind the archetypical sectarian*, which is in fact not a view that can be adequately sustained.⁶⁰ It signals the end of Jewish identity in any comprehensive understanding of the church, and makes Jewish 'Christianity' from the mid-fifties of the first century an anachronism to be withstood and relegated to the annals of past history. Such a theological rewriting of history is unacceptable in view of the now well documented fact of the continuance and often resilience of Jewish expressions of faith in Christ for several more centuries.

I have argued elsewhere that it is misleading to regard Paul as having advocated separation from the synagogue as a sectarian might do.⁶¹ Clearly, the glaring

---

57. Cf. the useful discussion of Gathercole who argues against (a) the idea of underlying *theological* differences between Peter and Paul before the Antioch incident, especially on the issue of table-fellowship, such that (b) the issue only first arises at Antioch, and that (c) the antithetical formulation of justification as 'not by works of the Law, but only by faith' was first formulated in the wake of that incident... (Gathercole 2005: 311–27).

58. 'The Incident at Antioch (Gal. 2. 11–18)' (1990a: 129–82 [161–2]). See further Dunn's assertion that 'The Antioch incident convinced Paul that justification through faith and covenantal nomism were not two complementary emphases, but were in direct antithesis to each other. Justification through faith must determine the *whole* of life and not only the starting-point of discovering (or being discovered) by God's grace' (Dunn 1990a: 162).

59. See esp. Ch. 12 of Dunn (1990a: 230–59).

60. It is quite clear from more recent scholarship that Paul does not fit the sectarian pattern, despite earlier suggestions to the contrary, see Watson (1989) and Campbell (1992: 122–31). Dunn notes, 'we may say that Paul stood for the reformation of Judaism, rather than its abandonment' (1991: 148). Cf. also Barton (1993: 140–62).

61. 'Did Paul Advocate Separation from the Synagogue?' (1990: 457–67), reprinted in Campbell 1992: 122–31. My view of sectarian mentality is based on Wilson (1970), and on the widely accepted

example of the Qumran sectarians demonstrates the possibility, however remote, of sectarian mentality in the variegated groups that constituted the Judaism of the first century.[62] But to interpret Paul primarily in the light of the Qumran community would be to greatly exaggerate its influence and also any apparent parallels with Paul.[63] If a sectarian perspective is defined as the perspective of those whose religious worldview portrays their group as the sole legitimate and exclusive arena of salvation and which thus sees all outside of that community as cut off from God's favour,[64] this is typical neither of first century Judaism nor of Paul.[65] Nickelsburg attributes this mentality only to the Qumran community and to the authors of many of the *Enochic* texts and *Jubilees*.[66] But Paul does not take the title Israel and claim it with its inheritance for those in Christ. His attitude is reformist rather than sectarian. In prophetic fashion, he seeks the renewal of his own people in the new era dawning with Christ, and his letters should be read in that light.[67] My contention is that a sectarian reading of Paul operates, whether consciously or unconsciously, with assumptions and analogies deriving from contemporary experience of, or theories about, sectarianism.[68]

1. A common presupposition is that Paul somehow operated and produced communities in complete isolation from all other groups in Judaism.[69] Wayne Meeks and others have maintained that it is clear that the Pauline communities were socially distinct from Judaism.[70] But to be socially distinct does not deny some contact, and could in fact even presuppose some positive links between diverse groups, as in the case of modern political parties.[71]

---

distinction between 'reformist' groups which seek to change a world that they see in need of changing and 'introversionist' groups which give up on the world and turn in on themselves.

62. Esler differentiates between reformist and introversionist attitudes within the Qumran literature; he is hesitant to describe those for whom CD was written as sectarian, and questions whether the Qumran community was sectarian vis-à-vis Judaism, but is nevertheless clear that introverted sectarianism was typical of the group (Esler 1994: 79–84).

63. Cf. Nickelsburg's comment 'Exclusivism and sectarianism in both Judaism and Christianity had ugly consequences in both communities and between them, consequences that were inconsonant with the heart of both religions' (2003: 200).

64. Cf. Watson 1983: 40, 69. Cf. also Nickelsburg (2003: 181–4).

65. Cf. Schwartz 2001: 59–69 and 91–9. Cf. also Eisenbaum 2005: 234–6.

66. Nickelsburg 2003: 182. The Christ-movement differed from the Qumran community in that whilst they claimed exclusive uniqueness for their status as God's people, they nevertheless had an open door and pursued a mission among gentiles. Nickelsburg (2003: 175).

67. As Nanos notes, the issues Paul faces are both halakhic and eschatological (2002: 396–407 [401]).

68. This does not overlook the fact that some of Paul's Jewish contemporaries may have regarded him as sectarian. Cf. Bockmuehl (1990: 130–2).

69. Cf. also the critique of this by Nanos (2005: 260–4).

70. Meeks 1983: 186. Similarly Sanders states, 'But it is equally clear that meetings of the church were not meetings of the synagogue… Gentiles who entered the people of God did not simply join Israel. There was a separate entrance requirement (faith), a separate rite (baptism), and a separate social reality (the church)', 1983: 176–8).

71. As Nanos has shown, Galatians can be better understood when intra- and inter-Jewish group

2. But even if a degree of separation between the Pauline groups and Judaism is allowed, there can be no denial of the fact that Paul himself sought, despite desperate conflicts, to maintain the link between his gentile communities and Judaism. The collection, taking up a large amount of his time and energy over a period of several years, is itself an abiding witness to Paul's concerns to link his nascent movement with Jerusalem and Jewish Christ-followers. The collection project witnesses against a sectarian mentality in Paul because in it he manifests hope rather than the despair typical of sects who withdraw from the larger group.

3. The fact that he himself maintained his links with synagogue worship, and, if Luke can be trusted, even with the Temple is further proof that Paul was no sectarian and should not be interpreted as such. As has been convincingly argued by Sanders and others, 'punishment implies inclusion', and 'Paul was not consciously aiding in the foundation of a new religion'.[72] That Paul suffered under Jewish discipline is one of the best attested aspects of his life and letters, indicating the apostle's rugged determination to cling to his ancestral faith. A sectarian apostle would have no such struggle.[73]

4. It is clear that in his use of scripture, Paul does not claim the scriptures for Christ-followers alone. He argues as a Jew of his own era, with the patterns and models of scriptural interpretation which he shares with those who do not share his view of the Christ. He has common ground with them and in his use of scripture he is wholly in line with contemporary Jewish practice. The apostle is obviously still engaged in dialogue with those who differ from him. But if Paul is not a sectarian, this comes as no surprise. To acknowledge his relation to contemporary Jewish thinking is merely to put Paul in his social context, 'to recognize the sociality of his reading and reasoning'.[74] Contrary, however, to such evidence, we do find Paul interpreted from a sectarian stance which somehow claims Paul's authority for its own separatist tendencies.

5. One point at which Paul seems guilty of presenting an 'Achilles' heel' is in his perception of Israel. If, as many assert, Paul regarded gentiles in Christ as Israel, then he is already responsible for having redefined the boundary between Jew and gentile. The interpretation of Gal. 3.28 is

---

boundary issues resulting from the formation of Pauline sub-groups are taken into account (2002c: 282–318 [289–91]).

72. Sanders 1983: 192. Sanders rightly asserts that 'both Paul and the Jews who punished him regarded the Christian movement as falling within Judaism', but he is in my view wrong to hold that Paul somewhat naively created, in his practice – against his own conscious intention – a church which was in important ways neither Jewish nor Greek: a third entity. Cf. Sanders (1983: 178–9).

73. Cf. Donaldson 1997: 302–3. Bockmuehl notes, 'Despite the acknowledgement of his pre-Christian persecution of the church... he sees no need to confess or apologize for his Jewishness *as such*' (1990: 130).

74. Cf. Ehrensperger 2004a: 142–6, and her 2004b: 32–52.

3. Paul's Theologizing Concerning the 'Other' 49

important in this respect. If there is in Paul no longer a distinction between Jew and gentile in Christ, then gentiles are also Israel and the ethnic and religious distinctiveness of historic Israel is annulled, and displacement theology is a valid option. However, textually, apart from an unclear statement in Gal. 6.16, there is no text in Paul, especially in Romans 9–11, which explicitly designates gentile Christ-followers as Israel.[75]

In Romans Chapter 9, gentiles are only introduced from verse 22 and are never explicitly called 'Israel'. Paul refers to all those who are being called, 'not from the Jews only but also from the gentile nations', *yet he never confuses gentiles with Israel, each retains their integrity.* What Paul does is to designate all Christ-followers as one entity. But that entity is the olive tree, not Israel.[76] We will return to deal with this topic in detail in a later chapter, but it is adequate for present purposes not to go into detail at this point. All are called, all are attached to the same tree, but the sub-groups of Jewish/Judean and non-Jewish/non-Judean Christ-followers remain separate socially identifiable entities.

Thus Paul, long after writing Gal. 6.16, still does not designate gentile Christ-followers as Israel, and with very good reason, because when gentiles are so designated, even if only in association with Jewish Christ-followers, they may then separate from Jewish Christ-followers and yet retain title to Israel and her heritage independently, a possibility Paul warns against in Rom. 11.[77]

In Dunn's scenario, faith in Christ became the inalienable essence of the new movement, and Paul was willing to separate from Peter and from Jerusalem and go his own way as an independent missionary. It would appear that Paul required only *initial* recognition by the other apostles for his gentile mission, but once it had been recognized, he felt free to renounce the earlier consensus. This version of events depicts Paul as the archetypal sectarian, and a model for all future sectarian Christianity. What is most deplorable is that it presents Paul as the *instigator* of division, contrary to much of the evidence of his letters which tend to portray him as *reacting* to incidents and events, making strenuous endeavours to maintain unity. The outcome of Dunn's theological emphasis is that Jewish identity and the markers associated with it were thereby rendered obsolete,[78] or at

---

75. On this issue see Campbell (1993b: 441–6). See also Campbell (1999: 187–211) and Dunn (1998: 504–6). Dunn is well aware that 'Paul's concern was not to merge "Jew and Gentile"' and that 'ethnic identity cannot be so simply changed' (506), but this does not prevent him from including gentiles in Paul's understanding of Israel, since in his view (and mine) 'Israel is defined by divine call' (1998: 514). This is clear in Dunn's assertion that 'The identity of Israel as defined by grace and faith, included both historic Israel and Gentiles' (1998: 526).

76. We will return to this topic in more detail in Chapter 8.3.

77. Dunn, writing of the emerging view in the second century of Christians as true or new Israel, rightly notes the link between this and anti-Judaism, 'Christianity began by rejecting the ethnocentricity of Judaism and of Jewish Christianity; but in coming to think of itself as a separate 'race', it opened the door to a different kind of racialism, where Christians defend themselves by *excluding* the Jews, making the very mistake against which Paul in particular protested so vehemently' (1991: 248). On this see further Rader (1978).

78. Similarly Thiselton, 2000: 551–2.

least became superfluous for Paul, and the Antioch incident sets him on a course that was to lead to the devaluation and eventual relinquishing of distinctly Jewish identity markers among all Christ-followers, at a much later date.[79]

Whatever the details of the scholarly consensus on the dispute at Antioch, it is not hard to see how Paul can be perceived as the champion of gentile Christ-followers who as such was led by the power of his Christ-given convictions into separation and independence. If Paul, the great advocate of gentile 'Christianity', was himself a separatist for the sake of the truth of the Gospel, then there is nothing to hinder anyone from following his example.

But this is, in my opinion, both an over-simplification and a somewhat anachronistic depiction of the Antioch incident. The historical evidence challenges this perception. Paul still continued with the collection for Jerusalem, and was under Jewish discipline, despite this face to face with Peter. Moreover, there is little other convincing evidence that, already in the early to mid-fifties, it had become clear that Jewish identity markers were in any way incompatible with Christ-faith.[80] It seems that a theological perception has become historicized into real history, and that later theological formulations indebted to Luther's insights have been retrojected into this early period.

3.6 Conclusion

Because scholars know the outcome of the conflicts in early Christianity, there is a dominant (anachronistic) tendency to read the Pauline texts in the light of theological doctrines and events that developed much later.[81] But it is essential to ask what could a separatist Paul (as frequently depicted since the Reformation), possibly have in mind in taking a collection from gentile believers to Jerusalem? Paul's life and actions are fortunately somewhat of a contrast to the history of interpretation of his thought. It would appear that in this portrait of Paul a distinctive theology has displaced history with its ambivalences and compromises to the detriment of our understanding of Paul both in his own day, and as a model for later Pauline Christians.

A later more doctrinally developed Christianity has been read back into Paul to establish his authority for what was to succeed him. Antioch thus becomes the 'watershed' in which Paul is represented as having, once for all, denied the relevance in Christ of Jewish identity as such – irrespective of the on-going disputes

---

79. Cf. Bockmuehl's discussion of Paul as 'Sectarian or Apostate'; although Paul in his own mind continued to be a faithful Jew, possibly as a result of unchecked rumours, 'It is therefore at least plausible that influential circles in the Jerusalem church had a sustained antipathy to Paul and his teaching; second century Jewish Christian evidence firmly establishes the existence of such a view' (1990: 130–2).

80. Cf. N. Elliott's corrective emphasis that Jewish boundary markers 'also defined modes of *inclusion* and *welcome* into the Jewish community' (2005a: 245).

81. Cf. Zetterholm, 'Paul was not involved in a process of creating a new religion where the torah was no longer valid for Jews. His mission was rather to emphasize that the torah was not for Jesus-believing gentiles. To state…that Paul thought it not possible to live at the same time "in Christ" and "in accordance with the law" is to invert the set of problems' (2002: 158–9).

concerning particular identity markers. He is depicted as thereby having clearly demonstrated the absolute incompatibility between Christianity and Judaism. Our contention is that this incident, whatever its significance, cannot possibly carry the weight attributed to it,[82] and that even many newer approaches still retain remarkable similarities with the emphases of F.C. Baur and historic Paulinism (e.g., Dunn and Boyarin, although in many details reading the incident quite differently). Moreover, if it is allowed to continue to carry this significance, it perpetuates the making of Paul into the sectarian founder of a sectarian Christianity in strong discontinuity not only with Judaism, but even more seriously, with Christ. The New Perspective, despite some of its opponents' exaggerated concerns, does not go far enough in its retreat from older antitheses and assumptions.

Modern conceptions of identity have made us aware that Paul's identity, even after his vision of Christ, is basically Jewish, and precedes the notion of 'Christian' identity proper. Christians cannot justifiably continue to use Judaism in a sectarian manner as a negative foil for Christian self-understanding.

The evidence within Paul's letters is clear when they are not read anachronistically from the disadvantage of hindsight, disadvantage because we find it almost impossible to envisage Paul writing before the eventual separation between Judaism and Christianity emerged. As we have demonstrated, *historically and theologically there is no need to locate anti-Judaism in Paul or to attribute the parting of the ways to his explicit instigation.* Anti-Judaism could and did develop in differing circumstances and at a later date without his express authorization.

The historical actualization of this possibility only originates with Justin around 160 CE. As Boyarin states, '*After the time of Justin and his promulgation of Verus Israel, becoming a Christian or (follower of Christ) meant something different – it no longer entailed becoming a Jew –, and once becoming a Christian became identified with "entering [the true] Israel", the whole semantic/ social field shifted. The boundary between Greek and Jew, the definition of Jewishness as national or ethnic identity, was breached or gravely threatened by the self-definition of Gentile Christianity as "Israel"*'.[83] So Boyarin correctly notes and, in my own opinion, once the door is opened to a definition of gentile 'Christians' as Israel, then theologically, Jewish identity is annulled, because Jewish Christ-followers are no longer essential in the church's self-understanding; gentile Christianity is no longer a branch, it can independently constitute the entire tree.

Some will find contrary evidence in the letters of Ignatius where the distinction between Jew and Christian apparently is already assumed to exist. The assertion by Ignatius that '*It is monstrous to speak of Jesus Christ and to practise Judaism*' (*Magnesians* 10.3) witnesses to Ignatius' desire for clear-cut boundaries but is simultaneously evidence that they did not yet exist unambiguously in Antioch – otherwise his complaint would have been purely theoretical. In my

---

82. Cf. Houlden 1983: 64–7.
83. Cf. Daniel Boyarin's recent book, which challenges much of the received wisdom in relation to the partings of the ways (2004: 73).

view, in the case of Ignatius and others, inner Christian debates were externalized and re-categorized along Jewish versus Christian lines.[84] This probably is again an incidence of early attempts to argue 'from theology back to history', an ideological construction developed where substantial evidence is frequently absent. Recent research[85] supports the thesis that *identity precedes theology and that in fact theological constructions emerge to solve the problem of identity rather than to create it*. In relation to Dunn's understanding of the Antioch incident, and true also of interpreting Gal. 6.16 as identifying gentile 'Christians' as Israel, the question arises, if this theological insight had already been realized, why then did it take the church so long to draw the perceived boundary?[86]

Finally, the question has to be asked, why is it so significant to continue to locate some basis for anti-Judaism in Paul? Historically and theologically, gentile Christianity did rightly or wrongly assume the heritage of Israel, and Jewish followers of Christ were eventually marginalized, but that does not mean that any or all of this process of development must be directly attributable to Paul, or that he would have approved of it.

Alternatively does the desire for clear-cut boundaries between Judaism and the earliest Christ-movement arise from a desire to establish and affirm the distinct identity of Christianity as a separate religion? Instead of 'iron boundaries and impenetrable ramparts', fuzzy boundaries now seem more credible. The analogy of the impossibility to denote clear boundaries between local dialects where two or more language areas intersect is a good illustration, offered by Boyarin,[87] of the difficulty of clearly delineating the borders of Christianity and Judaism. In any case it is decidedly immature and a sign of insecurity when adult Christians demand absolute distinctiveness for their religion. Contemporary society offers numerous examples that a healthy and confident identity is not dependent on such props.

Our conclusion is that only if the early 'church' had truly recognized diversity both in theological stance and lifestyle, that is, by giving it recognition and validity over a long period, could it have made the progress it did. To view Peter and Paul and their respective missions as in perpetual conflict not only contradicts Paul's own expressed statements, but even more so his frequently expounded theological understanding of 'the Other'. It is now becoming clearer that it was not simply Paul's theological innovation in the mission to the gentile nations in and by itself that produced the parting of the ways. This was to emerge slowly and at a much later date when social and political forces such as the

---

84. Luther's attitude to Judaism was coloured by the inner-Christian debate on grace and works originating with Pelagius and Augustine. Thus for Luther the Jews were eventually part and parcel of a theological category, rather than a people. Because they did not respond to his Reformation gospel, they represented in his view a type of Pelagianism. See Campbell 2000: 103–14; 109.

85. Cf. Lieu 2002: 297–313 and also 1996: 47–51; 277–90.

86. On this cf. also Gundry-Volf, who states 'Ephesians 2.20 contains the same key ideas as Romans 11.16ff.: Gentile Christians are saved by being adjoined to a Jewish remnant that exercises a foundational role towards these new additions...the language of co-participation does not obscure the abiding difference between the co-participants' (2000:13; 8).

87. Boyarin 2004: 19–20.

3. Paul's Theologizing Concerning the 'Other'

Jewish Roman War, the *fiscus Judaicus*, and the Bar Kochba revolt combined with the advent of the dissolution of the boundaries of Israel by gentile 'Christianity' defining itself as 'New Israel'. *But up until that time diversity in ways of life, and possibly theology, was not in itself an issue that separated 'Christianity' and 'Judaism' nor was Jewish identity universally seen as incompatible with 'Christian' discipleship.* Paul's own stance is absolutely clear in that he demonstrates that the 'other' in their difference is neither incompatible for him theologically, nor an insurmountable social problem.[88]

As Brigitte Kahl asserts,

> Within the framework of Jewish identity, Paul develops a concept of descent, nation, religion, and culture. By 'clothing' Paul with a Christian identity in the latter sense and after driving the circumcised out of the church, we have silenced and buried this highly challenging discourse on identity and difference, which today could be one of the most precious contributions of Paul to the dialogue of religions and cultures, especially to the Jewish–Muslim–Christian encounter.[89]

---

88. In this chapter I have used 'the other' to refer to non-Pauline Christ-followers – not to those outside of the Christ-centred communal movement of which Peter *et al.* were also a part. This is not to deny that it is in distinction and in opposition that identity is acquired. Cf. Boyarin (2004: 65–73). However, the opposition for Paul is not Peter and his mission, but the Roman empire, not Judaism *per se* but sin in all its ramifications and expressions. Cf. Horsley (1997: 6–7).

89. Kahl 1999: 70–1.

Chapter 4

PAUL'S PECULIAR PROBLEM:
THE CREATION OF GENTILE IDENTITY IN CHRIST

If there is any one dominant image of Paul in Christian tradition, it is that of doing a new thing, announcing the dawning of a new era and the creation of a new people.

As the hero of gentile Christianity, as with other heroes, legendary accretions and exaggerations surround such an innovator, so much so that he is sometimes regarded not only as the champion of the gentiles but also as the scourge of Israel. This is very much to do with the delicate task which Paul felt himself called to undertake.

Despite his careful approaches, his letters did prove difficult for some to understand and it seemed he was doomed to be misunderstood and to alienate either Jews or his own communities or both of these.[1] This was primarily because Paul was doing a new thing.

4.1 *Paul the Innovator*

This new thing was for him a direct outcome of the Christ-event. In one reading of this event, Christ is the inaugurator of a new creation symbolized by the church of Jews and gentiles. In this reading the barrier that separated Jew and gentile in the previous era is broken down. Christ ends the Law and with it the distinction between Jew and gentile. Paul was seeking to relate gentile Christ-followers positively to the traditions of Israel and yet attempting, nevertheless, to prevent them becoming proselytes to Judaism. Since on this scenario, all differentiation between peoples is abolished, then the way is open for an entirely new creation, sometimes termed a third race, that is neither Jewish nor gentile. The ongoing contact between Judaism and Hellenism especially in the Diaspora, already offered examples of how gentiles in varying ways could positively relate to Judaism whether as God-worshippers or proselytes or simply as benefactors.

---

1. 'There is a sense, then, in which Paul can be seen as a tragic figure. On the one hand, he was prepared to endure hardship, calumny, and eventually death, because of his concern that the gospel continue to be seen to be good news for Israel... Yet at the same time, his prodigious labours, both as a missionary and as a thinker, helped to create conditions conducive to just the type of gentile triumphalism foreseen and warned about in Rom. 11.17–24. The success of his gentile mission helped to ensure the eventual "Gentilization" of the church...'. Donaldson (1997: 306).

4. Paul's Peculiar Problem

But Paul's new communities of varying social levels of gentiles did not quite fit in or easily relate to the known patterns of the ancient world. Sometimes it seemed as if this Diaspora-born Jew understood neither his own people's nor the gentiles' traditions.

If, in accordance with the traditional perspective, Paul had operated on the view that the Christ-event ended the Law and thus the distinction between Jew and gentile, the way would truly have been open to create a new entity. Likewise, if Paul had simply wanted to forge a new movement without any affiliation to, or positive appreciation of, Judaism things would have been much simpler both for himself and his communities. He could have broken away completely from the synagogue and its discipline and avoided all the beatings and persecution[2] he was prone to as a Jew who apparently associated with gentiles in ways unsupported by normal Jewish patterns of life. He could also have avoided much misunderstanding in terms of the proposed way of life of his communities. They would have had no obligation to try to relate to synagogue communities in any meaningful way. Nor would they have had any pressure upon them to accommodate those with abiding Jewish scruples who wished to be part of their community. They would thus also have been free from the interference of those opponents of Paul who sought to make them into law-observant proselytes in the traditional pattern. Whether these opponents were Jewish Christ-followers or unconvinced Jews, the Pauline communities could simply have responded negatively to their demands as those who remained attached to a pattern of life rendered redundant by the coming of Christ. They could also have temporarily tolerated some Christ-followers with residual Jewish sympathies knowing that these must inevitably soon disappear; they would truly have been law-free gentiles.

However conducive such a scenario might prove to modern liberal thinking, it is not, however, in this perspective that Paul deserves the image of an innovator.

The older paradigm as sketched above was seen as axiomatic, so clearly visible in Paul's gentile mission, as to require little justification. However, the recovery of the relevance of Romans 9–11 for Paul's mission, and with this a fresh understanding of the central place of Israel in his thought, has rendered the old universalistic paradigm redundant or at least severely impaired as an instrument to elucidate contemporary understanding of Paul.[3]

Instead, it has now become clear that Paul's vision for gentiles originated from his understanding of the divine purpose for Israel and the nations. Since his vision was Israel-oriented, so too was his mission. He was not intending to offer an alternative vision to that of Israel (nor was he seeking to displace Israel).[4] Basic to Paul's theology was the Shema. God is one and therefore he is the God

---

2. 'Punishment implies inclusion'. Cf. A.E. Harvey 1985: 79–96 and also Sanders 1983: 192.
3. Terence Donaldson has usefully outlined the changes that the coming new paradigm for understanding of Paul is already demonstrating (1997: 3–27). In the years since the publication of Donaldson's book, a number of the features he notes have emerged more clearly, and in that respect, we are now much nearer to a radical new paradigm.
4. 'Paul's apostolate involves an expectation of salvation for Israel'. Käsemann 1980: 305.

of both Jew and gentile.⁵ There can be no separate or isolated destiny for the one apart from the other. Moreover since his conception of God's relation to Israel was one of faithfulness to his own character and promises, for Paul it was inconceivable that this God would reject his people Israel whom he foreknew. The route of replacement or displacement of Israel in the divine purpose by gentile Christ-followers was therefore not a viable option for Paul. The demanding task facing the apostle to the gentiles was to work out how his mainly gentile communities should develop their own gentile-in-Christ way of life in relation to the ongoing life of traditional synagogue communities. What could and should these gentile communities take over or adapt from the synagogue or other associations and what would or should be their appropriate ensuing identity? This was the particular and peculiar project of the apostle to the gentiles and it was sufficient to fully occupy him most if not all of the remainder of his life.

In the period prior to the Christ-event, the Jewish view of gentiles who wanted to be associated with Israel was quite clear. Gentiles were perceived as being under the Noachide Law and by obedience to this a gentile became a *Ger Toshav* and was ensured of a portion in the world to come, but remained a gentile. Such obedient gentiles were in some sense associates of Israel, but were clearly distinguished from the *Ger Tzedek* who was regarded as no longer a gentile because he had accepted circumcision and Torah, and was now perceived as being reborn into the household of Israel. In Paul's perspective, the Christ-event offered a new option to the *Ger Toshav*. Because of faith in Christ, this gentile could now assume the status of an adopted son and be regarded, by Paul at least, as a member of the house of Abraham whilst retaining his status as a gentile. As Michael Wyschogrod states, 'What was new about Paul's view…was the belief that the Noachide Laws combined with faith in Jesus as the Messiah brought into being a new category of persons, associate members in the house of Israel'.⁶

It would appear that Paul won many adherents to his movement from the *Ger Toshav* group attached to synagogues. It is easy to understand how opposition to the Pauline mission would arise as a result of this winning of such gentiles. But even more trouble lay in store for him, since he was not only creating a new group of those traditionally attached to synagogues, but he was also in conflict with some other Christ-followers who held that the former patterns of conversion to Judaism that operated prior to the Christ-event should still be followed. Scholars differ substantially concerning the strength and extent of such opposition, but that it existed need not be questioned. Paul's problem was that he did not want gentile Christ-followers to become Jewish proselytes. To continue in this pattern would be to deny the ultimate significance of the Christ-event as the inauguration of a new age and to make the God of Israel the God of Jews only. But since his most typical converts already had an association or at least an acquaintance with Jewish patterns of life,⁷ Paul had both advantages and dis-

---

5. As Nanos maintains, 'His oneness has been compromised if he is *only* the God of Israel, *only* the God of Torah and not *also* the God of the nations' (1996: 184).
6. M. Wyschogrod 2004: 188–201 (193).
7. Cf. Nanos 1999.

advantages in dealing with them. He could, for example, presume that they would know something of the scriptures of Israel.

On the other hand, they might be tempted to accept circumcision and continue on the path towards full membership of the house of Israel, despite his continued opposition to such a move. After all, motivated by a profound interest in Judaism, such converts had certainly already adapted to some extent to a Jewish way of life. They certainly did not want to separate from Judaism entirely. Quite the contrary, one of Paul's major problems was to prevent gentile Christ-followers from becoming Jews.[8] Paul and his associates did not reside permanently with the Pauline communities and this left these communities open to the influence of other interpretations of scripture and patterns of life which challenged, if they did not sometimes undermine, the Pauline pattern for gentile Christ-followers. It would have been much easier if Paul had simply and starkly contrasted everything in Judaism with the new life in Christ, leaving no bridges open that might encourage compromise between following Christ or being a Jew. But Paul's inclusive mission that embraced both Jews and gentiles did not lend itself to such facile solutions, and this left Paul with huge and sometimes insoluble problems.

The tensions resulting from such challenges would be most significant where Pauline Christ-followers were in close contact with large synagogue communities as seems to have been the case in Rome, and probably also in Antioch according to Galatians. And yet it would be quite reckless to assume that there were judaizers in all such contexts. As we have already maintained, we are not suggesting that Paul's mission to the gentiles was everywhere in direct conflict with the mission to the circumcised. But neither are we proposing that Paul operated in a vacuum, or that there were not ongoing contacts with non-Christ-following Jews and their leaders. Such was the delicate situation Paul typically addressed. But having no official status other than that given to him by Christ as apostle to the gentiles, and the recognition of this at the summit meeting in Jerusalem, it is understandable that his letters are sometimes strongly worded and that the burden of his churches sat heavily upon him.[9]

4.2. The Scriptures of Israel and the Formation of Gentile Identity in Christ

Nowhere would the liminal state of the Pauline communities be more apparent than in their development of scriptural understanding. Because they faced continuous debates about the way of life appropriate to those in Christ, and because such

---

8. Cf. Zetterholm 2003: 161.

9. Ignatius is interesting in that though he does not say much about Peter and not a great deal more about Paul in writing to the churches of Smyrna and Rome, like Justin and Serapion, he can refer to a shared 'catholic' memory of Peter. Peter's status seems to have been taken for granted in East and West alike, whereas Paul in his lifetime at least could not enjoy the status of being both a disciple of the earthly Jesus and of the risen Lord. Bockmuehl's comment in relation to Ignatius is interesting 'In the memory of Matthew and the Syrian church at least, Peter's Christianity exemplified neither autocratic leadership nor a radical break with Jewish identity and praxis. Ignatius, by contrast, may well have been Antioch's first gentile bishop' (2003: 142).

issues were decided by Paul and others in the context of the scriptures of Israel, in teaching his communities these scriptures, Paul was in some sense drawing them closer to synagogue influence since it was there that the scriptures would be available and always under discussion. If Paul and other leaders had, as has sometimes been proposed, simply used the scriptures as proof-texts to support their own novel interpretations arising as a result of the Christ-event, then the challenge they faced would have been much less demanding. But the earliest Christ-followers such as Paul never presumed they could simply take over the scriptures and wrest them from the people of Israel. In Paul's view these scriptures belonged primarily to Israel (Rom. 3.2, 9.4). Since Paul was no sectarian, he did not separate himself from the synagogue, nor isolate himself and his communities from alternative interpretations of scripture. Another major factor operating in Paul's thinking was that he was still optimistic about the future of his own people. He can hardly bear to consider the possibility that God may cast them off (Rom. 11.1, 11.11).

The significance of this hope, Israel's possession and interpretation of the scriptures, and the relationship of these to the Pauline gentile Christ-followers was great. Paul continued in dialogue with those Jews who as yet were not Christ-followers and the common ground for this dialogue was the scriptures. If Paul had given up hope for Israel, he could have disregarded the synagogue's views of scripture and also have ignored the requirements that enabled his community members to enjoy some social relations with Jews. But, as already argued, Paul did not regard his gentile mission as the only herald of the good news concerning the Christ. The apostle desired and also enjoyed the approval of Peter and others who operated in the mission to the circumcision. In order to maintain full fellowship and harmony with them, Paul and his communities had an obligation to live a way of life that did not completely cut them off from relations with the Christ-followers in the mission to the circumcised as well as from all other Jews. Thus Paul does not reject halakhic requirements and judgements for his gentile communities.

This is in accordance with the Noachide Laws which traditionally were designed to regulate the association of gentiles with Jewish communities. The peculiar problem of Paul is that he is apostle to gentiles, who remain gentiles free from the obligation of Torah-keeping (though under the law of the Christ)[10] and do not become proselytes, but who must observe such requirements as enable voluntary social relations with Jewish Christ-followers. Thus issues concerning the scriptures and the way of life of Israel could not be avoided, even by gentile Christ-followers in the Pauline communities. We are presupposing here that Paul accepted the Apostolic Decree which was probably a prevalent halakhah regulating the commensality between Jews and God-fearers which also included a general recognition that male circumcision and obedience to Torah were not to be imposed on the Christ-following gentiles.[11]

---

10. This may be described as the 'halakhic' will of God for converted gentiles and might consist of the 'words of the Lord' as filled out by a body of Torah-based ethical teaching related in some way to the notion of Noachide commandments (which in Jewish tradition applied to *all* the nations). Cf. Bockmuehl (1990: 155).

11. See Zetterholm 2003: 156–7.

4. Paul's Peculiar Problem

Gentile Christ-followers were considered to have through Christ, a place in the renewed covenant as gentiles. But this created some confusion since, in Jewish tradition, circumcision for males was the mark of the covenant. What was agreed by Paul and the other leaders at Jerusalem is that there is now a place for gentiles in salvation by their being allowed through Christ a place in the covenant and yet without having to conform to a Jewish way of life.

But even the concept of sharing in the covenant was not unproblematic. If gentile Christ-followers are within the covenant, how can they be allowed to differ from their fellow covenant members? And why should they not be regarded as Israelites if they share in the covenant with them? Donaldson suggests that following in the 'righteous gentile' and proselyte traditions in Jewish thought, Paul's gentile converts should be regarded as proselytes in a reconfigured Israel.[12] This view overcomes the problem noted above of gentile Christ-followers being members of the covenant but not becoming Jews. Such a tension would no longer exist. But, despite its apparent advantages, this view has serious limitations in that it sets at risk the distinct identity of Israel since Israel is reconfigured to include proselytes without circumcision.[13] Also it annuls the promise to Abraham that he would be the father of many nations; in this view he is still only the father of Jews. But even more it destroys the distinct identity of gentiles in Christ, since they enter the covenant only in the category of proselytes. Paul however was clear, if not always apparently consistent, in his understanding of the place of the gentiles. They entered the covenant as gentiles, and not as prospective proselytes to Judaism and so, however tempted to conform to prevailing Jewish norms for proselytes they must retain their gentile status in order to retain their sharing in the covenant, cf. συγκοινωνός, Rom. 11.17.

It is small wonder that Paul's gentile mission had a stormy passage in the earliest days. He was in many respects apparently moving simultaneously in two differing directions. He claimed through the Christ-event a share in the covenant for gentile Christ-followers and argued for their new way of life from the scriptures and traditions of Israel, especially as these indicated the obligations of gentiles in any association with Israel. Yet he fought fiercely against their full assimilation to Judaism and opposed all who dared to impose the full demands of the Torah upon them. In terms of their identity in Christ, Paul also included an understanding of the great haggadic drama of divine election with its concomitant obligations. It is difficult for us today to assess what this must have meant for gentile Christ-followers. As a disciple of Paul's explains, no longer were they strangers and sojourners, alienated from the commonwealth of Israel but fellow-citizens with the saints and members of the household of God (Eph. 2.19–20). They had a new ancestor in Abraham and belonged to his house. And yet, despite all this, in Paul's understanding, they were not Israelites even though they shared in the symbolic universe of Israel.

12. Donaldson 1997: 236–48.
13. This is not to overlook Donaldson's careful and reasoned argument which offers some very interesting insights into the issue, nor the fact that he himself is careful not to 'abandon ethnic Israel' as he accuses Dunn and Wright of doing (1997: 156–7; 341 n. 154–7).

How Paul relates his mainly gentile communities to the scriptures is illuminating. It is not only in Romans and Galatians that Paul grounds his arguments in scripture, but in some of his other letters, especially the Corinthian correspondence, his dependence, whether explicit or implicit, is easily demonstrable. Surprisingly then, even his gentile congregations are expected to be rooted in scripture. He assumed some of them at least to be familiar with scripture as is evident from his repeated questions and assertions using differing verbs ἢ ἀγνοεῖτε (Rom. 6.3, 7.1), οὐκ οἴδατε (Rom.6.16), οἴδαμεν γὰρ, οἶδα γὰρ 7.14,18 ('do you not know…'). More significantly Paul takes it for granted that the authority of scripture extends to his gentile Christ communities and that it should be formative for their identity in Christ. As Stanley perceives it, it is beyond any doubt that 'Paul regarded the words of Scripture as having absolute authority for his predominantly Gentile congregations'.[14] Paul expects gentiles who live in Christ to enter the symbolic universe of the scriptures. More to the point however and even when he differed from his Jewish contemporaries, Paul's reliance on the authority of scripture is something he shares with and that is wholly in line with contemporary Jewish practice.[15] Sameness or uniformity are not ideals of early Jewish interpretation nor of later rabbinic interpretation.[16] That Paul and contemporary Jews disagreed over certain issues in relation to the status of and contact with gentiles is no reason for a 'parting of the ways' as this was essentially an element of their common tradition of scriptural reasoning.

This means that in relating the ethical conduct of his gentile communities to the scriptures Paul may have come into conflict with Jews who disagreed with this practice. Their opposition would probably have been based on the view that gentiles must either live an entirely gentile way of life apart from Jewish norms and procedures, or else become proselytes. Paul's problem is that he does expect gentile Christ-followers to observe halakhah inasmuch as it is relevant to them, (as is increasingly being recognized in recent research).[17] Since Paul's 'opponents' also defined themselves and their way of life within the horizon of the scriptures, Paul could not avoid dialogue and interaction with them and their perspective on the scriptures. Thus Paul is not only in dialogue with Peter and Apollos but he cannot operate in isolation from contemporary Jewish exegesis. Essentially what this means is that 'scriptural reasoning' for Paul is necessarily a social and communal activity rather than being purely individual and personal.

---

14. Stanley 1992: 338.

15. Cf. Nanos, who sees Paul's discussions about the status and conduct of his gentile congregations as part of the Jewish debates about the relationship of gentiles with Jews (1996: 50ff.).

16. Cf. Patte, 'In other words what is essential is not a correct (orthodox) theological doctrine but an openness to Scripture, a "listening to Scripture" in the context of actual life. This in fact results in "a multiplicity of theological conceptions" not necessarily fitting with each other…' (1975: 75).

17. Nanos has shown that the issues Paul faces in Romans 14–15 are basically halakhic. 'Christian gentiles may be free from embracing Torah fully as Jews, but they are not free of the halakhah of the "righteous gentile" seeking association with Israel' (1996: 198). On this issue see also Tomson (1990) and Bockmuehl (2003). Sanders claims, 'Paul hands down no halakhah, only ad hoc decisions' (1983: 144).

It relates him to other Christ-followers both Jews and gentiles, as well as to non-Christ-following Jewish groups which as synagogue communities, despite their divergence in faith perspective, nevertheless also centred around the text of the scriptures.[18]

4.3 Abraham, the Father of Us All, the Locus of Shared Identities in Christ

As a result of Paul's own scriptural argumentation about the identity of Abraham's children which in turn reflected contemporary Jewish interest in the founder of their faith, Abraham and relation to him became a contested issue in the Pauline communities. 'The figure of Abraham could simultaneously serve as the ultimate symbol of Israel and the point of contact between Israel and the rest of the peoples of the world'.[19] Paul's mission proclaimed that 'in Christ Jesus the blessing of Abraham' comes upon the gentiles (Gal. 3.14). This indicates clearly that for Paul and his contemporaries the figure of Abraham is central to any discussion of gentiles and Israel.[20]

In Jewish thought, there was a tradition which, though not always emphasized, denoted Abraham as the father of gentiles. The image of one who left his land and the idolatry associated with it made the patriarch an excellent model for gentiles and also for Jews who were tempted to compromise their monotheism. The author of *Jubilees* portrays Abraham as one who practised the stipulations of what became known as the Mosaic law, and thus as a fitting exemplar for Jews. He is also the only one from the descendants of Noah – the entire gentile population of the earth – who worships the true God.[21] Thus in *Jubilees*, 'the worship of the one God and the separation from idolatrous gentiles characterized Abraham as God's own and should still characterize the readers of Jubilees'.[22]

In the works of Philo, Abraham is portrayed as one who stands for those things that make the Jews of Alexandria distinctive from their gentile neighbours, monotheistic faith and obedience to the Mosaic law. He is the first monotheist and the first member of Israel, the first gentile to leave idolatry behind to serve the one true God. He is thus the model for gentile proselytes to Judaism, as well as for Jews in his worship of the one God through obedience to the law.[23] In the late first century context of Pseudo-Philo's *Biblical Antiquities* Abraham's monotheism is again central and because of this God bestowed a covenant upon him and his descendants for ever. Abraham is depicted as one who refused to assimilate to the self-aggrandizing intentions of idolatrous people and thus he functions here as one who separates Israel from assimilation to gentile life

---

18. Cf. Ehrensperger 2004b.
19. Eisenbaum 2000: 145.
20. On this see Calvert-Koyzis 2004: 6–84.
21. Cf. Calvert-Koyzis 2004: 8–10.
22. Calvert-Koyzis 2004: 18.
23. So Calvert-Koyzis 2004: 40.

patterns.²⁴ Josephus, on the other hand, in his *Antiquities* presents Abraham as an example for the proselyte but, according to Louis H. Feldman, without any real missionary function.²⁵ Abraham was virtuous before the law was given, he was obedient to the essence of the law as exemplified in Josephus's claims that he married his niece rather than his daughter and that he first practised circumcision. Abraham is apologetically depicted as a Hellenistic philosopher who on sound philosophical principles is a practising monotheist.²⁶

In *The Apocalypse of Abraham* the apparently recent Roman destruction of the Temple is perceived as divine judgement because of Israel's idolatry. The true people of God will however eventually be vindicated over their oppressors if they maintain faithfulness to the one creator God as did Abraham their forefather. Abraham is perceived as 'the point of division between gentiles and his descendants and also the point where God divides gentiles into those prior to Abraham and those who came later' (who will receive harsher judgement). Thus the rejection of idolatry for monotheism after the example of Abraham is the ultimate criterion for those who are faithful to God. They will find their reward but those who do not follow Abraham's example, by participating in idolatry or forsaking their Jewish monotheism, these bring about their own destruction.²⁷

These varying portraits make Abraham an excellent model for Paul's gentile communities, and most significantly where the context involved debates about membership of the covenant and the conditions for entry to this for gentiles.

Paul's linking his gentile communities to Abraham as their father could however lead in two diverse directions. If Abraham is their father, and Abraham accepted circumcision, then his gentile children could legitimately be expected to follow his example. This form of argument could in fact represent faith in Christ as but the first step on the route to becoming proselytes to Judaism. But Paul's use of the Abraham tradition could also be used in another direction. Abraham is the prototype of the believing individual demonstrating that faith alone is what counts before God. This could be used in an anti-Jewish argument to deny any role to Judaism after Christ and to claim only individual linking to Christ by faith alone without any communal influence being necessitated. In this scenario, Abraham would most accurately be depicted as father of gentile Christ-followers.²⁸ Such a stance is strengthened by Paul's description of Christ as the singular seed of Abraham in Gal. 3.16 (the scripture says that the promise was to Abraham καὶ τῷ σπέρματι αὐτοῦ, not to καὶ τοῖς σπέρμασιν). Paul can go on to argue that if the Galatians belong to Christ, then they are seed of Abraham and heirs of the promise (3.29).

---

24. Calvert-Koyzis 2004: 49.
25. Feldman 1998: 162; 157–9.
26. Cf. Spilsbury 1998: 92.
27. Calvert-Koyzis 2004: 83–4.
28. So Michel, who despite his excellent discussion on 'Abrahamskindschaft', and his profound understanding of Judaism, claims that in Romans 4 Abraham is primarily the father of gentile Christians (1955: 14).

4. Paul's Peculiar Problem

Paul's discussion of Abraham in Romans gives a fuller picture of Abraham's significance for Paul.[29] The question asked at the beginning of Chapter 4 concerns what Abraham found and the implied answer is that he found grace, ἵνα κατὰ χάριν (4.16). Abraham is thus brought into the picture not merely as an example[30] of a believing individual but as the recipient of that grace, promises, etc. which were to make him the first of the faithful, the promise-bearer who as such occupied a unique role in the history of Israel. In Romans the issue concerns Abraham's faith but much more – who are the children of God and how is Israel constituted.[31] The election of Israel stems from Abraham, who as the promise-bearer is the founder of his people. Thus in Jewish perspective, which Paul shares, Abraham is first and foremost father of the Jewish people, as indicated by e.g. the οὐ τῷ ἐκ τοῦ νόμου μόνον (4.16) (cf. also 4.9). For this reason it is wrong to stress Abraham purely as an individual.

But in linking his gentile communities to Abraham, Paul links them particularly to one aspect of Abraham. It was not just that Abraham received the promise but it was also the content of the promise that was crucial. He was to become 'the father of many nations', πατέρα πολλῶν ἐθνῶν (4.17) not just of one. So in using the narrative of Abraham, and in locating his communities within that narrative, Paul uses it both to relate gentile Christ-followers to the Jewish symbolic universe, and also to claim that Christ confirmed these promises to Israel as well. Paul's use of Abraham in Romans is inclusive thus depicting him as the father of both gentile and Jewish seed, 'the father of us all' (4.16). What is noteworthy in Romans 4 is the clearly ordered parallelism between two groups who can claim Abraham as ancestor (4.16). Paul leaves no doubt that he sees Abraham as linking in a common paternity two groups who differ in their relation to him. As Stowers notes, Paul 'assumes that Abraham is father of the Jews', for him, the ἔθνη are 'the other nations', the gentile peoples, and he is the apostle to the 'other nations'.[32] Abraham is the father of both the descendants by his blood and also those by adoption through incorporation into Abraham's blood descendant, Christ.[33]

---

29. In Paul's midrashic use of the term, σπέρμα, to reach differing outcomes in the differing contexts of his argument in Galatians and Romans is not necessarily from a first century scriptural perspective, a contradiction. Romans, however, prevents the dissolution of Israel into the church as seems to be the essence of Tom Wright's use (1991: 246–51) of Gal. 3.16 in which 'Christ gathers up Israel's story so completely that he and those "in him" constitute Israel without remainder'. Cf. Donaldson's critique (1997: 191–2), cf. also 155–9; similarly Wagner (2002: 278–9).

30. The relation between Romans 3 and Romans 4 is confused when Abraham in 4.1–22 is treated merely as exemplifying what has already been asserted in Chapter 3. Stowers claims the emphasis is more on Abraham as ancestor rather than as example (1994: 227–50). Similarly Eisenbaum (2000: 136).

31. The tradition of Abraham as the first believer may derive from Joshua 24.2–3, cf. Kugel (1997: 133–4), cited in Eisenbaum (2000: 133–4).

32. Stowers, 1994: 246.

33. Stowers notes that the very first lines of Romans signal the motif of descent in relation to Christ, ἐκ σπέρματος David and ἐξ ἀναστάσεως son of God (1994: 240). Stowers suggests that this lineage emphasis means that 'Christ brought an end to his Davidic line and to a messianic dynasty when he allowed his death but founded a new form of kinship through the resurrection'. Cf. also 1994: 243–50 and Eisenbaum (2000: 136).

In making Abraham the father of both Jews and gentiles in the Christ-movement, Paul found a means to give gentile Christ-followers a specific identity that located them meaningfully 'in a larger cultural story' within his understanding of the divine purpose for the world.[34] Through the preaching of the good news, gentiles come into Christ and receive adoption into Abraham's lineage. This likewise made a link between two differing groups in the Christ-movement and thus stressed commonality despite difference. Again, in relation to our discussion of the difficulties Paul faced with gentile Christ-followers, we note that even this linking with Abraham could have resulted in or proved amenable to attempts to persuade these to become proselytes to Judaism. But as we will argue in detail later, this common linking to one ancestor was still meant to substantiate abiding differences between these two groups in keeping with the promise that Abraham should become the father of many nations, and not just of one.

4.4 *In What Sense Were the Pauline Communities Socially Distinct?*

The fact of sharing scriptures despite differing perspectives concerning their interpretation meant that whether individual Christ-following gentile groups had any real or close contact with synagogues as such did not necessarily mean they were completely isolated from their influence. Even where there was dispute and differing degrees of hostility, Jewish Christ-followers remained a potential link and point of contact between gentile Christ-followers and the synagogue.[35] What must also be recognized is that when one lives in opposition and denial of the 'other' who is different, this 'other' can still exert a powerful influence. Even in negative self-definition, the negated other(s) and their values continue to exercise a certain influence whether recognized or not.

Thus, although theoretically we can envisage the Pauline communities as possibly living in isolation from the synagogue, in practice in many areas, such complete isolation was well-nigh impossible. In the liberal view of Paul, he seems to operate in splendid isolation or at least independently from every possible influence from the synagogue. If the above argument is correct, however, it must be acknowledged that if, as we know, Paul was sometimes engaged in conflict with opponents from the synagogue, even this allowed some mutual influence and prevented insulation and isolation. And if, as may legitimately be claimed, both Paul himself and his communities were very much in contact with the diverse patterns of Judaism of that period, then the task of the apostle was made even harder. Those in the Pauline communities – and there may have been very many of them – who were formerly attached to the synagogues as God-fearers, may have retained in some instances a high regard for Judaism, and

---

34. Wagner refers to Paul's construct of a larger cultural 'story' that lies behind Paul's appropriation of Isaiah in Romans to speak *both of his own mission to the gentiles and of Israel's present and future relationship with their God* (emphasis mine). This construct forms the context for his reflections (esp. Isa. 49), on what God is doing in the world (2002: 31).

35. See Boyarin 2004: 1–33.

4. Paul's Peculiar Problem

also possibly did not want to separate from Judaism completely since they had already gone some way to adapt to a Jewish pattern of life.[36] As we have argued above, Paul was not undertaking an easy task. He was at one and the same time making links via the interpretation of the scriptures to living Jewish communities, and also probably through Christ-following Jews where these existed locally, but yet arguing vehemently, and acting in accordance with, the belief that gentile Christ-followers should remain gentiles-in-Christ and not become proselytes. Paul does stress the distinctiveness of gentile Christ-followers but it cannot be presumed that distinctiveness in this case implies complete separation from the synagogue communities.[37]

In respect of their pagan environment, separation from their previous way of life was demanded as the model of Abraham indicates. Now they must undergo a process of resocialization as Christ-following gentiles. In some sense they are a new creation in that Paul was doing a new thing in creating gentile identity in Christ. If the language of new creation means anything, it is in this context. These Pauline communities were not synagogues inasmuch as they did not demand full obedience to Torah. Nor were they simply pagan collegia, since they remained gentiles, but not pagans, as Nanos reminds us.[38] Significantly, Paul in his use of the Abraham tradition, does not use it to disinherit Jews and to replace them with gentile children of faith, but rather to stress Abraham as the progenitor in faith of both Jews and gentiles. In this respect Paul's new creations of gentile Christ-following communities are called not to an entirely new way of life, but to one significantly related to the God of Abraham and the people of Israel.

But what should this way of life consist of? The righteous gentile in Jewish perspective was the nearest relevant model on which to build. This explains the perceived connection between the Apostolic Decree and the Noachide commandments. For gentiles to join the Christ-movement was a life-transforming event, particularly for those few who had had little previous contact with Judaism whether as God-fearers or proselytes.[39] That conversion is not simply individual transformation, but a social process is being increasingly recognized.[40] Thus for a gentile to convert to the Pauline community, meant a complete upheaval in their social network and activity, particularly since Hellenistic religion was a basic and inherent part of the framework of society. This need not imply a rejection of all

---

36. Cf. Zetterholm 2003: 161. Nanos 1996 and 2002a.

37. See the chapter 'Did Paul Advocate Separation from the Synagogue' in Campbell 1992: 122–31. This study has now been superseded in some respects by new research such as Nanos, 1996 and 2002a and 2002b, but it represents an early attempt to relate Paul more positively to his Jewish heritage, and to situate his communities more closely to the synagogue.

38. Nanos, 1996: 168. 'Gentiles turning to faith in the Christ of Israel need not (must not!) become Jews; however, *equally important*, they must not remain pagans, nor offend their Jewish brothers and sisters by disregarding purity behaviour operative for guiding "righteous gentiles" in their midst' (1996: 197).

39. That affiliation of gentiles to Judaism was not always or necessarily religiously motivated has been argued by Cohen (1989: 13–34).

40. Cf. Taylor 1995: 128–36.

the values of the Graeco-Roman world. Christian understanding of conversion requires a complete re-evaluation of one's previous way of life, not its eradication.[41] However, the question of eating meat sacrificed to idols at public festivals and such like caused enormous conflict between the old way of life and the new.

There was great disparity in the degree of commitment to the norms of the Pauline communities and this made the maintenance of discipline extremely difficult as the Corinthian context vividly illustrates. But when we consider the values and norms in such communities, it becomes clear that whilst gentile identity in Christ remains paramount, Paul's ethical concerns closely resemble those of his ancestral faith. Gentile Christ-followers are thus being resocialized into an identity related to the God of Israel. For Jewish proselytes and for God-fearers, the process of resocialization into Jewish patterns of life was already in process.[42] For these some of the difficult breaks with previous patterns of life had already been achieved in varying degrees and it is not surprising that many of them joined the Pauline communities. Nevertheless the Pauline communities were difficult to locate socially. As noted above, they were not a synagogue community, though some may have retained links. They were no longer pagans in the sense that they had given up idolatry and its social manifestations in festivals etc. Unlike Jewish Christ-followers, whilst they could participate in Jewish life as righteous gentiles, they could do so only as non-Jews. Thus Pauline Christ-followers were at one and the same time related in some sense to a Jewish symbolic universe but simultaneously, required to remain distinct from Jews.[43] This was essentially the crux of Paul's problem as we understand it.[44] But even as presented in this way, this does not mean that Paul wished his communities to develop an entirely separate identity from Judaism.

41. Cf. Rambo (1993: 5-19). The significance of Rambo's typology is its breadth of perspective in which great diversity of 'conversion' is considered, thereby enabling some sort of link between studies that refer to Paul's Damascus road experience as a 'call' and those that see it as a 'conversion', cf. also Segal's view of Paul as a 'convert' (1990). Since Stendahl's emphasis on 'Call rather Than Conversion' (1976: 9), the issue is often clouded by tendencies to view Paul's Damascus experience as indicative of other stances, e.g. as to whether this view negates or supports individual conversion today or a mission to Jews whether in the first century or the modern world.

42. We are thinking here of an ongoing process and seeing this as varying for differing groups. We are not denying that a Jew such as Paul did in fact experience 'a resocialisation process in which "one universe of discourse" or set of shared social meanings was replaced by another', cf. Campbell (2004: 81), but we are also asking for more differentiation such as e.g. Richard Travisano (1970) who distinguishes between conversion as a radical change in universe of discourse and what he terms as 'alternation', a less radical form of identity transformation and conversion. Segal states that 'the degree of resocialization depends on the distance the convert must travel between the old and new communities and the strength of the new commitment. Conversion can take place within a single religion, where less resocialization is needed.' Segal (1990: 74).

43. If Paul recognized the right of Jewish Christ-followers to retain their Jewish identity, this might have had the effect of giving added significance to Jewish identity in Christ, even for gentiles, tempting them to judaize.

44. Dieter Mitternacht argues that the conversion of gentiles to faith in Christ led to their marginalization 'from both their potential social and religious homesteads', i.e it resulted in distancing from their former social location yet also failed to gain them status equality on prevailing Jewish communal terms unless they became proselytes, 2002: 411.

This is primarily because they shared a fundamental aspect of their identity with Jewish Christ-followers as with Paul himself. In Paul's perception, as we have already argued, Christ-followers had no option but to recognize one another since the God of Israel is God of both Jews and gentiles. Whereas gentiles were obligated to renounce fundamental aspects of their former way of life with resultant wide-ranging social implications, Jews or those partially socialized into the faith, did not need to repudiate their ancestral faith, but rather to transform it from a Christological perspective. One aspect of this must have involved their view of gentiles in Christ. The only option available for a complete dissociation from Judaism would have been a sectarian, supersessionist Christ-movement, which took over what it believed to be the essentials of the Jewish faith, reformulating these in a claim to be the only valid heir to the inheritance of Israel. This is precisely the option Paul explicitly rejected, and the reason why the term 'New Israel' is absent from his letters.

Thus the Pauline communities had a distinct identity but one which was developed from and in relation to a Jewish symbolic universe. These communities may or may not, depending on their social or geographic location, have been separate from Jewish communities. Whatever their location, their identity was not formulated in contradistinction to Judaism, but rather in association with it. They were not in opposition to Judaism, nor did their self-understanding involve the view that they had displaced it. It was their liminal social location, on the borders of the Jewish world, but not quite part of it, and yet retaining significant aspects of its self-understanding and identity that constituted the peculiar problem of Paul in the guidance and development of his communities.[45]

---

45. The situation at Rome where Paul had not yet visited may have been very different from the pattern common elsewhere. Nanos's proposals in this respect are exceedingly significant in that he envisages that the gentiles addressed are still meeting in the synagogues of Rome and that they are considered part of the Jewish community(s) as 'righteous gentiles' who within this Jewish context are developing a subgroup identity and beginning to disregard the Jewish behaviour required of them. This perspective brings Paul's teaching in Rom. 14–15 into the sphere of halakhah and demands a complete rethinking of traditional views of the relation of gentile Christ-followers to the synagogue and of the demands that may thus have applied to them. Nanos, 1996: 13–20. But cf. also Nanos 2002a and 2002b where similar discussions are developed in respect of Galatians.

Chapter 5

THE TRIPARTITE CONTEXT:
PAUL'S MISSION BETWEEN SYNAGOGUE AND STATE

In Chapter 4 above we have emphasized the continuing diversity exemplified in the varieties of Judaism of the first century CE, of which nascent Christianity was a dynamic part. In contrast to older paradigms of two opposing missions, we have stressed diversity within one movement with at least some degree of mutual recognition within its varied manifestations. We have sought to resist a simplistic conflict-focused schema based on two missions with two opposing identities and corresponding agendas in which gentile Christ-followers were involved in endless conflicts with Christ-following and other Jews.

In the course of researching this topic which extended to almost a decade, I became more convinced that a major weakness in the older construction of the development of the Christ-movement was that the opposition was almost universally depicted as coming from Jews and Judaism. That there was conflict between these two entities need hardly be disputed; it is only the extent that must be more precisely delineated. But what was missed in the depiction of the relations between the Christ-movement and other forms of Judaism of that period was that both of these entities had to relate to each other within the context of the all-pervading dominance of the Roman Empire. The conflict was not one of two opposing parties, it was rather tripartite in nature. This recognition changes our perspective on the development of the Christ-movement in the first century. The image of a tiny Christ-movement persecuted everywhere by Jews who opposed it, continually under threat from the Temple or synagogue, omits the fact that whilst Jews were present in large numbers only in certain centres such as Alexandria, Antioch or Rome, Roman power and influence was universal, though varying in its degree of effectiveness and immediacy in differing contexts. At best Jews could do only what Rome or alliances with local gentiles permitted. They cannot then, whatever their frequent resistance, be depicted as the real enemy of the Christ-movement.

Proceeding from this starting point, a more realistic assessment of the historical reality of Paul's missionary outreach indicates that it took place in a politically and religiously sensitive environment where all *collegia* and synagogues were obligated to forever keep in view the oppressive power of the state and the penalties resulting from antagonizing the authorities whether wittingly or unwittingly. The options available to Jews and Christ-following gentile communities were dependent not merely upon their relations with each other but above all on their common subservience to a cruel and dominating power. Thus the patterns of life that were developed within the Christ-movement and the outcome of these in subsequent circumstances cannot be regarded simply as what Paul or the Jews planned or permitted – rather it was what was feasible in the context of Roman imperialism. The recognition of this fact will enable us better to perceive the Christianity which emerged from the early Christ-movement as the product not simply of Peter or of Paul but of complicated and diverse historical forces that have left their indelible mark upon both the constitution and the doctrines of the church. In the previous chapter, we have emphasized that Paul should not be depicted as always the initiator of conflicts or division, but rather as reacting to a combination of people and circumstances. To this image of Paul in reaction to other leaders and sporadic opposition from Jews, we now add the more significant element that all his mission activity took place in a context in which he was forced also to react to the constraints of civic authorities in the Roman empire.

5.1. *'Christians', Jews and Civic Authorities in Interaction*

The focus of this chapter is therefore on the interaction between the Christ-movement, Jews and civic authorities in the course of Paul's mission activity. A recent study offers a convenient starting point for our discussion. Mikael Tellbe attempts to reconstruct the interactions between 'Christians', Jews and civic authorities in Thessalonica, Rome, and Philippi in the middle of the first century CE and investigates how interactions in this tripartite relation shaped the self-understanding and identity of the 'Christian' communities in these places.[1] The author argues that the need for socio-political legitimacy in Graeco-Roman society was a pressing issue for the Christ-movement already in the middle of the first century and that the interactions between 'Christians', Jews and civic authorities played a vital role in forming a specific 'Christian' self-understanding in the Pauline 'churches'.

Tellbe's reconstruction of the Christ-movement in Thessalonica is of a community in conflict, confronted with hostility from two directions: the synagogue community and the civic authorities, but also suffering from hostile fellow residents who suspected them of undermining the values of Graeco-Roman society in their neglect of the traditional and civic cults of the Graeco-Roman gods and benefactors. Paul responds to this situation in which his community's honour has been challenged and negated by reinforcing the boundaries between the group of believers and the outside world. Believers are called to please God – the 'church' of God is the only essential 'court of reputation'. A contrast seems deliberately drawn between Paul's eschatology and imperial ideology. Believers belong to another βασιλεία from which they can expect their saving κύριος. Paul thus gives the Thessalonians a spiritual identity with distinctive political connotations particularly in the use of eschatological terminology. However, whilst reinforcing

1. Tellbe 2001.

the 'church's' self-understanding, Paul does not explicitly criticize the state, but warns against extremist tendencies within the community which might lead to strife with the authorities.[2]

In response to the previous clashes with the Jewish community, Paul depicts the latter as outsiders, thus strengthening the inner cohesion and identity of his own group. Tellbe notes that Paul does not refer to the Christian community as συναγωγή but as ἐκκλησία. This arises 'probably from Paul's concern to reinforce a distinct self-understanding'.[3] Their identity as the people of God is also reinforced by terms drawn from biblical language referring to the divine election of Israel as e.g. 'For we know, brothers, *beloved* by God, that he has *chosen* you' (1.4) and again the Thessalonians are '*called* by God into his kingdom and glory' (2.12). By a repeated use of kinship language in a remarkable intensity of images, Paul evidences his concern to knit together the social and religious identities of the Thessalonians as a distinct group. This language of belonging plays a powerful role in the process of resocialization and in creating an exclusive sense of group identity as distinct from all outsiders (cf. οἱ ἔξω, 4.12). From this Tellbe concludes that in this letter, '*Paul draws new boundaries between Christians and non-Christian Jews as well as between Christian and non-Christian gentiles that would ultimately have legitimated a separation from the local Jewish community*'.[4]

Tellbe finds both points of similarity and contrast in comparing the three local settings of 1 Thessalonians, Romans and Philippians. He finds that though the Roman presence and influence was strong in all locations, the clash with imperial ideology was more pronounced in Thessalonica and Philippi than in Rome. In Romans Paul gives a positive assessment of the state and does not explicitly warn of the risks of Roman propaganda, although he regularly reverses terms and symbols employed in imperial ideology. The most explicit demarcation against imperial ideology is made in 1 Thessalonians, where Paul warns them not to put their trust in the false pretensions of Roman ideology and propaganda (1 Thess. 5.3). Tellbe suggests that 'the further away from Rome Paul comes, the more explicitly he expresses his distance from and criticism of Rome'.[5] It would appear that '*the varying degrees of Roman and Jewish presence and influence at the three locations in focus evidently affected the local interplay between Christians, Jews and civic authorities*'.

However, no clear homogenous pattern emerges for the interactions between Christ-followers, Jews and the civic authorities. Probably Christ-followers who operated outside Jewish communities and without Jewish identity markers were more exposed to conflict with their wider civic societies and the civic authorities

---

2. Tellbe 2001: 136–40.
3. Tellbe 2001: 134. Reference to Christ-followers as 'called' also occurs in 2.12; 4.7 and 5.24.Whilst it is clear that Paul is drawing parallels here with the call of Israel, this by itself should not be viewed negatively as diminishing the status of Israel but rather positively as reinforcing the identity of gentile Christ-followers. Cf. Campbell 1993a: 150–54.
4. Tellbe 2001: 135.
5. Tellbe 2001: 284.

in Graeco-Roman society. Tellbe does note some general similarities between Paul's comments in 1 Thessalonians and Philippians but this indicates no development in Paul's thought and theology concerning issues relating to these interactions; it was primarily contextual factors that explain how Paul reacted. Early interactions between Christ-followers, Jews and civic authorities thus belonged to what Beker termed the contingent factors of Paul's theology.[6] The latter is in fact 'an outcome of the complex interplay between ideas and social structures, theological concepts and socio-historical phenomena'.[7] In Tellbe's view, Romans stands out since it seems to lack any open conflicts between the house churches and the Jewish communities or between the 'Christians' and the civic authorities. But even though the most explicit assertions concerning the state are in Rom. 13.1–7, '*it is not correct to let this highly "contextualized" passage alone determine our perception of Paul's theology of the state*'.[8]

So much for a comparison between the three communities Paul addresses. There is much in the above with which we can concur, particularly Paul's pastoral concern for his converts. However, we would wish to add certain caveats. That Paul wanted his mainly gentile group to have a strong and distinct coherence and identity is beyond question. Since they were mainly gentile, this meant they did not constitute a synagogue, so it is not surprising that Paul should not urge them 'to maintain connections with the local Jewish community or to uphold certain Jewish identity markers'. It is not at all surprising that they differed and were distinct from Judaism.

It is also understandable and justifiable that Paul should indicate his gentile communities' place in God's purposes by describing them in terms of God's elect as recipients through Christ of divine grace. However, it must be significant that Paul does not explicitly call gentiles Israel nor does he imply a replacement of Israel by them.[9] What is lacking in Tellbe's conclusions is a recognition that the *Pauline communities did not constitute the whole of the Christ-movement*. If his argument is that Paul's views were meant to be, or simply that historically they eventually came to be, the universal norm then this needs to be clarified. Paul was an activist and certainly not neutral in any dispute concerning the security and identity of his communities, but that does not mean that he believed that his communities constituted the only true Christ-followers or that Peter and the other Jerusalem leaders and their pattern of life were either in error or only temporarily justifiable. This is basic to any discussion of whether Paul was preparing for or desired his communities to separate from Judaism.[10] But as we have already

6. Tellbe 2001: 296. See also Beker 1991: 24.
7. Tellbe 2001: 296. Concerning this aspect of Paul's theologizing – this interactive element in the creation of Paul's writings – I would very much wish to concur with Tellbe (and Beker). There has been, and often still is, too much concentration on Paul's conceptual thought as if it were an abstract entity, entirely divorced from his contextual activity and social location. On the nature of Paul's theologizing, see Campbell (1993a: 246–54) and also Chapter 10 especially 10.1–2.
8. Tellbe 2001: 288.
9. On this see Campbell 1993b: 441.
10. See Campbell 1992: 122–31. I mention this because I get the distinct impression that Tellbe holds that Paul is somehow preparing his gentile communities for a complete separation from

noted, to claim that the Pauline communities were socially distinct is not the same as arguing that for Paul, there was only one possible genuine form of identity in Christ, that of the believing gentile. We must resist the temptation to generalize Paul's statements to a particular gentile community into a universal norm to apply to the whole church.[11] On the contrary, we have in Paul's own words a recognition of diversity within the early Christ-movement in that he himself speaks without qualification or criticism of 'the churches of Christ which are in Judea' (Gal. 1.22), and as already noted, Paul commends the Thessalonians in that they had become imitators of the 'churches' of God in Judea which are in Christ Jesus (1 Thess. 2.14). Few scholars would argue that these churches in Judea would fit into the pattern determined by a universalization of gentile norms and patterns.

Secondly, to apply to gentile Christ-followers the promises of God to Israel need not in and of itself signify that these believers were the true Israel in such a fashion as to deny any validity to the way of life or status of Jewish Christ-followers. To maintain as Paul did that gentiles are truly God's people without observing Torah, and equal in Christ with Jewish Christ-followers, does not mean that they (gentile Christ-followers) were the only true people of God,[12] or that it is no longer legitimate for Jewish Christ-followers to keep Torah. What Paul is insisting is that these gentile Christ-followers are truly God's people – true people of God, distinct but not unique!

What everyone can readily acknowledge is that by the mere fact of including gentiles within the promises of God in any fashion Paul thereby began an erosion of the tightly drawn boundaries of Israel. The formation of a distinctive (gentile) Christ identity in the Pauline 'churches' would eventually have repercussions on the process of the 'parting of the ways'. But this does not mean that Paul foresaw or deliberately worked towards a breakaway movement from Israel, which in time would replace it. In other words, we are insisting that there is no direct and continuous development from Paul to the 'church' of gentiles only of a later time. For the emergence of this historical entity, Paul deserves neither all the credit, nor all the blame!

5.2. Paul's Goal for his Communities in the Promotion of Solidarity in Christ

The eventual historical outcome of the gentile mission must not be equated exactly with Paul's conscious or unconscious intentions. We are not wishing in any way to deny Paul's influence and responsibility for the mission, but rather to distinguish between intentions, however laudable, and their outcome in the communities in relation to whom they were directed. At this point what we are

---

Judaism. I see this in his claim that there is an inherent tension in Paul's strategy for the Thessalonians which would lead to further tensions and conflicts (with the local Jews, the civic authorities, and gentile society in general) (2001: 140).

11. Cf. Elliott 1995: 68. See also Ehrensperger 2004a: 179–80.
12. See Campbell 1999: 204–8.

5. *The Tripartite Context*   73

opposing is certain problematic views as to Paul's own desired goals for his communities. Did he build them up in order to make them independent of the synagogue and did he thus consciously or unconsciously contribute to the eventual gulf between them? Did Paul actually encourage animosity to Judaism and to the Jerusalem authorities, whatever their attitude to his mission to the nations? Even more extreme, did Paul discourage all links with the synagogue with the goal of building a separate entity, a brand new creation in Christ? Historically we know how things eventually turned out, but our question here is whether this was what Paul intended.

Our approach to this issue is to affirm Paul's positive goals in relation to the growth of his communities. They are his pride and joy, they are the cause of endless concern to him, they are the evidence of the legitimacy of his apostolate. As their nurse, father and mother, pastor and judge, these communities were the focus of all his interest and activity and occupied all of Paul's time. The evidence would suggest that he would not manipulate them for other goals that would diminish their well-being and development. In other words, the communities were for Paul an end in themselves, not a means to an end. Of course we recognize that they were regarded as a new creation in Christ and they were destined to grow together and towards Christ. But this makes their well-being even more important and determinative. Hence Paul's purposes for them are not designed to eventually cause separation from Judaism or opposition to Roman imperial power.[13] Such secondary goals would hinder their sole allegiance to Christ and his kingdom, and nothing must stand in the way of this.

This is merely to affirm that Paul's greatest good is Christ and his kingdom. Also it is affirming that Paul's first priority in all his activity is to serve Christ in the building up of his followers. Paul, as a good pastor, needs to scold, cajole, encourage or discipline his communities, but the declared purpose of all this is not that these communities become or do something in and by themselves but rather that both Paul and they should together realize the ultimate goal of conformity with Christ and the claims of his kingdom. And the people of Israel are not outside the scope of this kingdom since the kingdom of Christ has universal significance. Thus the vocation to which both Paul and his communities are called together in Christ is so determining and so demanding that they must not be side-tracked by lesser subsidiary goals that might jeopardize their development or success for Christ.

To ensure the growth and development of his communities, Paul seeks in diverse ways to increase their sense of belonging, to encourage solidarity and harmony together in Christ. We do not see such concerns as having other motivations than dedication to the work of Christ. To build up solidarity is to develop these communities as strong cohesive units that will enable them to survive in spite of all kinds of opposition or even persecution. Wayne Meeks has given an excellent account of the strong cohesion and intimate ongoing social interaction

---

13. This is not to deny the validity of Elliott's case arguing that in Romans Paul opposed Roman rather than Jewish ethnocentrism (2005b: 22).

that typified the Pauline communities.[14] In our opinion, Paul's concern for their unity and growth is an end in itself that can only be adequately explained as an attempt to live in accordance with Christ and in keeping with the demands of the Gospel such as witness and evangelization.

Thus as Meeks asserts, it is clear that the Pauline communities were socially distinct.[15] But although to maintain separation from other groups or even a negative relation may assist in some ways in the construction of a distinct identity, it is not the only route to this desired end. A positive relation can also reduce hostility and thus avoid hindrances to growth. Nor should such a positive appreciation of some aspects of the life of the other be regarded as militating strongly against a distinct identity. To be socially distinct by no means rules out some form of social intercourse – it could rather be argued that it presupposes such.[16] To be a distinctive or a true people of God, a group is not necessarily required to be unique.[17] Our proposal on this issue is that we must presuppose diversity in differing contexts, partially dependent on the number of Jews in any locality and on the existing relations with the gentile community. For example, the Roman situation differed from others in that Paul was not the creator of the Christ-following communities there. Similarly, Magnus Zetterholm has drawn attention to the history of strife between the two communities of Jews and gentiles that no doubt eventually contributed to 'the Antioch Incident'.[18]

It may, however, be questioned to what extent Paul's conscious and deliberate creation of group solidarity and particular identity was itself a negative influence in relations with the synagogue. Meeks, as we have observed, shows how powerful a force this developed sense of belonging to a new family could actually be. The new set of relationships supplant natural kinship structure into which the person had been born and which previously defined his place and connection with the society.[19] Does this also involve the 'creating an exclusive sense of group identity distinct from "the outsiders" '?[20] We have already maintained that Paul was not a sectarian and it is not our intention to detract from Meeks' helpful insights in this area. However it has also got to be recognized that real life does not correspond exactly to the neat categories of sociology, helpful though these certainly are. Overlap in membership of differing groups may seem to be ruled out entirely by an image of ideal group solidarity, but the fact that some Christ-followers continued to participate in synagogue life, in some areas at least, demonstrates the contrary. Thus though it cannot be doubted that the intensification of the language of belonging creates and sustains the organic life of a group, it

---

14. Meeks 1983: 85–90; Banks 1994: 108; see also Chapter 3.2.

15. Meeks notes that 'Socially the most striking thing about the communities revealed in the Pauline letters is that there is no visible connection or even contact between them and the synagogues... (They) were entirely independent of the synagogues', Meeks (1983: 168). See my critique of sociological understandings of sects, in Campbell (1992: 149–50).

16. Ehrensperger 2004a: 192. Also the work of Levinas e.g. 1969: 194–6.

17. Contra Stendahl's opposition of 'Unique Rather Than Universal' (1976: 67–77).

18. Zetterholm 2003: 112–28.

19. Meeks 1983: 88.

20. Tellbe 2001: 135.

needs to be questioned whether stress upon internal group solidarity *necessarily* creates an exclusivity that is alienating in relation to all other groups especially where the author of this has no sectarian intention and actually opposes such attitudes as in the case of Paul.[21]

We will now consider in more detail Paul's interaction with the situation of the Christ-followers at Rome with particular reference to Paul's interaction in relation to the formation of gentile Christ-followers' identity.

5.3. *Paul's Interaction with the Situation at Rome*

In focusing on the Roman context and those local issues addressed by Paul we will be able better to recognize the particularity of the letter to the Romans and thus guard against ever-present universalizing tendencies in its interpretation.

Of primary significance is the fact that unlike the communities referred to in his other letters, Paul had neither founded nor even visited as yet the Roman Christ-followers. He has known for some time of their faith and seems well informed about them but has not yet been able to make a long-planned visit even though Rome lies within the scope of his mission to the nations (Rom. 1.5–10). Whatever the origin of the Christ-movement in Rome it seems likely that it would not necessarily conform to the pattern of the Pauline gentile communities elsewhere. There are strong indications that at least some of the Christ-followers in Rome maintained links with the synagogue and followed a Jewish way of life.[22] Paul's gentle and cautious approach in his letter demonstrates his respect for a community he did not found and which does not necessarily follow his pattern for gentile Christ-followers (Rom. 1.12; 15.14–21). Some interpreters have anticipated that Paul would sooner or later advise Christ-followers to break their links with the synagogue in order to develop their own separate identity. There is, however, no evidence for this in the letter. We can agree that Paul did not aim '…primarily to encourage separation from the synagogue or to keep old structures unbroken but rather to keep the Roman house churches together as a community comprising both Jews and Gentiles'. However, it reads very much like special pleading when Tellbe continues that '…in order to unite them, Paul repeatedly defines what honour and shame are with reference to Jesus Christ, and not with reference to Jewish identity markers'.[23]

Confirmation that Paul is not attempting to impose a particular pattern upon the Romans is evidenced in the emphasis he lays upon 'each being fully con-

---

21. See Zetterholm's comment on *collegia* 'Normally there was little risk that they would conflict with each other: the *collegia* did not represent a sectarian way of life but rather confirmed the social order' (2003: 27).

22. The tradition reported in Ambrosiaster's commentary on Romans (ca. 375) is that 'the Romans, …without seeing any of the apostles nevertheless accepted faith in Christ, although according to a Jewish rite (*ritu licet Iudaico*)', as cited by Weddderburn (1991: 51). See also Campbell (1992: 14–16), Judge and Thomas (1966: 92). Brown and Meier (1983: 110) argue that the dominant strand of Christianity at Rome had been shaped by the Jerusalem church, was appreciative of Judaism, and loyal to its customs. For an overview see Nanos (1996: 30–40).

23. Tellbe 2001: 208.

vinced in their own mind' ἕκαστος ἐν τῷ ἰδίῳ νοὶ πληροφορείσθω) (Rom. 14.5). In a previous essay on this topic I discussed the view that Paul was dealing with a continuum of stances varying from close adherence to Jewish practice to gentile life 'apart from the Law'. I rejected, however, this scenario because it appeared to offer so many options to individual Christ-followers that Paul's statements concerning the weaker brother's danger in Rom. 14–15 were rendered meaningless. If there had been sufficient diverse groups for many differing forms of 'life in Christ' the problems between weak and strong as Paul presents them should not have arisen.[24] My conclusion is that Paul in these chapters is dealing not simply with individuals and their concern to live according to their conscience. Paul's concern is that some individuals may perish (14.15–20) because they do not fit into the limited options that differing groups offered them in Rome.[25] The significance of this for our understanding of Paul's response to the situation at Rome is that he not only recognizes the legitimacy of differing individual patterns of life but rather that he recognizes the legitimacy of differing groups of Christ-followers and their corresponding pattern of life (Rom. 15.14).[26] Although Paul does not explicitly mention the synagogue in this respect it can be readily inferred that groups retaining their affiliation were recognized along with others.[27]

This is a very significant feature of Paul's interaction with the Christ groups in Rome. If as we believe it is probable the Christ-movement at Rome developed in or around Jewish synagogues and if they prior to the time of Paul's writing had provided a source of nurture for those in the Christ-movement despite Paul's apostleship to the gentiles it would have been arrogant and unfruitful for him to advocate separation from the synagogues. It would in any case have been difficult for someone who had never visited Rome to impose what some hold to be his own solution on groups that he did not found. Faced with such a situation Paul wisely advocates that each group continue to practise their way of life in accordance with their own convictions regarding meat, special days, festivals, etc. (Rom. 14.5–13). This is nothing less than a wholehearted endorsement by Paul of Christ groups that he did not found and whose ways of life he had not determined. It was enough for him that their faith was recognized by other Christ-following communities. The demands that Paul places upon them is that they refrain from judging and that they take care of the weak (Rom. 14.22–15.3).

It could be argued that Paul had also long-term goals for his communities which meant they should grow stronger and more mature in Christ. But this tells us nothing about whether he would have preferred a uniform pattern of life in all the communities at Rome. How they would grow up in Christ Paul is content to leave open (unlike those interpreters who find it hard not to envisage an implicit agenda for separation from the synagogue). Paul seeks essentially

24. Campbell 1995: 76–86.
25. On this see also Clarke 2000: 189–91.
26. Esler 2003: 86–108.
27. Nanos 1996: 74–84.

5. The Tripartite Context

for peace in the midst of diversity for the sake of the total well-being and future of the communities.[28]

If in fact Paul had advocated separation from the synagogues he might thereby have drawn attention to the existence of the Christ-movement in a way that prevented it from any longer being protected as part of the status granted to the Jews under Roman rule.

Despite this status, the history of Jewish communities in Rome had been turbulent. During the reign of Tiberius and Claudius Jews were twice expelled from Rome in a period of some thirty years (19 and 49 CE). Even though Paul writes to the Romans almost two decades after the threat posed to Jews under Caligula, he would still have been aware that at the centre of Roman administration and the visual embodiment of the imperial ideology any group, especially a Jewish one, which appeared to challenge Roman cultural and political domination would be in great danger.[29] This risk would be greater if there had been, as appears to be, strong divisions among the house communities[30] with links to ongoing cultural differences between 'Jew and Greek'.[31] Although on a social and political level Paul apparently urges the Roman Christ-followers to submission and political quietism he nevertheless asserts divine authority over imperial power[32] and whilst affirming the political rights of the authorities he seems intentionally to redefine and challenge central concepts and values in imperial propaganda.[33] Terms such as εὐαγγέλιον, πίστις, δικαιοσύνη, εἰρήνη must have invoked allusions to Roman imperial ideology as Georgi contends.[34]

Since Paul needed a base in the Roman Christ-movement for his proposed future mission to Spain (Rom.15.23–24;32), he had a vested interest in the future peace and prosperity of the communities there. To invite the wrath of Rome on a tiny Christ-movement by strife within the communities or against the synagogue

---

28. Haacker 2003: 116–19.

29. We are mindful here of Horsley's political reading of Paul which draws attention to the fact that Paul's letters arise out of and address an imperial situation the significance of which should never be minimized. Cf. Horsley (1997: 142–5). Similarly Elliott (1995: 11–15).

30. We use the term house communities here due to the uncertainty as to whether the προσευχή were purpose buildings or merely the homes of Jewish families. The existence of a synagogue at Ostia should not determine entirely our perception of the scenario in Rome itself. For full discussion see Esler (2003: 86–108), and also Mitternacht (2003: 521–71).

31. This includes the fact that the households of Aristobulus (Rom. 16.10) and Narcissus (16.11) were probably linked to the imperial household since this Aristobulus was likely the grandson of Herod the Great and brother of Agrippa I (cf. Stowers 1994: 76–9) As Lampe notes, an analysis of Romans 16 shows that Paul greets primarily slaves and freedpersons, (2003: 182–3). Stowers says that Lampe overdraws the picture of Roman Christianity as a slave religion (1994: 340 n. 94) 'Some are also likely to have been members of the most socially mobile group in the Empire' (1994: 79). On the diversity of the names noted in Rom. 16 see most recently Judge 2005.

32. Κύριος occurs fifteen times in Romans 12–15 with reference to Christ rather than to the Emperor.

33. Georgi claims that Paul's argument in Romans, particularly the frequent reference to Christ as Lord could, when used in the seat of imperial power, had it been decoded, have led to a charge of treason (1991: 103). Cf. also Tellbe 2001: 206–8.

34. Georgi 1997: 148–57. Elliott 2005b.

or even in a refusal to pay taxes would have put both the existence of the communities and Paul's future plans in jeopardy.

To conclude that since '...the temple tax functioned as a distinctive religious and social identity marker for first century Diaspora Judaism, it is remarkable that Paul does not mention the issue when he deals with the Christian obligation to pay their taxes, in particular since his argument directly turns to conditions for fulfilling the Torah in Rom. 13.8';[35] this is building too much on an argument from silence. The primary focus of Paul's argument in Romans 13 is the relationship with the authorities in Rome not with the Temple authorities and Jewish obligations. There is no need to deny that the payment of the Temple tax was 'the best statement of Jewishness for a diaspora Jew in the pre-70 CE period'.[36] But Paul's silence in Romans concerning the payment of Temple tax by Diaspora Jews may simply indicate that a majority of the Roman Christ-followers were gentiles and it would have been surprising if he had advocated that they pay such a tax in view of his steadfast resistance to their acceptance of circumcision and other Jewish identity markers. As such the Christ-followers had no option but to pay their taxes and Paul does not want them to draw undue attention to themselves by becoming involved in public resistance to the authorities. We do not see the relevance of making a link between payment of Roman taxes and payment of the Temple tax. One possibility is that although Paul does not directly ask the Romans to participate in the collection for Jerusalem, perhaps indirectly he hoped they might be persuaded to do so.[37] This offering on their part could well be viewed as a gentile equivalent to the Temple tax indicating their awareness of their indebtedness to the Jewish roots of the gospel.[38] But it is wrong to insist that in seeking '...to resolve fiscal tensions between the Christ-movement and the Roman authorities Paul potentially creates new tensions between them and the Roman authorities by creating a self-definition whose fiscal application allowed Christians to be distinguished from Jews'.[39] Despite later accounts of the persecution of 'Christians' at Rome in 64 CE we are not convinced that at that period it was as 'Christians' *per se* (rather than as Christ-following Jews) that they were persecuted.[40] (But if there had been a recognition

---

35. Tellbe 2001: 208. We cannot agree with Tellbe's view that Paul's silence concerning the temple tax seems implicitly to affirm the autonomous religious identity of the Roman Christians vis-à-vis the Roman Jews.

36. Cohen 1993: 35 n. 141.

37. Jervell contends that the safe delivery of the collection has as much reason to be regarded as the occasion for the writing of Romans as the proposed visit to Rome and Spain (1971: 66).

38. Georgi sees Paul's collection as having a symbolic significance which the aid envisaged by the Jerusalem agreement did not. Georgi suggests that it was a sign to Israel (1965: 84–6). Similarly see Wedderburn (1988: 37–40; 70–3; 80–2; 141–2). Wedderburn considers it noteworthy that Paul's plans for the collection did not involve the Antioch church but only those churches he had founded (39).This might be related to the territorial dimension of the missions of the apostles. See Chapter 3.3 above.

39. Tellbe 2001: 209.

40. Contra Walters 1993.

that the riots instigated by 'Crestos' in 49 CE were Messianic in nature this might explain why certain Jews were persecuted a decade or so later).[41]

Far from escalating the process of self-definition and precipitating the final separation between the synagogues and the house churches, Paul's theology in Romans is designed to have the opposite effect. By allowing groups of Christ-followers to continue to differ in practice and by maintaining the rights of the weak in particular Paul's primary aim is shown to be the immediate and long-term welfare of the Christ groups in Rome. There is nothing clearer from Romans 11 than that Paul is entirely in opposition to a gentile Christ-movement that prides itself on its independence of Israel. A process of self-definition was doubtless ongoing in the Christ-movement at Rome but the image of the olive tree which Paul sets forth in Rom. 11.17–24 as a model takes full account both of the nature of the commonality and diversity that then existed in the Christ communities at Rome. The groups may differ but they are branches of a common tree and should not boast over their differences from one another. Paul's strategy in dealing with the Roman Christ-following groups is to seek to build them up in their own self-understanding in Christ in such a manner as to promote harmony within the communities, and the avoidance of strife with the Roman authorities through their continued submission.[42]

5.4. *The Function of the Pauline Legacy in the Formation of Christian Identities in Antioch*

If, as we have maintained, Paul himself was neither the originator of division, nor the advocate of separation from the synagogue, an explanation is required not only as to why subsequent separation emerged as and when it did, but especially why the name and activity of Paul is usually associated with it. It is with the latter that we are chiefly concerned since we are seeking to clarify the role of Paul in the creation of Christian identity.

It was in Antioch that the name 'Christian' originated and it was in this city that differentiation in identity for gentiles-in-Christ first became meaningful. What is important for us is to ascertain as far as is possible to what extent Paul and his legacy contributed to the eventual differentiation and subsequent separation between groups of Christ-following Jews and gentiles in this city. Tellbe claims that the designation Χριστιανός shows that the difference between Jews and 'Christians' (or alternately of Christians as a distinctive Jewish faction) was publicly known in Eastern parts of the empire already in the beginning of the 40s CE because Christ and 'Christians' in non-Christian first century sources are constantly associated with public disorder and crimes.[43] Zetterholm is not convinced by this very early date and points out 'that Christianity eventually became a non-Jewish, separate religion does not mean that this separation has already

41. Nanos 1996: 372–87.
42. Cf. I.E. Rock forthcoming 2007.
43. Tellbe 2001: 65–6.

taken place by the first time we hear the term "Christian". The sources actually indicate the opposite.'[44]

Relations between Jews and gentiles in Antioch had often been strained in the period since the Maccabean revolt.[45] The relative proximity to Judea and the fact that Antioch was a leading hellenistic city with a provincial administration were factors in creating animosity towards Jews, especially since Jonathan the Hasmonean ruler got involved in supporting Demetrios in sending 3000 soldiers to maintain order in Antioch. The resulting deaths of many of the inhabitants at the hands of these soldiers and the plundering of the city by them probably 'influenced the formation of a generally negative attitude towards Jews'.[46] The large Jewish population enjoyed special privileges and influence in the city, but in times of conflict these privileges were sometimes revoked, though usually subsequently reinstated. Attitudes reflecting animosity to Jews are well illustrated in Titus' visit to Antioch en route for Egypt after having captured Jerusalem. Twice the people of Antioch approached Titus with the request to expel the Jews from the city but their requests were ignored.

It is in this conflictual context that the 'Antioch incident' involving Peter and Paul is to be viewed. It is also not entirely surprising that in a later post-Pauline period the Pauline legacy is reappropriated in a conflict between Jew and gentile at the time of Ignatius.

Our interest at this point is not in this 'Incident' as such, but only in as much as it is a part of troubled relations between Jews and gentiles at Antioch. We have already maintained that this 'Incident' is much too early for the explicit formulation of a stark opposition between living 'in Christ' or 'in accordance with the law'.[47] We have also argued that the differences between the apostles were not primarily theological but halakhic. Recently Zetterholm has argued that the conflict at Antioch ultimately concerned different ideas of how the gentile nations would be embraced by the eschatological salvation of the God of Israel.[48] For the purpose of this discussion, we will work with the scenario he presents in which he concludes, 'Using his authority as the brother of Jesus, James demanded a separation of the community into two commensality groups, one for Jews, the other for gentiles, since too close social intercourse would have confused the boundaries between Jews and gentiles.'[49]

It is important to recognize that the probable outcome of the Antioch dispute in two separate Christ-following groups was by no means the result of purely

---

44. Zetterholm claims that none of the texts referred to by Tellbe can be used to indicate that the designation 'Χριστιανός' in Acts was given by the civic authorities at the beginning of the 40s as a result of association with public disorder. Tacitus' text indicates that 'Christians' in Rome in the 60s were associated with Jews (2003: 95). On the origin of the designation, if it is a fact that it was in use as early as the 40s, then 'it is possible that we have here an intra-Jewish designation for a Jewish Messianic synagogue in Antioch' (2003: 96).

45. Zetterholm 2003: 113–21.

46. Zetterholm 2003: 23.

47. On this see Chapter 3.3–3.4 above.

48. Zetterholm 2003: 163.

49. Zetterholm 2003: 166.

theological or even halakhic factors. As noted above, there had been a long history of poor relations between Jews and gentiles in this city and there were enough significant ongoing issues to reactivate and perpetuate the conflicts. These conflicts had a strong political dimension in which both Roman imperial policy as well as local provincial administration were involved. The fact that the large Jewish population enjoyed special privilege and influence, even if intermittent, meant that ethnic and cultural issues were a continuous source for potential conflict. Close interaction between groups with a history of mutual animosity within an unstable political environment is always difficult. But whenever there emerged a perceived crossing of traditional group boundaries, as in the early Christ-movement, disputes such as the 'Antioch incident' were almost inevitable and always bitter.

It is not surprising then as we believe that Paul probably lost the argument at Antioch. But this means that the outcome in two separate Christ communities and their subsequent history cannot be attributed to the Pauline gospel and his missionary policy. If he had been able to have his way one strong community encompassing people of diverse identities would have been the result. But as we have seen a multiplicity of factors rendered this outcome unlikely.

One outcome was that Ignatius some decades later seems to provide evidence that the distinction between Jew and Christian apparently is already assumed to exist in Antioch. His assertion that 'It is monstrous to speak of Jesus Christ and to practise Judaism' (*Magnesians* 10.3) witnesses to Ignatius's desire for clear-cut boundaries but is simultaneously evidence that these did not yet exist unambiguously in Antioch otherwise his complaint would have been purely theoretical.[50]

Thus, if Ignatius at a later period in the same city arrives at an anti-Jewish self-understanding this is no evidence that Paul should be credited with this. He was neither the founder of the community nor the instigator of its division. The latter is to a great extent the result of social and political factors, both at the time of Paul and in the intervening decades. If the Antioch community did split and separate the immediate results of the division would have left the gentile Christ-followers weakened in social influence and politically in a vulnerable situation since they would then be unable to claim the legal privileges of assembly enjoyed by the Jews. This possibly would eventually lead to an identity crisis.[51] They had been forced into a situation where association with Jews was no longer feasible and they were thus faced with the task of creating a new independent self-understanding. Previously they had been part of a larger community in which identity 'in Christ' had a basic Jewish orientation even for gentiles. No doubt for such a community Paul's gospel for gentiles would have been a significant resource. Zetterholm suggests that both Christ-following communities in Antioch used Christ traditions, e.g. the Gospel of Matthew, to help formulate their respective identities. In his longitudinal study of the Christ

50. On this see Bockmuehl 2000: 57 n. 32.
51. 'The outcome of the incident in Antioch had resulted in the separation of the community into two commensality groups and the status of the Jesus-believing gentiles had been reduced to that of God-fearers' (Zetterholm 2003: 223).

communities at Antioch he claims that whether or not the Gospel of Matthew originated in Antioch, it is a historical fact that Ignatius not only knew but also used it in some form in the situation in which he lived. Zetterholm claims that there is general agreement that the Gospel of Matthew represents a church in transition '…from a predominantly Jewish Christian church to an increasingly gentile church'.[52] His thesis includes the view that '…the presence of the Jewish Gospel of Matthew in the hands of the gentile non-Jewish and even anti-Jewish community of Ignatius in some way represents the culmination of the process of transition from a Jewish to a gentile setting'.[53] Of particular interest in the discussion here is how the text of the Gospel of Matthew could have functioned '…as a cultural resource in the social conflict between the community of Ignatius and the Jesus-believing Jews'.[54] Zetterholm concludes that '…the Gospel of Matthew could serve the purpose of both creating group solidarity and legitimating the interpretative authority of the bishop'.[55]

Thus it is evident that this Gospel, despite its Jewish orientation, could be used as an instrument in the process of mobilizing resources both inwards (creating a group with a shared identity and characterized by solidarity) and outwards (in the conflict with the Christ-following Jewish community).[56] Since Christ-following gentiles probably used the same Gospel after a radical break as they had used before, this would explain how Ignatius' community came to be in possession of it.[57] Thus Ignatius claims not only the Gospel of Matthew and the scriptures but also the authority to give the correct interpretation of these. This represents no less than an appropriation of Jewish traditions on the grounds that they had misunderstood their own scriptures and thus had lost the right to them. Ignatius' exhortation not to be led astray by doctrines and fables can be read as a warning against Jewish interpretation of the scriptures. 'The ideological message is clear: the Jews do not understand what their sacred texts are really about.'[58]

> What we find in the conflict with the Jews and in the 'Christianization' of Jewish traditions is *the mobilization of ideological resources to be used in the struggle for a position in the polity*. The Jesus-believing gentile movement had been forced voluntarily to place itself outside the polity – this was as a result of the separation from the Jesus-believing Jewish community: now was the time for the struggle for a position in the polity – but now on their own terms.[59]

It would appear that Ignatius' community now sought for recognition as a (non-Jewish) collegium which nevertheless claimed the heritage of antiquity which the Jews no longer could understand.

Zetterholm concludes that 'Probably during the reign of Domitian, there emerged in the Jesus-believing gentile community a leadership that formulated

52. Zetterholm (2003: 211) citing Senior (1996: 19).
53. Zetterholm 2003: 212.
54. Zetterholm 2003: 212.
55. Zetterholm 2003: 213.
56. Zetterholm 2003: 215.
57. Zetterholm 2003: 215.
58. Zetterholm 2003: 220.
59. Zetterholm 2003: 221.

a separate theological programme, presumably based on a one-sided understanding of Pauline ideology about Jews, the covenant, the torah, and the eschatological destiny of the Jewish people.'[60] Although generally supportive of this reading, we would stress the fact that when Paul came eventually to be used as a weapon in the struggle to separate from Judaism, the use of him is recognized as one-sided. It is only when Paul is misused and misrepresented in ideologies that often have their origin in political and cultural factors rather than in his theology that he can become an instrument in promoting or facilitating an anti-Jewish identity for gentile Christ-followers. But it is illuminating to note that already with Ignatius, the apostle and his writings are used (and misused) in the service of providing a desired identity, and that not necessarily in keeping with the apostle's pattern.[61]

5.5 The Significance of the Tripartite Context for the Formation of Christian Identity

To study such issues is exceedingly valuable in that by stressing the tripartite involvement of synagogues, Paul and his communities and the state, we are enabled to reconsider the actual dynamics of the situation in which Paul had to operate. This causes us to acknowledge the limited options available to Paul in each context and offers a more realistic assessment of how much or how little of what eventually emerged is directly attributable to apostolic effort and influence.

Secondly, the tripartite emphasis assists in diminishing the image of Christian origins and development as being constituted by an endless conflict between Paul and Jerusalem or Jewish 'Christians'. We should now recognize more clearly how both Jews and Christ-followers were subject to the overriding power of imperial Rome and all that that involved for each of them separately as well as in their relations with each other.

Thirdly, the effect of imperial policies and power upon both 'Christian' and Jewish communities is shown to have been much more significant in its influence upon the eventual formation of gentile 'Christian' identity than might otherwise have been realized. This should result in less emphasis being put upon gentile 'Christian' identity as being formulated in reaction to Judaism, which tends to give it a permanent anti-Jewish element of a sectarian character,[62] and more emphasis being put upon it as the outcome of a number of varying historical factors and processes, some beneficial, some detrimental to its mission.

---

60. Zetterholm 2003: 223.

61. Despite this acknowledgement we wish to stress that whatever the precise outcome of the 'Antioch incident' and whether a separation took place even as early as 70 CE, 'this certainly did not mean the once-for-all isolation of the Judeo-Christians from gentile Christians nor of Jews from Christians. The active influence of Judaism upon Christianity in Antioch was perennial until Christian leaders succeeded at last in driving the Jews from the city in the 7th century'. Bockmuehl 2000: 57 n. 32.

62. As e.g in the equation Christian *versus* Jewish Identity of Holmberg (1998). Käsemann's laudable efforts to relate righteousness to the whole of creation also had the effect of leaving Israel at the periphery of the divine purpose (1980: 79).

Fourthly, since on this scenario historical factors played a dominant role, we can now be much more critical about the course of Christian development and doctrine since we can no longer view it as being exactly what either Jesus or Paul might have planned or even envisaged. The nature and character of Christian identity needs also to be subject to this analysis and criticism, otherwise we are at risk of assuming that what happened was entirely in accordance with divine intention, in other words 'what is is best' or that we live in 'the best of all possible worlds'. The conflicts which surrounded the birth of Christianity were by no means neutral or negligible in their effects. 'The blood of martyrs' may be 'the seed of the church' but persecution also leaves its mark in other ways, sometimes contributing to a Christian imperialism and a corresponding disregard for minorities or to a hardening of attitudes to the other who was and who remains 'different', whether Jew or Muslim, humanist or atheist.

5.6. Conclusion

To conclude I wish to emphasize that in discussing conflicts in Christian origins we are inevitably dealing with Christianity's relation to Judaism including value judgements concerning old and new. This means that we must not presume that when Paul in a particular context reinforced or sharpened a specific 'Christian' identity, he had in mind eventual separation from Judaism rather than simply the building up of the communal life of his community against whatever adversity and whatever its source it might yet have to face. Whether it was unsympathetic Jews or Greeks alongside and against whom Paul defines gentile believers, his primary interest is not in them or even against them. As Wayne Meeks has noted, 'Sociologically, outsiders are often a negative reference group, yet the Pauline stance is not simply counter-cultural...however dualistically Paul can somehow portray "this world", it remains the creation of God that "groans in travail" for the liberation...in which the hopes and efforts and the inner life of the Christian groups are implicated.'[63]

Moreover, Paul's intense up-building of his mainly gentile communities is not designed to make them less Jewish or to prepare them for eventual independence. The recognition and acceptance of diversity by Paul takes place in a period when such a final, complete separation was not yet really envisaged as a valid historical possibility. As we have shown, the diversity of situations in each local context often determined the relations between the Pauline communities and all other groups in the Roman Empire. In this situation, Paul operates as a flexible pragmatist under the control of the gospel, rather than as an ideologist seeking conformity to some universal concept. He does not see it as his duty to make the church more or less gentile or Jewish,[64] but rather by any acceptable means to

---

63. Meeks 1991: 305-17 (317).
64. This is not to overlook the important insight of Elliott that the Roman gentile-Christian ideology of supersession which denies the value of Jewish identity was linked to prevalent Roman views of the Jews as a subject people which Paul certainly opposed (2000: 35).

enable both Jew and gentile within their given ethnic and social situation to give glory to God through Jesus Christ.

Paul's peculiar problem, the creation of gentile identity in Christ was not solved by his life or even by his death. This issue continued to disturb relations between Jews, Jewish and gentile Christ-followers for the next century or more. It became more difficult to solve in a Pauline manner, the more distant the knowledge of Paul and his letters actually became.

Chapter 6

'I LAID THE FOUNDATION':
PAUL THE ARCHITECT OF CHRISTIAN IDENTITY?

In reaction to Apollos' apparent interference in the life of the Corinthian community Paul reminds the Corinthians that he is the founder or planter of the church in that place. As such he retains an indisputable status in relation to his converts. He pointedly reminds them, 'For I became your father in Christ through the gospel' (1 Cor. 4.15). If Paul has successfully established a new community in Christ then subsequent developments must be consistent with the contours of that initial design; as Paul asserts, 'Let each man take care how he builds upon it' (1 Cor. 3.10).This need not imply that Paul was so controlling that he would allow no freedom in the life of the developing community or that he wanted them slavishly to follow his example.[1] Nor does it appear that he resisted the visits and influence of other evangelists. He accepts that others will influence his converts – the Corinthians may have 'countless guides in Christ' (1 Cor. 4.15), though he alone is their father. These apparently were not a problem, so long as what they were proclaiming was in accordance with the way of Christ for gentiles, and in accordance with agreements about their particular territorial assignments (2 Cor. 10.13–16). In another context, however, Paul claims his own policy was that he actually refused to 'build on another man's foundation' (Rom. 15.20). In Corinth, whether it was Apollos' message itself or the Corinthians' (mis-)understanding of it is unclear, but in either case Paul felt that this was having a negative influence upon the life of the Corinthian community, hence his application of the architectural image.[2] In Christian history, however, Paul is perceived as more than the architect of this particular community. He is perceived rather as the architect of Christianity itself.

Whether Paul actually perceived the church as anything like what it was eventually to become is very unclear. He had no precise blueprint of the edifice he was constructing. We say no precise blueprint, but that does not mean that he was tentative or confused.[3] Quite the contrary. As noted in the previous chapter, Paul was consciously creating and developing new communities of Christ-followers with a very strong solidarity and sense of belonging. As we will argue

    1. On this see Ehrensperger 2003: 247 contra Castelli 1991: 32. Cf. also Bartchy 2005: 60.
    2. On the church in Corinth, see the recent volume of essays, edited by E. Adams and D.G. Horrell 2004.
    3. We will argue later that the future for Paul was open-ended. On this see Chapter 10.5. But he did have his strong convictions within an Israel-centred symbolic universe.

in more detail later, although they were to some extent socially distinct, these communities were not perceived by Paul as self-standing independent entities, but as groups loosely related to Israel. 'All the churches of the gentile nations' (Rom. 16.4) is how they are usually described, and although 'people of God' might have offered Paul the title he needed, for various reasons, this was not his preferred option.

The reasons for regarding Paul as the architect of the whole church are several. Firstly, *Paul is credited with being the architect of gentile inclusion in Christ.* Although it is likely that he was by no means the first to preach the gospel to gentiles, there is no debate that he was the theologian who justified their inclusion. He provided the rationale for a church of Jews and gentiles, and that unquestionably based on being in Christ.

Secondly, *it was Paul also who fought continuously for the inclusion of gentiles on equal terms with Jews* and resisted all attempts to treat them as proselytes or potential Jews. Gentile Christ-followers are equal with Jewish, all are heirs of Abraham, and are one in and through Christ.

Thirdly, *the Antioch incident is perceived as Paul's triumph over Jewish influence in the church.* It is in fact as the champion of gentiles that Paul is most revered in Christian tradition.

In the vicissitudes of the first centuries of the history of the church, Jewish Christianity became less significant and, with the recognition of the church in the Roman Empire, to all intents and purposes, the church became a gentile church. This seemed to signify the triumph of Paul's foundational design and original intention. But what we wish to maintain is that this represented in fact a universalizing of one particular form of Christian faith as the norm for all. If Paul were to return to gaze at this edifice of gentile Christianity today would he be satisfied with the outcome or would he caution again as he did to Apollos and the Corinthians, 'every man take heed how he builds'? Is the church building that materialized in history really what Paul intended, and was he in fact responsible for it?

6.1 *Paul's Own Self-Understanding and Identity*

The focal points for any discussion of Paul's understanding of his identity are that his own mission lists Jerusalem as its starting point (Rom. 15.19), that he received from the Lord what he delivered to the Corinthians and others, and that he 'was set apart' to a prophetic vocation before he was born and called to preach Christ among the gentiles, going up to Jerusalem to meet the apostolic leaders there on at least two later occasions (Gal. 1–2). For Paul, Jesus is Jesus the Christ, the Messiah of Israel[4] (Rom. 9.4, 2 Cor. 1.5). The fact that he was called to work among gentiles was due neither to his own preference nor experience, though both of these may have some relevance. In his own self-understanding, he identifies himself as a 'Hebrew of Hebrews', as an Israelite (Rom. 11.1, 2 Cor. 11.22),

---

4. On the political implications of this conviction see N.T. Wright (2000: 166–7) and 1991 chs. 2–3.

willing to be cast off from God for the sake of his kinsmen (Rom. 9.1–5). He can refer to himself (and Peter) as a Jew by nature, and not a gentile sinner (Gal. 2.14).

However, Paul's encounter with Christ had meant a complete rethinking of his previous value system: compared with being found in Christ, all previous potential grounds for boasting are now regarded as dung (Phil. 3.4–8). There is general scholarly agreement that this new perspective 'radically relativizes' everything for Paul, and that this is the key to all his subsequent thought and action. But without in any way diminishing the significance of Paul's Damascus road experience, we must be careful that we do not claim more than Paul's own evidence allows or suggests. It is clear that the encounter with Christ would not obliterate all social and historical categories despite Paul finding therein a new self-understanding.[5] A transformed identity in Christ is not one entirely in antithesis to everything one previously adhered to, particularly since, in Paul's case, this was Judaism. Paul did not set his understanding of the power and grace of God specifically in contrast to his own former life. Barclay, however, argues that Paul's 'role as apostle to the gentiles presupposes that his theological categories have been changed at the most fundamental level. Being called by God is not just a "vocation" but involves "a complete reconception of the self".'[6]

According to this perception, Paul is regarded as the ideal paradigm of the 'new man' in Christ. His past history in Judaism is negated and a complete new identity is supplied in Christ. The effect of this conception of Paul is that it enables him to be the paradigm of all Christ-followers whether Jew or gentile. Previous socialization and cultural identity are obliterated. Paul's experience of Christ is thus universalized to provide the template for one undifferentiated identity in Christ.

This has a corresponding outcome in the view that Paul consciously designed the church as a new creation where, in parallel to his own experience of life in Christ, old things that formerly had great value and significance no longer counted. In this church ethnicity has disappeared – there is no longer Jew nor gentile. Nothing is clean or unclean, and the slave-free, male-female distinctions are annulled, because the law itself has been *annulled* in Christ. In such a church, a Jewish way of life with all that went with it is prohibited because these things are no longer valid. There is one *universal* church, one and the *same* way of life for all its members, and particular circumstances or history are of no relevance. And, of course, in this view of the church, there can be only one form of Christian identity for all are *one* in Christ. Thus, it follows that a Jewish identity is *necessarily antithetical* to a Christian identity.

But it must be recognized that this is only one reading of the significance of becoming new persons in Christ, despite its widespread acceptance as normative Paulinism. If, alternatively, we utilize a model of transformation in Christ rather than of 'new creation' it does not follow that to be in Christ involves 'a complete reconception of the self'.

---

5. Contra Barclay 2002: 133–56 (139–40).
6. Cf. Barclay 2002: 149.

David G. Horrell suggests that 'the fundamental story of God's gracious dealings with humanity reach their zenith in the Christ-event, itself the generative centre of this story, which then provides the paradigmatic story with which Paul shapes his telling of any other stories, including those about himself'.[7] This reading suggests a reconfiguration of the history and identity of those in Christ rather than simply the obliteration of their past. In the case of Paul this would involve a re-evaluation of himself in the context of his Jewish heritage. This would consist of a transformation of a person and their self-understanding rather than the creation of a totally new person with a new identity. Thus Paul, as transformed in Christ, can still call himself an Israelite. In this respect Paul is the paradigm only for those whose former life was in Judaism rather than for gentile Christ-followers. Despite the fact of all Christ-followers sharing in the experience of being transformed in Christ, and sharing this aspect of their identities, in other significant respects they were and do remain different. This is not to suggest that the experience of Christ as Lord does not influence every part of their existence but rather that everything is relativized by being in Christ.

6.2 *The Relativization of all Things in Christ*

What is being expressed in this assertion is that the only ultimate value for Paul and other believers is Christ and his coming kingdom. All else has only relative significance.[8] We need, however, to be aware of the complexities of our modern English vocabulary which has diverse ways of describing and interpreting transformation in Christ. We can, for example, express the change in Paul's self-understanding in this way – for him the law, ethnicity and all other human distinctions can never again be regarded as *absolute*. This means in effect that they can and must be regarded very differently from previously. A major change in their status has been effected, they have been *annulled* in Christ. It can thus be claimed that these categories, regulations, demands, have now all been *transcended*.[9] This is because for Paul circumcision or uncircumcision are 'nothing'. According to Anthony C. Thiselton, 'in the terminology of Pauline studies new creation terminology affirms an eschatological status for believers on the basis of which issues of circumcision and "Jewishness" have become obsolete'. However, although these things have now been rendered *obsolete* '...they are not *abrogated* wholesale'(emphasis mine).[10] In the expressions of other NT voices such as Matthew, it can be claimed that the promises have been *fulfilled*,[11] and that

---

7. Horrell 2002: 157–71 (168). Similarly, Ricoeur, 'I see in the plots we invent the privileged means by which we reconfigure our confused, unformed and, at the limit, mute temporal experience' (1984: ix–x).

8. According to Boyarin, Paul's adiaphorization of circumcision/works of law amounts precisely to the *erasure* of the difference between Jew and Greek (1994: 156). We disagree with Boyarin, and argue that Paul was by no means indifferent to his Jewish heritage hence our preference for the term 'relativization', contra Deming 2005: 394–6.

9. As e.g. D.G. Horrell 2000: 320–44 (338).

10. A.C. Thiselton 2000: 550–2.

11. The most frequent use of fulfilment terminology (πληροῦν) in relation to scriptural texts is

therefore new options for all are now available. Paul does not tend to use this vocabulary in relation to promises or scriptural texts, but rather in relation to the law being fulfilled in believers (Rom. 8.4), or by believers loving their neighbour (Rom. 13.8, cf. Gal. 5.14). In Paul's own terms, the more precise description of promises from the past impacting on the present is indicated in the verb βεβαιῶσαι, to *confirm* (Rom. 15.7 but cf. also Rom. 4.16 and 2 Cor.1.21) which does not necessarily imply the same negative view of the past.[12] In personal terms, this more positive image of continuity would appear to negate extreme claims that imply a total demolition and reconstitution of the self.[13] We now need to look more carefully at some examples of Paul's statements on the significance of the new status of believers in Christ and what this entails, particularly in terms of behaviour and way of life.

It might be claimed that in this vocabulary of transformation or relativization of the past, we come face to face with what some scholars regard as Paul's understanding of the church as a new creation, in the sense of Rev. 21.5, 'Behold I make all things new'. As J.M. Barclay says,

> Paul makes it as clear as possible that he no longer regards himself as living within 'Judaism'. But this is not because he has entered some other cultural medium, with its own rules of human tradition, but because he now sees with utterly different eyes, from a perspective that radically *relativizes, if it does not wholly obliterate*, all social and historical categories (emphasis mine).[14]

Paul's foundational design would thus appear to justify a universal church, rising above the particularities of Jew/gentile, race and gender as well as local or particular situations and circumstances. But we need to pause and ask whether in the light of Paul's own statements this really does constitute Paul's vision for the *ideal church*? Is this not rather an *idealist interpretation of Paul's view of the church*?

If we look in more detail at, for example, Thiselton's excellent commentary on I Corinthians, the issue becomes clearer. Despite his use of such words as 'obsolete' or 'abrogated', he quickly returns to speak of 'Paul's paradox'.

> In this sense, Paul's paradox offers both an explicit affirmation of the salvific aspect of eschatological belief at Corinth: yes, the Corinthian believers are part of God's new creation in which former distinctions are placed within a new frame and relativized. *But no, this does not mean an eschatological perfectionism in which commands and constraints no longer apply, for the church is still en route to becoming what God has made it to be as the new creation*[15] (emphasis mine).

So according to Thiselton, Paul is apparently saying two things at once – the church *already is* but also is *not yet* living in and by the new creation, a very

---

found in Matthew's Gospel, which seems to have provided the normal nomenclature for Christian understanding of the relation of the New Testament to the Old Testament.

12. By this we mean that if the promises to the fathers are *confirmed*, this gives more substance to these in themselves, whereas *fulfilment* implies more provisionality. Contra Dunn 1998, who speaks of 'Israel fulfilled in Christ' (725). See Chapter 10.5.

13. Cf. Horrell's critique of Barclay in this respect (2002: 157–71 [157–59]).

14. Barclay 2002: 139–40.

15. Thiselton 2000: 551–2.

difficult stance in view of the perfectionist tendencies apparent in the Corinthian Christians. And because Paul is saying two things at once, commentators very rapidly divide as to which one most needs to be emphasized – the already, giving an over-realized eschatology – or a not yet, giving a more futuristic eschatology, and it is tempting to choose the option that suits one's preference or argument.

It is easier to be more idealistic if one desires merely a convincing set of theological concepts or coherent ideas. On this level, the 'already' makes for a distinct and appealing argument especially for those Christian commentators who wish to strongly emphasize the difference that being in Christ actually makes. After all, the ultimate reality is the fact of the dawning new creation and our participation therein, since this world with its social systems and patterns is beginning to pass away (1 Cor. 7.31). We note though that Paul does not here (in 1 Cor. 7 but cf.also 2 Cor. 5.17) use explicit 'new creation' terminology as he does in Gal. 6.15; in both instances we have the same formulaic assertion that neither circumcision counts for anything, nor uncircumcision, but in 1 Corinthians, instead of 'new creation', he stresses 'keeping the commandments of God' (1 Cor. 7.19). Should circumcision (for Jews) be considered as included in these? The fact that there is no uniform emphasis on 'radical newness' in two passages, both offering an apparently similar relativization of circumcision suggests that we must be careful in assuming some generalized concept of newness as always and everywhere operative in Paul's letters.

This is borne out by the guidance Paul gives in 1 Cor. 7.17–24. Instead of ignoring situation and circumstance, what may be termed one's social locatedness, Paul surprisingly asserts, 'Each person should remain in the situation in which she or he was when God called them' and this after a previous statement, 'If anyone was circumcised already when he was called to faith, let him not cover over his circumcision. If anyone was uncircumcised at the time of his call, he should not be circumcised' (1 Cor. 7.18, 20). And lest there should be any doubt, Paul repeats his exhortation in almost identical wording in v. 24.

Thus despite the relativization of everything in Christ, the situation (the point of receipt of call – κλῆσις) in which one received the call to faith has a specific significance in Paul's ethics. This remains a vital factor in determining future conduct even in issues as significant as whether or not to accept or reject circumcision. One's situation may not be the decisive factor, but it is still significant. So circumcision or lack of it still plays a role in the ethical decisions of those in Christ. Horrell says that there is no need to remove the marks of circumcision simply because for Paul circumcision or lack of it are truly nothing (οὐδέν). But what does Paul mean by 'nothing' or of no account? Is it absolutely or only *comparatively* nothing?[16] As Thiselton states,

> In one sense, the new eschatological reality of the gospel abolishes 'human' categorization; but in a deeper and more realistic sense, it relativizes and redefines them. The logic of eschatological perfectionism (to use Schrage's term) would abolish

---

16. Horrell 2002: 338. Whilst Horrell agrees that Jews need not remove the signs of circumcision and that gentiles should not be circumcised, the reason for this is simply that circumcision and uncircumcision are nothing.

physical intimacy and prior mutual obligations concerning race, status, and gender. Paul's difficult pastoral task is to show in what sense this is true and in what sense it is false.[17]

So even if, as some would hold, ethnic issues – Jew or gentile – are not quite so pressing in Corinth as sexual matters, our discussion thus far confirms that for Pauline ethics, circumstances form part of the criteria for ethical decision in Christ.[18] Whether we see Paul's ethic as leaning towards the rule to 'Remain as you were' (Fee) or conversely towards 'Eschatological freedom' (Conzelmann), the particularity of one's situation is crucial.[19] Whatever eschatological freedom Christ-followers may enjoy, this freedom is limited by one's situational starting point when called to faith, which Barth terms, 'the whole of the particularity, limitation and restriction in which every man meets the divine call and command'.[20] So if wives remain wives and slaves remain, temporarily at least, slaves even in Christ, one's status at the call to faith has abiding significance, it is certainly not *obsolete,* and cannot adequately be described as such without encouraging some of the very problems, emanating from an over-realized eschatology, which Paul was seeking to overcome in Corinth. The fact that Paul uses call/ 'κλῆσις' for the point of receipt of the call to faith indicates that he is in fact giving a Christological significance to the human status and condition at this crucial juncture. Those who are called must take into account and respect where they and others were when they were called. Thus although circumcision and uncircumcision are 'nothing', this means only that one's standing at the receipt of Christ's call is relativized, not removed or obliterated. Wives remain wives and circumcised remain circumcised also even though both are in Christ. The force of Paul's theologizing must not be overlooked. Calling takes place at a particular time and place and that status remains a given, an essential component of one's ongoing identity in Christ, subject only to the Lordship of Christ.

If this factor is considered in association with the stress on the particularity of each Pauline letter, viewing the address and the statements in each letter as applying in the first instance to those precisely addressed, then *particularity rather than universality* becomes the mark of Paul's ethical guidance. Thus his churches are not governed by universal generalized principles despite the fact that there are patterns that apply in all the churches of the gentiles (1 Cor. 7.17). So whilst, eschatologically, there is no longer Jew or Greek, this does not mean that these are not abiding realities in ethical matters in the everyday life of the churches. Thus Dale Martin, dealing with the issue of slavery in 1 Corinthians concludes,

---

17. 2000: 547.
18. As in Gal. 3.28, Paul works not only with the issues of gender, sex, marriage and celibacy but also with the parallel 'pairs' of Jew and gentile, slave and free. Following the emphasis of D.R. Cartlidge 1975: 220–34, Thiselton claims, 'Paul does not want the addressees who may have a lack of realism and unhelpful priorities in the first area to fail to notice how the same stance would impinge on the other two related categories', 2000: 544.
19. The main exponents of each of these stances are fully documented by Thiselton 2000: 544–66.
20. Barth 1951: 669–70.

Paul does not here destroy the divisions between persons of different statuses. He first redefines the arena for status by taking it out of normal discourse and placing it within the symbolic world of the household of Christ, then reversing the status giving higher status within the household to those who held lower status outside the household.[21]

We need to be more careful in Pauline studies in our use of words such as 'obsolete' or 'abrogated' especially in ethical contexts. This world may be passing away but even if it is, the whole of one's Christian calling has to be lived within it. We may, like the Corinthians, desire life on a higher plane, but rising to an idealist philosophy beyond the particularities of time and place is no solution. Thus whilst theologically, ethnic, gender and sexual issues are *relativized* by the call of Christ, they are neither *obsolete* nor *irrelevant* when it comes to real life situations, as liberation theology and other contextual theologies have long since stressed. As Thiselton himself notes, 'To *remain* Jewish or non-Jewish does not spring from general indifference, but from its *salvific* irrelevance. As in the case of gender, such distinctions are not abrogated wholesale... The new creation *transforms* and *relativizes* such distinctions, but they have a place'.[22] Our concern is to show that this place is much more significant than is often noted.

6.3 *Ethnicity and Paul's Construction of Identity in Christ*

So what does Paul mean when he insists that neither circumcision nor uncircumcision counts for anything but only keeping the commandments of God. We have already asserted that it is significant that in the similar passage on circumcision in Gal. 6.15 (cf. also Gal. 5.6), Paul stresses that what is important is 'a new creation'. But to the Corinthians with an over-realized eschatology, he stresses 'keeping the commandments of God'. Moreover, Paul does not make a separate statement saying simply 'circumcision or uncircumcision are of no account' as might be assumed if we split the two parts of Paul's single sentence in 1 Cor. 7.19. Rather, there is a strong element of comparison involved which functions to bring out the relative significance of the differing items noted. Some things now matter relatively little whereas others are of paramount importance. Whatever Paul meant by 'the commandments of God', at a minimum, even for those in Christ, this must include keeping at least some of the commandments of Judaism. The commandments do count for something since they still have a paraenetic function for Christ-followers.[23] Paul therefore does not make a bland, blanket statement that can be interpreted to mean that 'Jewish identity is of no account', or of no relevance whatsoever after one's initial call.

He certainly cannot mean therefore that 'Jewish identity' has become obsolete for Christ-followers. If Jewish identity raises ethical issues, then ethically it is far from obsolete as Paul, in the very different context of Romans 14–15, clearly

---

21. Martin 1990: 66.
22. Thiselton 2000: 550–1. Cf. Deming 2003: 394–7.
23. On this see M.N.A. Bockmuehl, 1995: 72–101 (98). Cf. also P.J. Tomson 1990: 281 and 1996: 251–70. Also Bockmuehl 2003 and Rosner 1994.

demonstrates. Recently, the ethical significance of Paul's counsel in this part of the letter has become more widely recognized as a coherent and inalienable element in the letter.[24] Paul, whilst heavily emphasizing that nothing is clean or unclean as such, nevertheless counsels the strong to give way to the convictions of the weak in not pleasing themselves – in accordance with the example of Christ (Rom. 15.1). Instead of being informed or governed by some other general universal principle, groups of believers are to be 'fully convinced in their own minds' (14.5) because otherwise if one is forced to do what one's convictions prohibit, one is led into sinning, since 'whatever is not of faith is sin' (Rom. 14.23). The respect advocated for the convictions of the other who differs in various respects should not be viewed in a purely individualistic manner as if Paul intended to allow infinite diversity of lifestyle among the Christ-followers. This might suggest that what is at issue is purely a matter of individual taste. This is far from being the case – it is a situation more similar to issues such as Sikhs not being allowed to wear a turban rather than whether one prefers a certain brand of tea! It has to do both with way of life and group identity, rather than with purely individual choice or preference. Individual identity is determined in the context of the group identity in which one is enculturated and is not simply the possession of the lone individual! Scholars who tend to think only or mainly in terms of the individual and their conscience miss out the group and cultural aspects of convictions and accompanying ways of life thus tending to trivialize the issue.[25] It is rather that the differing groups of Christ-followers must accept one another and respect the convictions and consciences of those who do not fit easily into the context in which they find themselves.[26] So far from opposing Jewish identity in Romans, Paul seeks to make space to allow it to continue indefinitely (and not simply to be temporarily tolerated).[27]

What is distinctive about the situation at Rome despite its diversity, and possibly also, despite its divergence from his own normal patterns,[28] is that Paul accepts what already exists, apart from divisiveness and anarchic tendencies. He is not simply advocating temporary tolerance of a diversity which he is forced to accept until such times as traditional Jewish sympathies are eroded with the passage of time and frequent contact with gentiles. Rather, Paul advises the acceptance of diversity,[29] not as a remaining vestige of human sinfulness, but as something perfectly in accord with the mind of Christ. To be more explicit, when Paul came in contact with Christ-followers in Rome who continued Jewish practices in an association in some form with Jewish synagogues, he is perfectly prepared to accept this. Jewish identity is affirmed and is to be maintained.

---

24. Philip F. Esler has sought to relate the theological and ethical dimensions of Paul's thought in a coherent pattern (2003b: 51–63). See also my chapter on '"The Rule of Faith" in Romans 12:1–15:13', in Hay and Johnson 1995: 259–86.
25. Contra Boyarin 1994: 32. Cf. also Barclay 1996b: 305–6.
26. See Campbell 1995: 259–86.
27. Cf. R. Jewett 1982: 62–7.
28. On the diversity of Roman house churches see P. Lampe 2003: 359–96.
29. Cf. M. Barth, 1968: 78.

This conclusion does not seem to fit with the 'normal' model of the Pauline community as one in which there is no longer Jew nor gentile. This is quite true because *what we find in Rome is not a typical Pauline community, and for the first time in his letters we find Paul in a situation in his own mission field where we can observe his attitude to Jewish/Judean Christ-followers and how they relate to his own (Pauline) communities.* Surprisingly, from some points of view, in the Roman context, Paul allows equal validity in practice to the convictions of both Jewish and gentile Christ-followers.

For those who hold that Paul's gentile mission existed in parallel to a mission to Jews led by Peter, this seems perfectly reasonable. In Pauline communities, a gentile-in-Christ way of life was the norm but Paul did not legislate for, nor would he oppose, Jewish Christ-followers in the mission to Jews continuing to keep Torah.[30] We are still very unclear as to the patterns of social relations between Jewish and gentile Christ-followers within the Pauline communities, but in my opinion there was much more flexibility and diversity than scholars normally perceive. It is also becoming clearer that there was considerable flexibility in the synagogues on how to relate to gentiles.[31] From a comparison of some issues in Romans and 1 Corinthians, it becomes clear that what Paul opposes in these differing contexts is not ethnic distinctions as such but rather discrimination against people by virtue of their ethnic background and issues arising directly from this.

If Jewish identity in Christ-followers is here affirmed or at least recognized, then it cannot be claimed that in New Testament times the Pauline 'churches' acknowledged only one undifferentiated identity; rather we have evidence here of a recognition of sub-group identities in accordance with convictions similar to, if not identical with, Jewish/gentile categories. According to Philip F. Esler, the category of all those who have faith is a category comprising two subcategories, Judeans and Greeks and that despite the new sense of identity within this new category, 'such identity will need to coexist with whatever remains of the members' original Judean and Greek identities'.[32] To insist that Paul did or would oppose 'Jewish identity' in Christ-followers is not only historically indefensible, but also contrary to Paul's own emphasis that circumcision is 'nothing'. If it were truly 'nothing' then it would be comparatively unimportant, not a threat to Christ-followers. To rule it out is to admit that for some scholars, it is far from being 'nothing' but 'something', still threatening their presuppositions as Christians about Jews and Judaism. As Cosgrove notes, 'When one's own treasured cultural identity is not threatened, it is easy to quote (and misuse) Paul's universalizing

---

30. See Chapter 3 above.
31. Cf. M.D. Nanos 1996, also 2002: 201–3. A number of biblical and extra-biblical Jewish traditions (e.g. Isa. 2.2–4, 56.3–7; Mic. 4.1; Zech. 2.11, 8.23; *Pss. Sol.* 7.31–41; Tob. 13.11, *Sib. Or.* 3.616, 724–725) suggest that when God establishes his kingdom these two groups will together constitute 'his people': Israel redeemed from exile and the gentiles redeemed from idolatry. Cf. Fredriksen 1991 now in Nanos 2002e: 246–7.
32. Esler 2003: 140. Whilst maintaining the existence of differing sub-group identities as an abiding reality, Esler also speaks of 'bringing Judeans and Greeks together in the overarching identity of the Christ-movement' (2003: 153).

rhetoric against the claims of others'.[33] We can contrast this with Paul's stance in 1 Cor. 9.19–23. Here he is able to present himself as a model of infinite flexibility for the sake of the gospel – 'to the Jews, I became as a Jew in order to win Jews'. If Paul had really thought that Jewish identity was obsolete in Christ, he could not have been as flexible as he claims. As noted previously,[34] Wayne Meeks reminds us that although 'outsiders are often a negative reference group, yet the Pauline stance is not simply countercultural' and that 'however dualistically Paul can sometimes portray "this world", it remains the creation of God...in which the apostle's efforts and the inner life of the Christian groups are implicated'.[35]

This stance which we have argued for in no way seeks to diminish or ignore the fact that believers are all 'in Christ', whether of Jewish or gentile conviction and/or way of life. But we do need to recognize that Paul's letters address gentile Christ-following communities – their sphere of reference at its widest includes all the 'churches' of the gentiles – no letters of Paul to Jewish-'Christian' congregations survived, if such ever existed. Particular address need not demand a limitation in Christology. Because Paul is not normally in close communication with Christ-following assemblies in Palestine does not mean that these did not exist, or that he did not recognize them as full and equal members 'in Christ'. So to insist that Paul's significant and original vision of believers as being 'in Christ' somehow rules out the possibility of his recognition of other non-Pauline believers with whom he and his adherents must share this foundational aspect of their identity is by no means warranted, especially since it seems likely that the concept of the universal church was not yet fully developed.

6.4 *Paul's Foundational Design for the Church: Potential Models*

As a result of Paul's pioneering work among gentiles and their full inclusion in the church, four differing scenarios of the church's identity become possible. Bearing in mind our earlier conclusion that for Paul Jewish identity is not obsolete for those in Christ, but constitutes a viable and recognized sub-group identity pattern, we will review these options considering which of them is most in keeping with Paul's foundational design as far as this can be discerned.

The Church as a Third Race

W.D. Davies maintained that 'In Christ Jews remain Jews and Greeks remain Greeks. Ethnic peculiarities are honoured'.[36] But E.P. Sanders responded by asserting that this recognition was honoured 'only so long as ethnic factors which separated Jews from Greeks did not come into conflict and that when they did, the factors which separated Jews from Greeks had to be given up by the Jews'.[37]

---

33. Cosgrove 1997: 75.
34. See Chapter 5.6 above.
35. Meeks 1991: 305–17 (317).
36. Davies 1977: 23.
37. Sanders 1983: 178.

For Sanders, 'Paul's view of the church, supported by his practice, against his own conscious intention, was substantially that it was a third entity, not just because it was composed of both Jew and Greek, but also because it was in important ways neither Jewish nor Greek'.[38] A major part of Sanders' argument was based on the fact that in concrete social reality, there could be no doubt that the church and synagogue were socially distinct.

Thus Sanders depicts Paul as reluctantly being forced into a theological stance in which he views the church as truly neither Greek nor Jewish.[39] In differing times and situations this view of the church as a third race has emerged in history. As W. Rader notes, already John Chrysostom stressed in relation to Ephesians 2.11–22, that in Christ the gentile is not joined to the Jew but both are lifted to a new status. The uniting of the two is accomplished by completely removing the differences between them.[40] F.C. Baur held that just 'as the distinction between Jews and gentiles was cancelled in the unity of the new man, so Christianity stands above Gentilism and Judaism as the absolute religion'.[41] The concept emerged again most notably before and during the Third Reich in the case of some German theologians to whom the concept of a new super race that was non-Jewish had great appeal. There are however strong arguments against such a view. Firstly there is too much discontinuity between this church and Israel, a stance too extreme to accommodate Paul's many statements to the contrary. Secondly, it is socially an impossibility for this third race to be devoid of cultural heritage, as if, magically to be in Christ were to live in a culture-free zone. Admittedly, Paul's own life narrative can also be used to support the image of the church as a completely new entity. So for example, it can be argued, as noted above, that Paul's 'conversion' was an 'event that owes absolutely nothing to upbringing, human development, or cultural tradition' but only to God who set Paul apart from his mother's womb. The latter

> expresses in the most dramatic form possible, the conviction that God's fashioning of history is independent of the normal channels of human causation. This 'setting apart' happens before birth, before human nurturing, before cultural socialization, and before Paul himself became a human agent. The only agency here can be that of God.[42]

But whether we like it or not, Christ-followers are of the family of Abraham, and not like Melchisidek apparently without historical originator. Moreover, where there is no adequate concept or awareness of cultural indebtedness, the outcome tends to be that such an organization simply reflects and, to some extent, becomes, an agent in disseminating the dominant culture in an imperialistic manner.[43]

---

38. Sanders 1983: 178–79.
39. Sanders 1983: 171–2, similarly Horrell 2000: 341–4.
40. Rader 1978: 32–5. Rader notes that Chrysostom's interest lay chiefly in the individual's relation with God.
41. Baur 1864: 45. Cf. also W. Rader 1978: 171–2.
42. Barclay 2002: 139.
43. Elliott 2005b: 11–14.

It seems reasonably clear to me that once interpreters choose a reading of Paul that minimizes if not denies completely the significance of one's previous life and identity prior to joining the Christ-movement, then it is almost inevitable that there is a tendency towards something akin to a 'Third Race' theology. If previous life and culture is annihilated, obliterated or simply disregarded, then the people of faith are all equally rendered 'rootless' and the stage is set for this 'new creation' because the past is theologically eliminated. When we look more carefully at Paul's comments such as 'to the Jew first and also to the gentile', and especially at his own self-assignation even after he joined the Christ-movement, it is plain that this does not do justice to his opinions and actions. Horrell argues very strongly that Paul's corporate Christology is the foundation for a new common identity which both Jewish and gentile Christ-followers share, and having focused primarily on this, notes not surprisingly that 'one might gain the impression that Paul perceived this body of people "in Christ" as a new entity, a "third race"'. But Horrell is forced to note that Paul himself 'did not see it in those terms', but claimed for those in Christ the privileged identity and descriptions which traditionally belong to Israel according to the flesh.[44]

The Church as New Israel
Both Paul's admirers and his critics agree that he himself is responsible for introducing the question in Romans 9 as to the identity of Israel by his statement that 'Not all Israel are Israel'. Important here, is the fact that Paul's assertion arose precisely because of the arrival on the stage of history of Jesus Christ and those who followed him. One of the purposes Paul had in Romans was to define the new group of Christ-followers in relation to historic Israel. It would appear that the identity of the two entities is somewhat intertwined and that in defining the one, we are also simultaneously involved in defining, redefining the other. As Charles Cosgrove notes, 'If the Hebrew scriptures present us with a God who chooses Israel for a special vocation and destiny, Romans requires that we interpreters choose the identity of Israel from a circumscribed group of plausible exegetical candidates'.[45] Hence it is no surprise that in considering Paul as the architect of Christian identity, we are at the same time discussing possible designations/theological descriptions of Israel. Both of these arise from, and are also related to, the fact that we are actually discussing how God works in the world and the degree of continuity/discontinuity that this involves or demonstrates.

Paul's inclusion of gentiles, as gentiles and as equal with Jews, within the people of God raised a host of new questions and it was imperative that Paul the troublesome innovator should seek to provide some explanation and rationale for the gentile mission and its successful outcome in 'all the churches of the gentile nations'.

The image of the church as 'New Israel' rightly stresses Paul's theological perspective that the 'church', even though comprising believing gentiles as well

44. Horrell 2000: 341.
45. Cosgrove 1997: 73.

as Jews, stands in the closest possible proximity to historic Israel. However, by taking over the honoured title 'Israel', this view actually identifies the church as Israel in such a way as to leave no space for any other 'Israel' except this one.[46] Historically, this kind of 'displacement theology' has led inevitably to boosting the image and significance of the church at the expense of historic Israel. It arises from what we might describe as a theology of reversal. Whereas the Jews were once God's chosen people and the gentiles regarded as sinners, now the situation has been reversed and God has created a new universal people for himself. The character of God, however, is greatly diminished in such a scenario. How can such a God be described as faithful? A theology of reversal of the status of Jews and gentiles actually destroys the credibility of God. Is this God not rather weak and limited compared with another possible vision of a God who would not fail in his original plans but would achieve what he first intended? God may have the power to make sons from stones, and 'New Creation' theology (properly understood) is certainly not un-Pauline. But it needs to be stated in a manner that does not set the church in antithesis to Israel, that does not encourage prejudice against the Jews and that allows for Paul's dominant theological tendency, a 'theology' of transformation, to be maintained.

The Church as Redefined Israel
We have noted above the need that Paul recognized – to keep the 'church' in close proximity to Israel whilst not displacing it. We also noted the need for God's character as faithful to be clearly demonstrated, faithful to Israel as the recipient of the promises. Regarding the church as redefined Israel, seems to meet these essential prerequisites. The main criticism that may be levelled at this view is that in it Israel includes gentile believers and not as traditionally, only faithful Jews. It could be claimed that in this respect the view is essentially un-Pauline in that he was always very careful to distinguish Israel and the nations. But it may well be asked, why is it so important for Paul to keep a separate identity for Israel and 'the church' of believing Jews and gentiles?

Basically, it is because, according to Paul, God's purposes for Israel are not yet complete. A redefined Israel, in which gentiles also have a share, does avoid many of the errors apparent in the past history of the church. Yet it deals only with the part of Israel that has responded in faith to Jesus the Christ, as if in this limited response all God's purposes for the world or Israel were already realized. J.C. Beker, in opposition to this perception, rightly stressed the eventual but not yet realized 'Triumph of God'.[47] There is general scholarly consensus that Pauline eschatology is not a realized eschatology but includes a strong 'not yet' element. To see the church as redefined Israel suggests more realization of God's promises than Paul's theologizing actually allows. In addition, emphasis placed on realized eschatology by Christ-followers frequently has a negative outcome for Jews who do not confess Christ because instead of waiting until the harvest when wheat

---

46. See Campbell 1993b: 440–6.
47. Beker 1980: 355–60.

and tares can be clearly identified, this stance tends to stress that those Jews who have not responded positively to Christ are judged already. In my opinion, in both of these instances of over-realized eschatology, wish-fulfilment rather than sober expectation plays too great a role and contrary scriptural evidence is disregarded.

The primary objection already noted above still holds, i.e that Paul himself did not explicitly (and I would argue implicitly also) designate the 'church' as Israel. One important reason for this is that if there was pressure, in certain regions at least, for Paul's gentile Christ-followers to become full proselytes to Judaism, to explicitly describe them as 'Israel' would encourage confirmation to existing conceptions of Israel, which of course included circumcision and full law-keeping. In this respect, it was not at all in Paul's interests to abolish absolutely and in practice the distinction between gentile Christ-followers and Israel.

To designate the church as Israel redefined to include gentiles, also tends to promote a predominantly gentile movement of Christ-followers. In the early period of Paul's gentile mission, as we have already noted, Paul had to fight hard to safeguard the identity of his converts as gentiles in Christ (rather than as potential Jewish proselytes). But a movement committed to safeguard the identity of gentiles as gentiles in Christ, would be essentially and clearly inconsistent in refusing to recognize diversity as an essential component since otherwise only one group's identity in Christ would be secured. Difficulties would certainly arise when Christ-followers of Jewish and gentile background met at the Lord's Supper. Paul saw it as his distinctive task to safeguard the identity of gentile Christ-followers. It was certainly not his particular task to safeguard the identity of Israel in quite the same way since the new entity consisted of gentile Christ-followers whose identity was now only in process of realization.

To return to our first criticism, does this perspective not confuse the church with Israel and is such a stance not entirely un-Pauline? It seems that Paul envisaged the 'church' as co-existing in close relation to, but also distinct from historic Israel until such times as Israel may be fully restored. Paul's view of Jews and gentiles is that they remain two distinct entities, a distinction that abides, even though all is relativized in Christ. As noted, a basic plank in this construction is that Paul would never confuse Israel and the gentiles, so that although in God's purposes, the two are intertwined and closely related, they remain related but separate entities.

The crucial text in the discussion is Romans 9–11, but especially 9.24, where Paul refers to 'us' whom God has called as being 'not from the Jews only but also from the nations'. Already in 1 Corinthians, Paul used καλεῖν frequently to refer to the call of gentiles implying that they too belong to God's elect people,[48] and thus linking the new people of God with Israel, in continuity rather than antithesis. But although at first glance Rom. 9.24 might seem to demonstrate that Israel includes gentile Christ-followers, there is little other evidence to support this. The argument depends on equating all the called with Israel, but this is to go

---

48. See Campbell 1993a: 234-54.

beyond what Paul's statements assert. It is one thing to claim, as most New Testament scholars would do, that all Christ-followers are called but the reverse does not hold since there are certain 'called' who although part of historic Israel, still fail to affirm Jesus as Messiah. So it would seem that we are not here dealing with a simple equation between two mutually interchangeable entities where if it is agreed that A is B, then it follows that B must also be A!

To argue that the analogy of the one olive tree of Rom. 11.17–24 is firm evidence for the opinion that the church is Israel redefined, is to overlook the nature of metaphorical or figurative language. In my view, the image of the olive tree should be interpreted as a metaphor rather than an allegory.[49] Such (metaphorical) language permits several diverse images of the same actuality without definitively confirming one meaning at the expense of another (or excluding the rest). That the olive tree image strongly supports some form of relation between gentile Christ-followers and Israel is beyond dispute, but the analogy by definition involves two differentiated entities and cannot be used simply to deny the existence of one at the expense of the other, or to allow one to swallow up, and thus to displace, the other.

Another issue in this view of the church is whether there remains any room within it for diversity. We do not propose to argue the case here, but it is amazing that in a church that sees itself as Israel redefined, there is no real space for Jewish followers in Christ continuing to follow their convictions alongside gentile followers who see no significance in food-laws etc. Where problems arise, Jews who are Christ-followers must always give up those things that offend others.[50] It thus becomes clear that the perception of the church as 'redefined Israel', tends to hi-jack the title and inheritance of Israel without any real concern for diversity within the 'church' – as such it clearly tends towards a gentile church rather than as a church of believing Jews and gentiles and as such has no real warrant for claiming the title Israel.

The Church and Israel as Separate but Related Entities
We will need to return to the discussion of the identity of the church as Israel in Chapter 8, where we will deal in more detail with the theme of the church and Israel as related but separate entities but we must now move on. Our view is that the church and Israel are related but separate entities which should not be dissolved or merged in such a way that the sub-group identity of the one is lost or unrecognized.

6.5 Conclusion

It is apparent here that in our search for Paul's understanding of identity in Christ, we are still dealing with a single topic with many facets – that of the continuity and discontinuity between Christianity and Judaism, evident in the use of

---

49. Esler 2003a: 298–305.
50. Thus E.P. Sanders 'the factors which separated Jews from Greeks had to be given up by the Jews' (1983: 178).

terms such as relativized, abrogated or even obsolete. Great feats of ingenuity have been displayed in attempting to fit Paul's scriptural understanding of Israel and the 'church' into modern philosophical parlance, some of which are much indebted to Bultmann's existentialist approach. The weaknesses of this in relation to certain aspects of Pauline theology were already apparent some thirty years ago, and scholarship seemed to have moved on from there. But apparently there is a deeper attachment by some to a triumphalist reading of Christian history and the corresponding denigration of Judaism than might have been anticipated. Possibly the dawn of the New Perspective has caused some scholars to react against what they perceive as too favourable an attitude to Judaism, by a return to older more traditional ways of thinking, precisely those which the New Perspective sought to overcome.

From this overview of recent discussion concerning the relation of Paul, the 'church' and Israel, it is easy to see how very involved he still is with his own people and their history. Nothing can displace Israel in God's purposes because he is faithful to his promises. So for Paul Israel abides as Israel despite the fact of a 'church' of Christ-following Jews and gentiles. As believers, gentiles are the called of God but although closely related to, they do not become part of Israel even though they are called to share in the inheritance of Israel with Israel and not simply by themselves as a separate entity. Paul can speak of an 'Ἰσραὴλ κατὰ σάρκα but 'Ἰσραὴλ κατὰ πνεῦμα is nowhere to be found in his letters despite the fact that sometimes he seems to come close to such a conception.[51] Paul avoids the twin dangers of identifying the 'church' with Israel – and thus displacing Israel – and the opposite tendency to so separate or distance the 'church' from Israel, that the church stands at risk of deteriorating into a 'Jesus cult'. The identity of the 'church' is thus not one single undifferentiated identity, but according to Paul's foundational design, the 'branches on the olive tree' have a differentiated sub-group identity as believing Jews or gentiles and they are one but not the same in Christ. Christianity is thus not best understood as a sectarian new religion, nor as a reaction to Judaism, defined in antithesis to it. It is rather a transformation of a (mainly) Pharisaic Judaism from which it borrows and affirms some motifs whilst rejecting others.[52] This is in accord with Paul's own understanding of new life in Christ. Although he asserts that both circumcision and uncircumcision are nothing, he does not mean this absolutely but only comparatively. Thus the Christ-follower's past life does count for something even if it is of relatively little significance compared with being in Christ. It is somewhat naïve to insist that Christianity as such is a brand new creation, coming straight from God out of heaven and having no cultural or religious roots. Of course, God could theoretically create a totally new people, an entirely new creation. But that would imply a failure to achieve desired goals and put divine faithfulness at risk. If 'salvation is of the Jews' (Jn 4.22), it would be truly inconceivable if Jewish roots were not essential for a true understanding of

---

51. Cf. Horrell 2000: 341–2.
52. Cf. E.P. Sanders 1983: 210.

Christian identity and if the New Testament were not read and interpreted in conjunction with the Hebrew Bible. As Richard Hays claims, 'If ethical judgements are inseparable from foundational construals of community identity, then any consideration of Pauline ethics must attend to the way in which Paul's understanding of the church's vocation is rooted in his reading of scripture.'[53]

---

53. Hays 1996: 35.

Chapter 7

PAUL'S ATTITUDE TOWARDS JEWISH IDENTITY IN ROMANS

When Paul in Romans contrasted the outward and inward Jew in his claim that one is not a proper Jew if they are only a Jew in appearance i.e. by virtue of circumcision, he could not have envisaged the can of worms he offered to interpreters down the centuries. Could this text be read as suggesting that the 'real Jew' might in fact be a gentile in Christ? Does Paul in fact have in mind something such as 'the ideal human' or 'the true believer'? In order to translate Paul's Greek in Rom. 2.28, translators have found it necessary to supply some additional word in English to clarify his meaning. Thus the RSV has 'For he is not a real Jew who is one outwardly...'. If Paul is defining real Jews, and not intending to refer at this point to gentiles, it would make even better sense to translate, 'For he is not a real Jew who is one *only* outwardly'. His contrast is intended to be between the Jew who is a real Jew in the sense of being both circumcised and living in the faith of Abraham, and the Jew who regards the mere fact of circumcision as adequate evidence of belonging to the house of Abraham. At least that has been a traditional reading though new and distinct options are now available.

7.1 The Identity of Paul's Addressees in Romans

In earlier research, I took the view that the addressees in Romans were mainly of gentile background, but living in an environment where Jewish identity and the way of life associated with it were still a burning issue. I was particularly interested in the possibility of there being a considerable group (or groups) of proselytes or God-fearers for whom the issue of Jewish identity, particularly after the arrival of the (Pauline) gospel in Rome, would be significant.[1] Recently I posited another version of this same hypothesis in the suggestion that if there were a majority of gentiles in the Roman Christ-movement, then there could well have been divisions particularly amongst those God-fearers who had already become proselytes prior to the advent of the Gospel in Rome.[2] If some of these had come to realize that there was now no need for God-fearers to become proselytes, then there might well have been a reaction from these against Jewish identity as a

---

1. Campbell 1992: 185–7.
2. On God-fearers and proselytes in Rome see Lampe (2003: 69–71), Feldman (1993: 331–41) and Davies (1984b: 157–8).

previously chosen way of life.³ If others of the same background opted instead to continue to adhere to their chosen way of life even after they had joined the Christ-movement, then we would have a situation in Rome where a mainly gentile Christ-movement was split over the issue of residual patterns of a Jewish way of life, perhaps even over the significance of Jewish identity in Christ. If Paul addressed his letter to such a situation, it could offer a good explanation for the dual character of Romans as a letter addressed to gentiles, but which discusses Judaism and its place in the divine economy as well as the relation of gentile members of the Christ-movement to Abrahamic faith.⁴

Such a context would inevitably include an ethnic element and value-judgements would also be involved especially where a change of a way of life from one sub-group identity to another within the Christ-movement took place or was contemplated. Political factors would accentuate the differences between groups if these included, as we suspect, an element of cultural superiority in some gentiles over against Jews (as a by-product of Roman imperialism).⁵ A debate about whether certain foods could be eaten⁶ and which special days should be observed would in all probability involve expressions of gentile attitudes to Judaism, which were not necessarily favourable. This would be the more pronounced if some of the Jewish synagogue communities were, or became, resistant to the Christ-movement. Some such sentiments seem to surround the scornful words of Rom. 11.13–24, 'Branches were broken off so that I might be grafted in', which are perhaps an indication of self-definition in the face of the 'other'.

Such a statement implies a very specific context because it presupposes both a connection to, or a relationship with, the Jewish community and simultaneously a distancing from it. This paradoxical situation would give added support to our hypothesis concerning proselytes and/or God-fearers, though it need not be limited to these. That the situation posited was regarded as a serious issue is demonstrated by the attention devoted to it by Paul in Romans, particularly in chapters 9–15. It was all the more serious because references to boasting over the discarded branches, implies the existence of a perceived gentile superiority in relation to Jewish identity and practice as noted above.⁷ Thus the animosity between Jew and Greek that frequently surfaced in the Mediterranean world of this era appears to be emerging also within the Christ-movement.⁸ Since mutual hostility between Jews and Greeks would have formed part of the living memories of most of the Christ-followers in Rome and some of them may also have experienced it in other cities of the Mediterranean region, it is highly likely that Jewish and Greek converts brought heavy loads of ethnic prejudice with them

3. Campbell 2004a: 74–7.
4. Campbell 1992: 53–5; Thorsteinsson 2003: 113–14; Kümmel 1975: 309.
5. Cf. Elliott 2000: 35.
6. Cf. Feldman 1993: 167–70.
7. Cf. Feldman 1993: 123–76.
8. As Davies states 'Although many of them had doubtless been proselytes and God-fearers, the Roman Christians to whom Paul wrote, conscious of belonging to no mean city, would find it easy to carry over into the church the contempt that their neighbours felt for Jews' (1984b: 158).

into the new house-churches.⁹ Such prejudice indicated a conformity with the world in antithesis to the gospel of Christ as Paul understood it. But for Paul this dispute represents not simply an ongoing conflict between cultures and social levels¹⁰ (which it probably is) but more significantly, a failure of love, in that it was putting at risk the faith of weaker 'brothers' in the movement who were caught up in the conflict but were unable to cope with the pressures. The movement as a whole was thus being put at risk in Rome.

However, it is gentiles *as gentiles* whom Paul specifically and directly addresses at this point in Romans, 'Now I am speaking to you gentiles...' (11.13–24). This may possibly hold for the entire letter since those whom Paul addresses in 8.15 are those who have now received 'a spirit of adoption' and thus apparently gentiles (since in 9.4 he refers to the Jews' adoption as sons). Although he says in Ch. 7.1 '...for I am speaking to those who know the law...', this is unlikely to indicate Jews but rather those gentiles or former gentiles who have been catechized in the Torah. It would have been superfluous to mention to Jewish addressees that they know the law.¹¹ In any case, it is clear that Paul is not addressing Jews in Romans. This is not to deny the possibility that Paul may be addressing gentile Christ-followers still in contact with Jews who had not yet fully committed to the Christ-movement in order that these gentiles may not prove a 'stumbling-block' to their coming to full commitment.¹²

Whether the gentiles Paul addresses can be more precisely defined is difficult to determine. Is he addressing loosely related groups of gentiles all of whom, or some of whom, have close links with synagogues?¹³ Or is he addressing only the gentiles because they are within his sphere of mission, and does he know of Jewish Christ-followers who may still worship with their fellow Jews and maintain their distinct Jewish identity?¹⁴ It seems reasonable to claim that 'Romans is

   9. Esler 2003: 75–6.
   10. Reasoner 1999: 57.
   11. Thorsteinsson 2003: 119.
   12. As ably developed and argued by Nanos (1996: 85–165).
   13. We use the term 'synagogue' as implying a worshipping community of Jews, and possibly other adherents, not necessarily as yet having a designated community building in which to meet. If both Jews and gentile Christ-followers each met in the homes of some of the members, this would make it still more difficult to distinguish Christ-followers from other Jews and from gentile Christ-followers (contra Esler 2003: 344–5). In our opinion, the evidence at the moment is still finely balanced for or against community synagogue buildings in Rome in parallel with the synagogue at Ostia, on which see Runesson (2003: 63–89) and Richardson (2003: 90–117). It is significant that there is epigraphic evidence in the Mediterranean in the first century which shows that Jewish congregations referred to themselves as synagogues, but to the buildings in which they met as προσευχή. Esler argues that even though the word προσευχή has not turned up in the Judean catacomb epigraphy from Rome, its occurrence in an epitaph of a gentile fruit seller whose place of work was identified by reference to it, shows it was already in the public domain and distinctive enough to require a Greek loanword to designate it (2003: 94).
   14. Is this diversity of Christ-following groups perhaps the reason why Paul avoids designating all the Christ-followers at Rome as an ἐκκλησία? Cf. its use in 16.5. Cf. Lampe (2003: 359). In any case, differing places of meeting need not imply differing theologies any more than differing historical and geographical roots. As Judge and Thomas have stressed, immigration to Rome had played a role in the diverse origins of the Christ-movement there (1966: 81–94); see also Lampe 2003: 55–66.

7. Paul's Attitude Towards Jewish Identity in Romans

addressed to non-Jews, but precisely those non-Jews who had been or still were operative within a Jewish community in Rome'.[15] I would wish, however, to stress that the letter may also specifically have in mind gentile proselytes to Judaism[16] who, having responded to the gospel, and because of cultural conflict between Jews and Greeks with its political implications for minorities, and ongoing contact with gentile Christ-followers were prompted to reassess their affiliation and identity.[17] For just such people, Jewish identity and its relevance would be a significant issue. With this in mind, we will now consider the address to a Jew in Romans 2 and its contribution to the issue of Jewish identity.

7.2 The Identity of 'the Jew' in Romans 2

As noted above, English translators tend to add words to clarify Paul's meaning in this chapter, particularly in v. 29. Whether we support this addition or not, the discussion clearly centres on what constitutes a true or real Jew. So it essentially deals with the definition of Jewish identity, both positively and negatively.

A related issue surrounds Paul's attitude to Jewish identity in this letter which, as we shall maintain later, is extremely positive. To clarify this, it is necessary first to set Ch. 2 in context, particularly in relation to Ch. 1. There is general agreement that in Ch. 1 Paul describes the typical sins of the gentiles as seen from a Jewish perspective. Thus the catalogue of sins represents typical Jewish attitudes to gentile 'sinners', which Paul himself doubtless shared, as one who describes himself and Peter as a Jew by nature, and not a gentile sinner (Gal. 2.14). As Philip F. Esler has recently demonstrated, the background of this depiction of gentile shortcomings in Romans 1 is not the story of Adam and its consequences, but rather that of the biblical story of Sodom.[18] This is not, nor is it meant to be, a flattering image of gentile society. But having delivered a devastating critique of the gentiles in his first chapter, the almost universal scholarly opinion since Augustine is that Paul turns in Ch. 2.1 to address the Jews.[19] The reasons given for this are varied. Primarily they result from 'anachronistically reading later Christian characterizations of Jews as "hypocritical Pharisees"'[20] into the text. Thus the stereotypical Jew who judges others is recalled when in 2.1

---

15. Cf. Thorsteinsson (2003: 121) who also notes that of the 26 names mentioned in Romans 16, there are at least six Jews and one Jewish household.

16. Of the 534 inscriptions of Jews from ancient Rome, seven definitively belong to proselytes. The fact that five of the seven are in Latin whereas 76 per cent of all Roman Jewish inscriptions are in Greek (and almost all the others in Latin) led Leon to conclude tentatively that proselytes were more frequent in the more Romanized element of the community (1960: 256). For a detailed consideration of names and their significance for an understanding of the composition of the Roman Christ-movement see Lampe (2003: 164–83). Cf. also Feldman 1993: 331–2 and Judge 2005: 103–17.

17. On the tensions experienced in the Galatian context by gentile Christ-followers in relation to becoming proselytes see Nanos (2000: 147–9).

18. Esler (2003: 149–50), also in more detail see Esler (2004b: 4–16).

19. See Schelkle 1956: 70–1.

20. Stowers (1994: 13; 101). For an example of the tendency Stowers criticizes, see Dunn's linking this passage with Mk 7.9–13 (1988a: 79–80).

Paul in diatribe style attacks the one who judges others by means of an imaginary interlocutor[21] whom he addresses directly in the second person singular throughout the chapter.[22] More understandably, it is also based upon the address in 2.17 where Paul says, 'But if you call yourself a Jew...'. The latter interpretation is based on reading back the content of 2.17-29 into 2.1 which is not a problem for a scholarly or literate audience, but not plausible for an audience who did not have a text before them, and who had not previously heard the message.

Most noteworthy is the fact that Paul does not say that the person addressed in 2.17 is a Jew but only that he claims to be a Jew, wants to be called a Jew or simply calls himself a Jew.[23] This raises the possibility that the person is not actually a Jew as distinct from being a real Jew. The latter issue has been concentrated upon in Christian exegesis because Christian exegetes tend to stress the inward reality of faith in contrast to profession (whereas Jewish scholars would tend to stress actions as well as attitudes). But since 'inscriptions from the diaspora reveal that Ἰουδαῖος and its Latin equivalent "Judaeus" were sometimes used as surnames',[24] there is a real possibility that the person calling themselves a Jew is in reality of gentile birth. This might point towards proselyte or potential proselyte status rather than to a born Jew. The (partially) idealized view of Judaism given in the verses following (17-20) indicates a favourable view of Judaism such as a would-be proselyte might hold.

> ...if you call yourself a Jew and rely upon the law and boast of your relation to God and know his will and approve what is excellent, because you are instructed in the law, and if you are sure that you are a guide to the blind, a light to those who are in darkness, a corrector of the foolish, a teacher of children, having in the law the embodiment of knowledge and truth...

This particular version of a Jewish identity is however turned back upon the interlocutor in judgement because although he confesses such things, apparently, he does not do them. Thus, if this reversal represents a critique of Judaism, it would seem to fit in with the traditional interpretation of 2.1 whereby a Jewish person is encouraged to share Paul's critical view of gentile society as outlined in Romans 1. But in this traditional exegesis, the tables are turned because the one judging is trapped by his own expressed judgement on the gentiles, when Paul says that the judge does the very same things himself. According to this view Paul 'sets up' the objector (who has normally been perceived as Jewish) and then traps him by his very own judgements. Now if Paul traps the Jew in this way at the beginning of Romans this would introduce a very negative attitude towards Judaism in the letter. But, as we have discussed above, this is by no means the only reading nor does it find support in the grammar and rhetoric of the text.

---

21. See Stowers 1981: 79-81, 99, 114, 118-22.
22. 'Hence, the feature which both distinguishes and unites Romans 2 is Paul's use of the second person singular'. Thorsteinsson 2003: 152-3 (153).
23. Cf. Thorsteinsson 2003: 197-8. As Gorday has pointed out, Origen already noted this in his commentary on Romans (1983: 43).
24. Cf. Thorsteinsson 2003: 201.

Romans 2.1 does not fit neatly into the traditional view. The chapter begins with διό – therefore, implying that what is now being said follows on the basis of an argument about the failings of the gentile world already made (cf. vv. 24, 26, 28). It is beyond debate that the addressees of Romans 1 must be gentile and there can also be little doubt that the image of the gentile world is exactly as *Jews*, including Paul himself, would have viewed them. It is only in 2.17 that the Jew is first addressed as such. In view of the form of the transition between the first two chapters, it can confidently be affirmed that neither the grammar nor content of this section justify viewing the judging person as a Jew. As Esler says,

> for some reason that escapes me, there is a fierce debate as to whom Paul is addressing here. A large number of scholars consider that the ἄνθρωπος is a typical Judean… others see a non-Judean interlocutor. The latter position is correct, and the widespread support for the former is a cause for wonder.[25]

7.3 Jewish Identity in Romans: Negative Aspects?

As already noted above, if Paul in his rhetoric at the commencement of his letter to the Romans, sets a trap for a Jewish interlocutor, this would imply a somewhat hostile attitude to Jews and Judaism throughout the letter. But this presupposition is hard to maintain, particularly in view of Paul's frequent explicit declarations to the contrary. However, before we proceed to discuss the latter, we will look at indications that might suggest a critical if not hostile view of Jews and Judaism throughout the letter.

Several items are potential candidates for indicating a negative view of Judaism in Romans. In this letter there is an ongoing and strong emphasis upon the significance of the Christ-event. In 1.16, Paul stresses the new aeon that has now dawned with the advent of the gospel which includes both Jews and gentiles within its scope – 'it is the power of God for salvation to everyone who has faith'. But even the proclamation of this new universal message may carry a veiled critique of a Judaism which stressed that 'Salvation is of the Jews'. Again in Rom. 3.21–26 Paul asserts 'But now the righteousness of God has been manifested apart from law…'. The explicit contrast between the former era and the revelation of righteousness in Christ, especially since the latter is manifested 'apart from law', carries with it an implication that the law has been found wanting and therefore rightly bypassed in this new context. Similar conclusions may be derived from Paul's discussion of the weakness of the law in Romans 7 and the proposed solution to these deficiencies through the life-giving Spirit in Rom. 8.1. More serious still is Paul's clearly expressed regret in Chs. 9–11 that his own people as a whole have not yet responded positively to the gospel: they have stumbled, they have mistakenly sought a 'righteousness of their own' so that they have not recognized that 'Christ is the end of the law' (10.4). Also the traditional view of the weak, usually identified as Jews, in Romans 14–15 is that they represent a narrow-minded judgemental attitude which cannot abide the new freedom to be found in Christ.

25. Esler 2003: 151.

It is not surprising that by combining a selection of texts from this letter such as these, scholars have frequently arrived at the conclusion that Paul could not have held anything except a negative view of Jewish identity, and that viewed from this perspective, the outcome is not all that different from the critical view of Judaism already familiar to those acquainted with the dominant consensus on Galatians.[26] However, this would represent at best only a partial version of the position Paul outlines in Romans. What is noteworthy is that at almost every point where Paul apparently asserts or implies a critique of Jews or of Judaism, this is always tempered by a positive qualification so that readers or hearers do not rush to a too negative conclusion. This stance appears early in the letter with the very announcement of the gospel. It was promised beforehand through the prophets in the scriptures. It concerns the Son who was descended from David (1.2–3). Now the righteousness of God has been manifested 'apart from law' but Paul does not end with this but adds significantly 'although the law and the prophets bear witness to it' (3.21). Even the weaknesses of the law so clearly set out in Rom. 7.7–23 are accompanied by what may fairly be described as an apologia on behalf of the law, so that although in the new era in Christ the law by itself is inadequate for salvation, it is diagnosed as weak not because it is not God-given and holy and just and good but because of the sinful context it addresses (7.13–20).

The same pattern holds within Chs. 9–11. Christ is not simply described as terminating, or as the termination of, the law as some scholars have maintained,[27] but is more plausibly depicted as the 'goal' of the law[28] which has either purely positive or at worst both positive and negative implications for our view of it.[29] Paul's position becomes clearest in his statements concerning his people Israel. Even in what seems to be his critique of their failure to reach their desired goal, he bears them witness that they do have a zeal though it is not according to knowledge (10.2–3). When it is suggested by his interlocutor that God may have cast off Israel, Paul gives a horrified rebuttal 'God forbid' (11.1; 11.11). When it is acknowledged that it might seem as though God's word to Israel had utterly failed, Paul responds with the image of a righteous remnant, and this is not meant to indicate the poverty of Israel's response, but rather his hope for her future. The remnant for Paul is here not so much a saved remnant as a saving remnant, that witnesses to God's ongoing purpose for Israel[30] (9.27–28; 11.5–12). All of this culminates in Paul's asserted hope that 'all Israel will be saved', which is, however it may be read, a powerful and positive affirmation. It is no surprise then to find that in Chs. 14–15, it emerges that Paul does not take sides with those who regard Jewish identity as something to be rejected, or only temporarily tolerated.

---

26. Though Nanos 2002e challenges this, see especially Nanos 2002b, 2002c, and 2002d.
27. Cf. Bultmann 1952: 48; Käsemann 1980: 281–3.
28. Cf. my article, 'Christ the End of the Law: Romans 10.4'; Campbell 1991: 60–7; similarly also Badenas for whom 'Christ is the hermeneutical key which makes intelligible what was always the law's true meaning and purpose' (1985: 150); cf. more recently, Bockmuehl 1990: 150–2.
29. Cf. Beker 1980: 91, also 106–7.
30. We will return to this topic in Ch. 9.2.

Nor does he directly or by implication suggest that some should relinquish their Jewish identity and practice. Instead he takes fully into account the conscience of the weaker brother, including the risk of destroying 'the one for whom Christ also died'. Thus those within the Christ-movement are not to be forced into a conformity that is determined by another group; rather, in contrast to this tendency to dominate, Paul stresses the need for each to be fully convinced in their own mind, and to 'welcome one another fully'. We will need to deal with this latter element in more detail later, but for the moment it is adequate to affirm that Paul's attitude to Jews and to Jewish identity in Romans is far from universally negative.

Moreover when the fact is explicitly recognized and given due significance that Paul in this letter affirms the revelation of God in Christ, it follows that there must necessarily be both some qualification placed around the law as well as some positive affirmation of its continuity with his revelation to Israel. The mere fact of the Christ-event meant that Paul had to demonstrate the newness of the revelation in Christ as well as its continuity with that of the preceding era. But if we read Paul's intention in this way, and allow for the resultant qualification of all that went before, we are left with little in this letter that sets out to denigrate Jews or Judaism as such, and much more that indicates a contrary stance.

7.4 *Judaizers in Romans?*

Paul would not have been able to be so positive in his stance towards Judaism[31] had there been judaizers in Rome who could have used his pro-Jewish stance as ammunition in their own agenda. Older views of Romans were more likely to posit the existence of a substantial group of Jewish Christ-followers in the context Paul addressed.[32] Along with this tendency went another which anticipated the presence not only of Jews but also of judaizers.[33] If such did exist, we would have expected some sort of strong response to their views, but such is completely lacking. It can only be derived from Paul's statements about the revision of the role of the law in the light of Christ, such as e.g. Rom. 10.4. The disposition to anticipate judaizers is fuelled partly by too much attention to apparent parallels between Romans and Galatians, particularly in relation to the theme of justification by faith, and a corresponding disregard for the distinctiveness of the two

---

31. Käsemann (1980: 405) considers that Paul in Romans is so mild and accommodating to Jewish (Christian) concerns, such as observance of days, and bases his gospel and world mission very firmly on scripture because Paul hopes thereby to win a Jewish Christian minority.

32. Käsemann claims as irrefutable the fact that Baur was mistaken when he ascribed a dominant position to Jewish Christians in Rome (1980: 254).

33. We are deliberately using the traditional terminology here, but are aware of its limitations as noted e.g. by Nanos who depicts the Galatian situation as an 'intra-Jewish context' and uses the term 'influencers' to describe those who are influencing Paul's converts (rather than such terms as judaizers, opponents, agitators or trouble-makers, or teachers etc.). As Nanos notes, judaizing is something that gentiles seeking Jewish status may do, it is inappropriate for describing efforts to persuade gentiles to seek Jewish status. Following Cohen, he asserts that 'as a reflexive verb it is inappropriate as a label for Jews' (2000: 151); cf. also Cohen (1999: 175–97).

letters. This can result in a decontextualized reading of one or the other, possibly even of both. There is always a risk that emphasis upon theological themes or doctrines will displace or weaken a contextual reading. The emphasis on theological or any other thematic approach obscures the contextualized meaning of Paul's statements in favour of a generalized meaning imposed upon the text.[34]

Thus the apparent similarity between Romans 3–4 and Galatians 3–4 may be quite misleading in any attempt to reconstruct the contexts addressed. When similar arguments are found in two differing texts, the tendency to give a homogenized meaning, rightly rejected and deplored by Stendahl, is strong. In any case, the theological statement of a doctrine or a form of argument in one specific context does not preclude its re-use in a differing context to draw out different social implications, since there is no inherent function in any genre.[35] We must not assume that if the presence of judaizers is a strong possibility in the Galatian context, then the same must hold true for the Roman context. In Galatians the chief function of Paul's argument is to argue that gentile Christ-followers do not need to accept circumcision to facilitate table fellowship (commensality) with Jewish Christ-followers. But in Romans, circumcision is not in dispute to such an extent that Paul can acknowledge that circumcision indeed is of value (3.1–2) and can describe Christ as having become a servant to the circumcised (15.8).[36]

What is clear to me is that when Romans is viewed in light of the information *within* the letter, rather than from facts smuggled in from elsewhere, its contents are distinctly different from Galatians. Stuhlmacher, for example, claims that Paul had heard that there was criticism of his preaching and mission in Rome and that 'in all likelihood, this criticism derived from Jewish-Christian sources and was the result of disputes which Paul had to fight out in Galatia, Philippi and Corinth with the counter-missionaries who had appeared against him there'.[37] Other information from outside the text of Romans indicates a differing perspective – that of a strong Jewish presence from the earliest period of the Christ-movement. As noted already, Ambrosiaster reports this information without criticism or reference to judaizers. Thus we must distinguish clearly between the presence in Rome of Jewish Christ-followers and a judaizing movement, between respect for the law and Jewish practices and pressure on gentile Christ-followers to judaize. The probability that Jewish (and possibly also gentile) Christ-followers continued to have harmonious links with some of the synagogue groups[38]

---

34. See Beker's discussion of Galatians 3 and Romans 4 in relation to the disparity between them which he attributes to difference in audiences and contexts (1980: 98–100).

35. Cf. Kee 1989: 24.

36. D.A. Campbell has demonstrated that the baptismal formula in Gal. 3.11 is structured chiastically indicating that circumcision and uncircumcision are used metanonymously for Jews and 'Christians' there (1996: 120–36).

37. Stuhlmacher 1988: 31. In a more detailed presentation of this argument, Stuhlmacher asserts that the objections to Paul's doctrine and person emanate pre-eminently from Jewish-Christian sources (Stuhlmacher 1986: 191).

38. Cf. Nanos 1996: 13–20. Also Tellbe 2001: 169. We agree with him that it is probable that, since the Roman Christian movement originally seems to have been an intra-Jewish phenomenon, 'the Roman Christians organized themselves in a way similar to the Jewish communities…' (163).

demonstrates the absence of any split or division concerning the issue of circumcision. Likewise, Paul's straightforward and uncritical reference to those who 'know the law' in 7.1, followed by an apology for the holiness of the law in 7.17–19, would be most unusual in a context where judaizers were present. We are not convinced by the suggestion that possibly the fact that Paul does not refer to circumcision and uncircumcision in Rom. 14–15 in the same way he discusses food and drink is evidence that there may have existed only a moderate form of judaizing in Rome that made minimal demands on gentile Christ-followers in terms of fellowship with Jews.[39] What is evidenced in Romans is rather the normal problems that would arise where both gentiles and Jews in Christ interact without any pressure on gentiles to judaize.[40] There is no real evidence for such judaizing but more for the opposite kind of pressure, i.e. that gentile Christ-followers had both the power and the inclination to try to force Jewish Christ-followers to 'gentilize'.[41]

7.5 Judaism and Jewish Identity in Romans: Positive Aspects

At the very beginning of Romans, prior to being described as being designated Son of God in power by his resurrection from the dead, Christ is portrayed as descended from David by physical descent – κατὰ σάρκα (1.3–4). We note that Paul here did not feel it adequate simply to speak of Christ's designation as Son in power, but also included his physical descent from David. The notion of physical descent emerges again in reference to the 'seed of Abraham' (σπέρμα Ἀβραάμ) in Romans 4.11–16. Since Paul in this chapter is clearly arguing that the faith that Abraham exercised preceded his circumcision, the argument theoretically could have been completed by demonstrating that thus he was only truly the father of gentile Christ-followers rather than of those already circumcised.[42] But Paul in both verses 11–12 and again in verse 16, by claiming Abraham firstly as the father of two groups differing in relation to circumcision, and then as 'the father of us all', shows that although he wants to maintain the right of gentiles to remain gentiles within the Christ-movement, he is by no means unfavourably disposed towards those of Jewish descent.[43]

Because he asserts the entry of gentiles as gentiles into the Christ-movement, this does not necessitate a corresponding claim concerning the loss of the heritage of Israel for the circumcised. The nearest we approach to this is in the Pauline acknowledgement that 'not all Israel are Israel' (9.6), which some have

---

39. Contra Wedderburn 1988: 51–61 (61).
40. Cf. Tellbe 2001: 170.
41. Cf. Elliott 2005.
42. Cf. F.J. Leenhardt's criticism of Michel on this point (1961: 119). Michel's emphasis on 'Abrahamskindschaft' is however, an important correction against viewing faith only in relation to individuals (1976: 167–71).
43. To argue positively for the full inclusion of gentiles in Christ need not necessarily imply a negative view of Jewish identity. It is a conclusion drawn from what Paul does not say with the advantage of hindsight.

seen as Paul deliberately and foolishly driving a wedge within the people of God. In this and subsequent verses, Paul argues that in the divine design, God has always exercised a certain freedom within the people of Israel, thus subverting in prophetic style any presumption that physical descent is all that is required. As was noted by Johannes Munck, Paul does not deny the significance of physical descent, but merely denies the right of anyone to use it as a claim against God.[44] There is really not much that is radically new in Paul's statements here. The history of Israel had never been straightforward and there had always been prophetic voices warning against Israel's tendency toward presumption of divine favour. Yet despite that, there had never been any real consideration of the possibility that God might replace Israel with another nation; the discussion took the form rather of a debate about the role and extent of a righteous remnant (which we will consider in the next chapter). In Romans this theme centres not so much on the topic of a saved remnant, but rather on a saving remnant, thus indicating the apostle's hope for God's continuing purpose for his people. The continuity with Israel's previous history emerges more clearly when the first half of Romans 9 is viewed primarily as a discussion of Israel, an inner-Israelite discussion rather than one involving gentiles. Thus Paul is positing a reduction in the number of those who are Israel, but not a displacement of Israel as such. Viewed in this light, Romans 9 and Romans 11 do not offer two conflicting portrayals of Israel.[45] Both affirm in differing ways the continuing divine involvement with Israel, and through Israel with the gentiles.

Contrary to Sanders' view, and others who see Paul as contradictory at this point, there is no denial here of Israel's election,[46] as we shall note in more detail in the next chapter Israel remains within the divine purpose and witnesses to it both positively and negatively. Thus Paul's discussion by no means denies all benefits of physical descent but qualifies and refines its significance.

7.6 *The Affirmation of Jewish Identity in Romans 14–15*

In Romans 14–15 Paul addresses concrete issues of interaction between the diverse groups in the Christ-movement at Rome. That there is division with judgemental attitudes (ἐξουθενείτω, κρινέτω) and a power struggle which may endanger the 'weak' is evident. Paul is concerned lest the weak are destroyed in the conflict and is probably also aware that inter-group strife may bring the Christ-movement unfavourably to the attention of the authorities. To this end his goal is

---

44. Munck 1967: 138.
45. In Campbell (1999: 195–203), I consider a number of texts in Rom. 9–11 where some scholars maintain that Paul appears to contradict himself. A major part of my response is that Paul's method of arguing is often misunderstood because he is perceived, wrongly, to be writing abstract theology of a somewhat traditional kind as on e.g. law, election, predestination, whereas if Romans is read as a real letter addressing concrete issues, arising from within the community and in relation to his mission, his argumentation reveals a different kind of logic. For more on this see Ch. 10.1–2. Campbell 1992: 134, also Campbell 2000: 195–203.
46. Campbell 1992: 134.

to promote peace within the communities and indirectly with the authorities. I have argued elsewhere that it would be simplistic to see the conflict here simply in terms of two groups divided according to ethnic origin. There is more diversity than this; what is required to make sense of the content is not Jewish Christ-followers as such but a context in which Judaism plays a role. I envisaged a scenario where proselytes and former God-fearers interacted within a synagogue setting influenced in varying degrees by Jewish practices.⁴⁷ The groups obviously differ on matters related to food and drink and also to certain days. In 14.2–3 the text mentions meat and vegetables, 14.21 adds wine to the list, and 14.5 mentions regard for days. All this strongly indicates that Jewish matters are at stake, most likely halakhic issues about kosher meals.⁴⁸

Whatever their distinctive identities and practices, the groups are still interacting with each other in such a way that the quality of their relationship did actually matter since it impacted upon them both. 'Jewish affairs' still mattered to them,⁴⁹ since they were a matter for judging and disputes (κρίνων, διαλογισμῶν) which Paul fears will escalate, and thus endanger everyone.⁵⁰ The situation Paul addresses is one in which competing groups, critical and judgemental of each other⁵¹ were engaged in the process of group identity construction in order to preserve differing identities which would have been normally perceived as being in opposition in first century Rome. The problem was that there was so much diversity among the Christ-followers that there was not an adequate number of groups to allow everyone to find a group in which they could conscientiously participate.⁵² Some were at risk because their needs were not provided for by any of the groups. Paul's creative response is not to take sides even though he acknowledges links with the strong but rather he seeks to promote harmony.⁵³ This must not be overemphasized since Paul does not share their scorn for the

---

47. Campbell 1995: 267.

48. Although my view is that there was wide-ranging diversity in the Christ-movement at Rome I agree with Esler that 'although the weak and the strong did not represent a tidy split between Judeans and non-Judeans...it is likely that the core element of each group were Judeans among the weak and Greeks among the strong' (2003: 344). In my view, that is why Paul can so smoothly proceed from calling for the mutual acceptance of weak and strong in 14.1–15.6 to a paradigmatic description of Christ's service to both Jews and non-Jews in 15.7–12. Cf. Marcus 1989: 67–81.

49. Ehrensperger 2004a: 182.

50. The root 'κριν' becomes a *leitmotif* in Romans and thereby connects the judging in Ch. 2 with that of Chs. 14–15; see Meeks (1987: 290–300) esp. 296.

51. On inter-group relations generally see Henri Tajfel: 1978. On the relevance of inter-group dynamics as distinct from individual freedom see Campbell 1997; cf. also Esler 2003 for an excellent development and application of Tajfel's theories.

52. This does not conflict with the obvious fact that Paul refers to weak and strong as if there were only two groups; as Horowitz has noted, despite the plurality of ethnic groups in any particular environment, most conflicts involve only two groups, and participation by other groups tends to be minor (1985: 182). See also Ch. 5.3 above. For further discussion of ethnic conflict see Esler (2003: 50–2).

53. Not least does Paul seek harmony in attitude, he does not want them to think arrogantly (μὴ ὑπερφρονεῖν). As Jewett translates 'not to be super-minded above what one ought to be minded, but (to) set your mind on being sober-minded' (1982: 66).

weak. Also if Paul is expecting compromise from those with strength in the community he needs to emphasize common ground in order to progress from there especially since he goes on to side so obviously with the needs of the 'weak'. Paul's own attitude in relation to the strong must not be seen as indicating a negative verdict on the weak. It is probable that their stance concerning food and days coincided with past or present affiliation to, or participation in, synagogue communities and resultant convictions about Jewish identity and a Jewish way of life.

One strand of interpretation has tended to view Paul's call to bear up (βαστάζειν) the weak as indicating only a temporary tolerance rather than a full acceptance of residual Jewish tendencies in some groups. Thus, e.g. Barclay holds that what Paul demands of the weak is commitment to a 'church' in which the Jewish way of life is tolerated but not required. 'In demanding this toleration, Paul subverts the basis on which Jewish law-observance is founded and precipitates a crisis of cultural integrity among the very believers whose law-observance he is careful to protect. Such is the fundamental paradox of the passage...'[54] Barclay notes that Paul is actually relativizing the significance of the Israelite cultural tradition by advocating that Jewish Christ-followers associate freely with others who differ from them, thus undermining the theological and intellectual foundation of their tradition. But this does not necessarily follow from Paul's stance. Paul is concerned with practice not purely with theological stances and their consistency, though this practice is consistent with his theologizing. In any case whilst the *effect* of Paul's ethics may have been as Barclay proposes, this is certainly not what he *intended*.[55] Paul had to find a solution to a serious social and cultural problem which threatened the harmony of the Christ-movement at Rome and in similar situations elsewhere. And his solution was one which confirmed the differing identities of the groups involved. Post-Enlightenment scholarship would tend to view this as of less significance than the long-term goal of unity through sameness in Christ. But such a solution would have destroyed the weak and thus made unity possible only at the expense of destroying those who were different if they were not willing and able to conform.

If the issues at Rome among the Christ groups had been theological rather than halakhic, then a refusal to compromise might seem warranted, but Paul wanted the movement to flourish and to be a base for future expansion in Spain. To risk schism, and accentuating the divisions that already existed would have been catastrophic. If we perceive Paul's response from a pastoral perspective, the (limited) options available to him become clearer, and the solution proposed for harmony in diversity is evidence of wisdom.

As we have demonstrated, the main issues discussed in Romans 14–15 concern Jewish identity and self-understanding. Those who eat only vegetables are discernibly Jewish when it is recognized that the eating only of vegetables was a

---

54. Barclay 1996b: 308.
55. As Esler notes, 'What seems to us an awkward compromise, or even a paradox, does so with the benefit of hindsight' (2003: 355).

7. Paul's Attitude Towards Jewish Identity in Romans 117

Jewish form of accommodating to social relations with gentiles. This enabled Jews to keep Torah and still to socialize with gentiles.[56] Likewise not eating meat represents clearly Jewish concern to avoid anything associated with idolatry. It is also clear that the reference in Rom. 14.5–6a to observing the day refers to 'one' day and it is observed in honour of the Lord. Whilst this does not prove that the reference is to keeping the Jewish Sabbath, a comparison with 14.6b makes this more likely. In this verse both eating and non-eating are related to honouring the Lord. But no such parallel is found in relation to the day. If it is the Sabbath that is in mind, this is understandable. Only Jews would observe the Sabbath and those who did not observe the Sabbath would not do this in honour of the Lord. Taken together, these debated issues clearly indicate adherence to a Jewish way of life.[57] This is further evidence that the problems in Rome have a specific ethnic dimension.

What needs to be recognized in the light of the interpretation proposed above, are the norms for the believing community, the rule of faith,[58] that Paul enumerates as the solution to these conflicts. Firstly there is no suggestion, contrary to some scholars' views, that groups following a Jewish way of life should cease to adhere to it. Rather Paul requires that 'everyone be fully convinced in their own mind' (Rom. 14.5) and that 'no one judge or despise a brother' (14.10).[59] In addition he demands that rather than judging the strong should decide 'never to put a stumbling block or a hindrance in the way of a brother' (14.13). That here he is addressing the strong is evident from his declaration 'I know and I am persuaded in the Lord Jesus that nothing is unclean in itself'. But for Paul such knowledge is inadequate and he adds a significant qualification, 'but it is unclean for anyone who thinks it is unclean'.[60] Thus the demand to modify their social behaviour is

---

56. Bockmuehl notes 'As even the earliest evidence from Daniel (1.3–1.7), Judith and the *Letter to Aristeas* (181–4) shows, a good many Jews clearly *did* eat in the company of Gentiles or even accept food supplied by them, without thereby surrendering their Jewishness or their respect for the Torah. Attitudes to this question evidently varied a good deal, depending on one's halakhic stance and perhaps one's geographic location' (2003a: 58; also 60–2).

57. Cf. Reasoner who refers to a verse of Horace in which it is suggested that to observe the Sabbath is 'weak' (1998: 54). Reasoner also offers a useful discussion concerning the probability that the terminology of 'weak' and 'strong' was already current in Rome prior to Paul's writing (1998: 57; 61).

58. As developed in Campbell 1995.

59. The word for 'despise' used here ἐξουθενέω refers particularly in an intergroup context to the scornful rejection of another from a position of perceived superiority. As Esler notes 'The attitude condemned is cognate with the boasting by the non-Israelites over the Israelites that Paul disapproves in 11.18. In both cases, the motivation is likely to be Greek ethnocentric dislike of Israelites triggered by their distinctive customs that depend on adherence to the Mosaic law' (2003: 350–1).

60. Contrary to a wide spectrum of opinion (e.g. Barclay 1996b: 300) the view that nothing is unclean in itself does not necessarily represent a fundamental rejection of the Jewish law. Tomson cites Rabban Yohanan ben Zakkai's reason for the purity ritual with the red heifer (Num. 19) 'By our lives! A corpse would not render impure, nor water purify, were it not for the decree of the Holy One, blessed be he'. The implication of this Tomson holds to be that it is only through the law that one makes the distinction pure or impure rather than by nature. (Tomson 1990: 251).

addressed principally to the strong, and it is Jewish identity which is thereby protected. Such a conclusion varies greatly from the common tendency which views Paul as always supporting the more 'emancipated'. His position is in fact the reversal of this. The implication is that the strong have more power whether numerically, socially, or otherwise. They have resources at their disposal and they have space for movement whereas the weak had probably no such option of flexibility as it would mean that, to put it bluntly, they had to give up what they are, their Jewish identity. On the other hand they need to increase in faith as their father Abraham did. Paul hopes that by their being fully welcomed with an open heart, they will in fact do just this.

This is entirely in accordance with what we already noted in relation to 1 Cor. 7.17–24. To remain in the state of calling in which one is called is Paul's pattern for his converts. So there is no suggestion here that those with Jewish convictions should separate from the synagogue[61] or turn their back on their Israelite identity. Nor is this conclusion contradicted by a perceived link with Abraham's growing strong in faith already stressed by Paul in Romans 4. Some commentators draw implications from the Abraham narrative in Ch. 4 with regard to the weak in Romans 14. They hold that the weak must grow strong as Abraham did. But some of them presuppose that the weak will thus gradually dissociate themselves from their Jewish way of life and conform more to gentile Christ-followers' patterns.[62] But to grow stronger in faith as Abraham did does not imply growing out of one's traditional identity. It is rather to grow stronger in one's self-understanding in Christ and thus to become less judgemental and less vulnerable in disputes with others who differ. In the Roman situation this would involve 'welcoming one another' in the full acceptance of difference rather than a qualified temporary acceptance with an obligation to eventually surrender those practices that others find problematic.[63] This welcoming probably carries overtones of welcoming someone into one's household[64] possibly particularly the other with whom you are not already in close association, as Donfried has noted.[65] It is clear that Paul is referring here to relations between differing households where Roman family rivalries and antagonisms probably played a part. The precise reference in 14.4 to οἰκέτης meaning domestic servant or slave, and the reminder of his loyalty to the head of the house makes this clear. If groups of Christ-followers in 16.10–11 belonged to the households of Aristobulos and

---

61. Esler says that Paul's acceptance of those who continue to adhere to '…Mosaic food laws may seem odd on the lips of someone who expressed the negative views toward the Mosaic code we find in chap. 7' (2003: 352) Our view is that Ch. 7 is not so negative in this respect and therefore it is not so odd. See above Ch. 7.3.

62. Jewett offers an alternative reading that does not presuppose such dissociation (1985: 341–56)

63. Cf. also Ehrensperger 2004a: 187.

64. Fitzmyer interprets προσλαμβάνω as meaning 'take to oneself, take into one's household' and hence 'accept with an open heart' (1993: 689).

65. Donfried 1991: 110. Dunn says it has the force of 'receive or accept into one's society, home, circle of acquaintances' (citing 2 Macc. 10.5 and Acts 28.2) 1988b: 798.

Narcissus they would share their status and be involved in such loyalty.[66] The call to welcome one another would only have significance to those who had both the space and the authority to admit the other into their household and may well apply primarily to the leaders of the Christ groups.[67] The implication here seems to be that the call to welcome is addressed especially to the strong. If these did not follow a Jewish way of life (whatever their ethnic origins) the onus was on them to welcome Christ-followers who adhered to a Jewish way of life in such a way that their guests were not compromised or forced into exclusion.[68] Paul expects the strong to exercise ἀγάπη which he repeatedly emphasizes as the unique feature of being in Christ,[69] and thus not merely to tolerate but to 'carry' the weaker brother. Whether this is too idealistic to work may be debated but there was no inherent reason why it should not.[70]

7.7 Conclusion

The focus of our argument in this chapter has been to demonstrate that neither grammar nor rhetoric support the reading of Rom. 2.1 as Paul's setting a trap for a Jewish objector. This recognition changes our perspective on Paul's attitude to Jewish identity within the letter. We have argued that Paul's perception of negative aspects of Jewish identity such as are implied in statements concerning the law can be read more appropriately as his transformed explanation of the role of the law in the light of the Christ-event. Most telling of all is Paul's conclusion of his letter to Rome which affirms Jewish identity as an abiding reality in the Christ-movement which the strong are obligated to accept and protect. Since Paul fought an ongoing battle to preserve gentile Christ-followers' identity as gentiles in resisting pressures upon them to accept circumcision, it is of major significance that we have demonstrated that he likewise resisted pressures upon Jewish Christ-followers to cease adhering to their way of life. It seems that to grow strong in faith in Paul's terms is to be able to welcome fully those who adhere to a differing way of life in Christ.[71] It is the latter that is the primary link between the groups who differ and it is the compelling force that obligates those in Christ who are different to accept one another. But unlike earlier understandings of this

---

66. This would be all the more difficult where heads of houses were not Christ-followers as in this instance. See Lampe 2003: 164–5. Cf. also Esler 2003: 346–8.

67. Campbell 'The attitudes and activities of the leaders may have well have accentuated the differences between groups and thus led to the persecution and stumbling of individuals (1997: 276).Cf. Lampe 2003: 48–66. Cf. Jewett 1993, especially 29–30, for a different scenario.

68. If the issue had been that those adhering to a Jewish way of life were to welcome those not following this pattern, then the issue would not arise since the latter would have no problems of conscience.

69. Cf. Esler 2003: 339–40.

70. Bockmuehl 2003: 172.

71. We cannot be certain that this includes joint worship in one house though we would expect such to take place at some point, as Rom. 15.10 'Rejoice, o gentiles with his people' seems to imply. If joint meals are also implied then God is blessed at meals and to do so with an insecure or idolatrous conscience would be blasphemy. Cf. Tomson 1990: 256; also Ehrensperger 2004a: 185.

acceptance, it does not imply the giving up of one's particular identity in favour of a 'Christian' identity in which other identities are dissolved.[72] Thus there are differing identities in Christ but these are borne without being discriminated against because there is now no distinction amongst those who are in Christ.[73]

---

72. As Stowers recognizes 'Paul does not assimilate Jew and Gentile into a generic Christianity' (1989: 674). Esler concludes 'Their new common identity did not entail the dissolution of their valued sub-group identities' (2003: 355).

73. Wagner's thorough discussion of Deut. 32.43 LXX in Rom. 15.10 – εὐφράνθητε, ἔθνη, μετὰ λαοῦ αὐτοῦ – shows that Paul's citation of this text provides a deeply satisfying conclusion to his reading of Moses' Song in Romans 9–11. Paul appeals to Deut. 32.19–21 to show that Israel's present resistance to the gospel is an integral part of God's plan to effect the salvation of the gentiles and also to redeem Israel as well. Wagner views Paul's use of Deut. 32.43 as a striking confirmation that Paul reads the Song as a whole as a narrative of God's faithfulness to redeem Israel and, through Israel, the entire world (2002: 316–17). Viewed from this perspective, what Paul desires is the mutual recognition of Jews and gentiles in Christ rather than necessarily their united worship.

Chapter 8

SELF-UNDERSTANDING IN CHRIST AND THE PEOPLE OF GOD:
ISRAEL IN ROMANS

8.1. *Jews, Gentiles and Israel:*
The Implications of Paul's Terminology in Romans

In the previous chapter we have shown that Paul's attitude in Romans to Jewish identity is really positive. If this is accepted, then we would expect the same attitude to be clearly reflected in his understanding of Israel. It is this we must now investigate.

Paul's stance is well illustrated when he describes the purpose of Christ's mission in Rom. 15.8. In a main sentence with three subsidiary clauses he describes its significance.

Christ became a servant to the circumcised:

— to show God's truthfulness
— in order to confirm the promises given to the patriarchs
— and in order that the gentiles might glorify God for his mercy.

The description of Christ as διάκονος περιτομῆς is most significant.[1] Paul has earlier in Romans spoken of both Jews and of Israel/Israelites. It might have seemed more fitting that, at this point, he would refer to Israel or at least to Jews. But there is no mistaking the fact that Paul deliberately describes the mission of Christ as having this specific ethnic and particular frame of reference. It is apparent that the Christ of Paul's theologizing is not someone who shuns ethnic particularity or focus. Far from denigrating the fleshly history of Israel, Paul finds it an appropriate locus for the work of the Christ. Of course, this is but one element of Pauline thought, but nevertheless it is very much in keeping with his emphasis in Romans on 'the Jew first and also (to) the gentile'.

---

1. So long as Rom. 9–11 was neglected, being viewed as concerning only theodicy or predestination, as in the exegesis prior to F.C. Baur, this aspect of Christ's and of Paul's mission was neglected. F.C. Baur set Chs. 9–11 in the centre of the letter, but his own systematic conception of an antithesis between Jewish-Christian particularism and Pauline universalism prevented the theme of relations between Jewish and gentile Christians, supported especially by 9–11 and 14.1–15.13, from being adequately investigated, cf. Käsemann.1980: 403. Munck's combination of stressing the significance of 9–11 in relation to Paul's mission and eschatology offered the opportunity for a new view of the structure and purpose of the letter, and especially of Paul's attitude to Israel, cf. Donaldson. 1997: 17–21.

On the other hand, there is differentiation and nuance in Paul's varied terminology in Romans. On the ethnic level, the terms are clearly Jew and gentile or when describing differing cultural worlds – Jews and Greeks, or even barbarians. In the divine order of salvation, it is the groupings of peoples as ethnic entities that is listed – 'to the Jew first and also to the gentile'. Yet despite all this, in Romans 9–11, the emphasis seems to shift to Israel/Israelite rather than remaining within the purely ethnic or cultural realms/terminology. Already in Rom. 9.4 these are specifically designated as 'Israelites', and that immediately after a reference to being Paul's συγγενῶν μου κατὰ σάρκα (9.3).

Thus an analysis of Paul's terminology in Romans emerges as follows. The term Ἰουδαῖος is probably implied in Rom 1.14 in respect of Paul himself when he speaks of his indebtedness both 'to Greeks and barbarians'. Then in 1.16 we meet the typical coupling of Jew and gentile when Paul insists that the gospel is 'to the Jew first and also to the Greek' – Ἰουδαίῳ τε πρῶτον καὶ Ἕλληνι. This phrase is twice repeated in 2.9–10. But it is in 2.17 that we get a specific reference to self-designation as Ἰουδαῖος. Whether or not we insist that here we have an example of someone who is of non-Jewish extraction, wishing to claim to be a Jew, is not essential for our discussion at this point. From Paul's critical response it can be claimed that there might be such a person who is a Jew in name only, or in self-designation only. Paul criticizes this Ἰουδαῖος as not being consistent with his profession in that he does not practise what he claims to adhere to. In this argument, even circumcision does not constitute a Ἰουδαῖος. The Ἰουδαῖος is one who is one ἐν τῷ κρυπτῷ - whose praise is not from men but from God, i.e. one who is recognized by God as Ἰουδαῖος. So, on these premises, even the fact of becoming a proselyte does not in and of itself guarantee recognition by God.

It would appear that what Paul is moving towards is a definition of the people of God that gives primary recognition to the practice of Abrahamic faith as well as descent from Abraham. This becomes more apparent in Romans 9–11. The terms of Chapters 1–3, Jew–gentile, Jew–Greek/barbarian do not re-emerge explicitly until 9.24 (and then again in 10.12). But with 9.4, we find a new terminology. Paul's 'kinsmen by race – τῶν ἀδελφῶν μου τῶν συγγενῶν μου κατὰ σάρκα (9.3), are now redesignated, in Paul's words, *They are Israelites* and to them belong the sonship' etc. but this is almost immediately qualified by the verse οὐ γὰρ πάντες οἱ ἐξ Ἰσραὴλ οὗτοι Ἰσραήλ (9.6). After discussing in 10.19 whether Israel had not understood, Paul then proceeds to designate himself as an '*Israelite,* a descendant of Abraham, a member of the tribe of Benjamin' (11.1).

Interestingly, when in 9.30 Paul introduces a summary of the present stage of his argument, he does not return to the Jew/gentile couplet, but asserts that although gentiles have attained a righteousness through faith, *Israel* did not so succeed.

The last verse of Ch. 10 (21) concludes with a reference again to Israel, citing Isaiah 65, 'But of *Israel* he says, 'All day long I have held out my hands to a disobedient and contrary people' – λαὸν ἀπειθοῦντα καὶ ἀντιλέγοντα'. Ch. 11.1

continues in this vein with the question 'Has God rejected his people?', which is negated in 11.2, with the aid of the scriptural narrative of Ezekiel pleading with God against *Israel*, thus indicating clearly that the λαός intended in 10.21, and 11.1–2 is Israel.[2] The term *Israel* reappears again in 11.7, but then not again until 11.25.

The gentile nations–Israel couplet introduced in 9.30 is repeated in the summary of the argument at 11.11, 'through their trespass, salvation has come to the gentiles'. Only in a personal reference in 11.13 do we find an implicit reference to the term 'Jew'. 'Inasmuch as I am an apostle to the gentiles, I magnify my ministry in order to make my *kinsmen* (μου τὴν σάρκα) jealous and thus save some of them'.[3] From this point in the chapter, the discussion continues by means of the analogy of the olive tree, until in 11.25, the 'full number of the gentiles' (τὸ πλήρωμα τῶν ἐθνῶν) is positively linked to the claim that '*all Israel* will be saved' πᾶς Ἰσραὴλ σωθήσεται. What is most significant from our analysis of Paul's use of Israel terminology is that having made a distinction within 'Israel' between the 'remnant' and the 'rest' (11.7), he does not disinherit either group by employing the term to refer exclusively to one party or the other.[4]

So the three chapters end as they began – with a discussion by Paul about gentiles and the purpose of God for Israel. The latter is referred to in the third person '*they* are Israelites…to *them* belong the sonship'. '*They* have stumbled over the stumbling-stone…'. 'My heart's desire and prayer to God for *them* is that *they* might be saved…', '*They* have a zeal for God…', 'But I ask, have *they* not heard…?' 'So I ask, have *they* stumbled so as to fall?' ' For if *their* rejection means… what will *their* acceptance mean?' 'When I take away *their* sins' (11.27). '*They* are enemies for your sake' (my translation) 'as regards election, *they* are beloved for the sake of *their* forefathers'. 'Just as you… So *they* now have been disobedient…so that *they* might receive mercy'. In only one other passage in the remainder of Romans does Paul return to the third party references to Israel. Concerning the collection in 15.26, he reports that he is going with aid for (the poor among) the saints at Jerusalem. He indicates his view that since the gentiles have come to share in *their* spiritual blessings, they ought also to be of service *to them* in material blessings. Here again it is reasonably plain that the 'they' referred to is Israel (of whom the poor saints are a representative part).

What is noteworthy here is that apart from several brief comments emphasizing his own personal affiliation to Israel, the discussion takes place about Israel as a third party who is not actually participating in the discussion that is taking place. It is also significant that although Paul uses a diverse vocabulary in his

2. Cf. Campbell 2000: 198.
3. As Käsemann notes, 'If the recipients of the epistle are in the first instance the Roman (gentile Christian) majority… They are told that precisely Paul's apostolate involves an expectation of salvation for Israel'. 1980: 305.
4. Cf. Wagner (2002: 237 n. 65). Wagner also notes the ongoing significance of these careful references to Israel, 'This observation will prove crucial for what Paul means by "all Israel" in 11.26. Like Paul, the Qumran covenanters did not consider themselves the sum total of eschatological Israel' (2002: 237 n. 65).

discussion in Romans, concerning descent from Abraham, etc. there is a degree of precision in Chs. 9–11 in his designation of his own people as 'Israel'.

Thus it is apparent from Paul's use of terminology concerning Jew and gentile that he does not intend to denote the people of God as a purely spiritual entity nor to depict them as devoid of ethnic affiliation. Jesus Christ is presented both as descended from the house of David (1.5) or root of Jesse (15.12) and also designated Son of God in power by the Spirit (1.4). Abraham is not depicted as father only of the circumcision or father only of the uncircumcision, but specifically as father of both. Not all descended from Israel are Israel, but the discussion is centred within Israel and around Israel. There is divine selection within Israel and the gentiles are notably first referred to as being included at 9.24. The distinction between Israel and the gentiles remains constant throughout the letter.

The term 'Israel' is here limited to those who are descended from Abraham. But continuity with Abraham is not to be maintained or secured at the physical level only. Abraham's descendants should also share his faith. Thus although the focus is on continuity within the people of God, the ethnic dimension is not dismissed nor annulled. In light of this, Rom.9.8 could be translated as: 'For it is not those of fleshly descent alone, but those of fleshly descent and of promise who are Abraham's seed'. At this stage in his argument *Paul is not offering a general principle that any group of any descent could constitute the people of God* as the RSV translation might suggest. 'This means that it is not the children of the flesh who are the children of God, but the children of the promise are reckoned as descendants'.[5] In Paul's terms, the children of promise is here a sub-group within those of fleshly descent from Abraham, and at this point in Chapter 9 he does not yet (prior to 9.24) include any beyond this group. It is not warranted to simply generalize this sub-group to refer to gentiles who at this stage in Paul's argument are not directly in focus.

Moreover, the solidarity of Israel as a people is not sacrificed despite the wedge Paul appears to drive within his own people at 9.6b. A similar distinction appears at 11.23: 'and even the others, if they do not persist in their unbelief, will be grafted in...' But in his concluding verses of Ch. 11, the unity of Israel, 'all Israel', reappears. From this terminology, it seems that despite Paul's suggestive usage, Israel cannot be precisely limited only to those descendants of Abraham who share his faith. Such a view might prove enticing and convenient to Christian theologians since it would make feasible a definition of Israel which omits entirely to discuss those descendants who do not share their forefather's faith, and also leaps too easily from believing Israelites to gentile Christ-followers.

---

5. It is significant that Käsemann notes a similar point in relation to Rom. 4.11–12. 'His (Abraham's) example shows that everything depends only on faith. Becoming a proselyte is not a prior condition of this. In fact, then, Judaism is robbed of both Abraham and circumcision...' Käsemann, however, in view of this problem he has just noted, goes on to add, 'This roughness is softened in v. 12. As often, Paul hastens to qualify an exaggerated statement. An on-going relation of the patriarch to Judaism is now acknowledged. In fact the apostle is concerned to be able to call Abraham also the father of the circumcision, since any other course would take the promise away from Israel and contest its salvation history'. (Käsemann 1980: 116).

8. Self-Understanding in Christ and the People of God

Thus 'Israel' in this scenario would not be limited only to those who are Abraham's descendants but can include Christ-followers of gentile origin with no connection with Abraham except through faith in Christ. This is not the route Paul chose to follow in Romans. He is not content to salvage some remnant from the people of Israel and to sacrifice the rest. In this regard he sticks with the historical particularity of his own people Israel, and cannot be content even though at least some of them have found the new faith in Christ and shared it also with gentiles. A distinction remains in Paul's thought between Israel, whether or not it is faithful Israel or 'the rest', and those gentile Christ-followers who though not being Abraham's physical descendants become his lineage by virtue of Christ. It is not surprising then that later in Romans, Paul emerges as a defender of those who retained their Jewish sympathies and way of life.

In the light of our analysis of Paul's terminology, we have noted that ethnicity is not something to be left behind with the coming of Christ, nor to be replaced by a purely spiritual as distinct from a fleshly based reality. Thus Israelite identity whether of Paul or his fellow Christ-following Jews, is not to be seen as incompatible with, nor irrelevant to, the life of discipleship demanded of a Christ-follower. For the first time in his career as apostle to the gentiles, he finds it necessary to make a defence of a Jewish way of life within the Christ-movement and also to argue for the need for this movement to recognize its roots in the Abraham tradition. In defending the freedom of members of the Christ-movement to be fully convinced in their own minds as to the will of God for their way of life, Paul provides an argument for recognizing diverse ethnic identities within the Christ-movement and a corresponding argument against an imperialistic tendency to demand conformity to a dominant ethos. He also incidentally provides arguments for a (subsequent) gentile Christianity remaining self-conscious of its roots in Judaism.

But this depiction of Paul's attitude to the Jews in Romans may seem in sharp contrast to the traditional view of the apostle to the gentiles. This disparity arises partly from the fact that Judaism has been successfully stereotyped as a religion of salvation by works. The Reformation stressed the opposite, salvation by faith alone and good works as the fruit of faith rather than its substitute. Thus it seems surprising and inconsistent that Paul, the supposed opponent of all enemies of the gospel, can have a good word to say about Jews, whom the very tradition that introduced us to Paul, has depicted as being included in that same category. It thus emerges that what we are faced with is an inner-Christian conflict concerning which image of Paul and his attitude to Judaism we find most attractive or convincing.[6] Our response to this choice will depend to a great extent on whether in our understanding of Paul in Romans we view him as defending emergent 'Christianity' (over against Judaism) or, on the other hand, whether from within his ancestral faith he is defending and explaining the purpose of God for both Jew and gentile prior to the much later partings of the ways between Judaism and Christianity.

---

6. Cf. Elliott 1995: 66–72.

If Paul is operating within his own faith tradition and speaking critically from within this, then he cannot be viewed as suggesting that the true Jew might actually be a gentile Christ-follower. His critique is rather that the Jew who is faithful to his ancestral faith will not be a Jew simply by virtue of circumcision but by circumcision and accompanying faith. A parallel to this aspect of Paul's theologizing is found in Romans 9. Here Paul argues that the promise is effective only for Abraham's children (τέκνα) and not simply for all his descendants (σπέρμα).

Paul bases this argument on the fact that the scripture says, ἐν 'Ισαὰκ κληθήσεταί σοι σπέρμα, thus recognizing that the specific covenant referred to is not one including all Abraham's physical descendants, but only those whose descent is through Isaac and then Jacob.[7] But this represents a narrowing of the scope of the promise within the progeny of Abraham, not a transfer to some other unrelated group. Paul is arguing a case for divine selection within the descendants of Abraham (gentiles are not mentioned until 9.24). Thus it is to misinterpret Paul if we generalize and conclude on the basis of selection within the people of Israel that Christ-following gentiles may replace them in the divine purpose. The dilemma is clearly visible as already noted in the RSV translation of 9.8 – 'This means that it is not the children of the flesh who are the children of God but the children of the promise are reckoned as descendants'. Here Paul does contrast 'τέκνα τῆς σαρκὸς' and 'τέκνα τῆς ἐπαγγελίας' but to state that those of fleshly descent are not God's children is certainly not what he is asserting. As already noted, we need to paraphrase what he is saying as 'it is not those of fleshly descent alone who are God's children but those of fleshly descent and of promise'.

Of course this is only a section of a longer argument which goes on to speak of the inclusion of gentiles also in 9.24 and, when Paul comes to this, he will argue for an opening up of covenant promises to include the gentiles. The pattern is this: first Paul establishes that not all those of fleshly descent are children of promise and then he argues that the God who had freedom to select from within the historic people of Israel has the freedom to select gentiles also. But nowhere does he claim or assert that God has the freedom not to select any from within Israel – to do so would be to deny his own word of promise to Abraham and through him to the nations. Even divine freedom is limited by divine commitment.[8] Thus divine freedom is freedom to include Christ-following gentiles along with those who are both of flesh and promise, i.e from within Israel. There is freedom to choose from within Israel but not freedom to reject all Israel since God has freely decided to commit himself in his promises. Thus, already there is a remnant (ὑπόλειμμα) for 'though the number of the sons of Israel be as the sand of the sea, a remnant of them will be saved' (9.27 omitting the gratuitous 'only' of the RSV).

Paul's apologetic stance in Romans cannot be in doubt. Although it may have the appearance in certain sections such as 1.18–3.20 of being a general treatise on

---

7. See Crüsemann 2003: 23–7.
8. Contra Käsemann's claim on Rom. 9.6ff. that the omnipotence of the creator is not restricted even by promise and grace but precisely remains free from restriction (1980: 286–7).

8. Self-Understanding in Christ and the People of God

the equal sinfulness of both Jews and gentiles, the last half century of scholarship has revealed the subjectivity and inadequacy of such an opinion. In this letter Paul does not set out to speak even-handedly of Jew and gentile as if he needed to demonstrate his impartiality.[9] Instead he speaks of a divine impartiality which somehow encompasses an historic role for his people Israel. God's impartiality means he can have no favourites, but that does not mean that he has rejected his people Israel. Election is not to be confused with favouritism. The problem with our modern post-Enlightenment language is that we conceptualize differently from Paul and perceive contradictions from our oppositional form of thinking which put Paul in an either /or dilemma that was quite foreign to his thought.[10] We tend to argue – either A or B but Paul's approach is more inclusive, not only A but B also. So for Paul, it is not a question of Jew or gentile but to the Jew first and also to the gentile.

This form of argument is also demonstrated in Rom. 4.16 – where Paul maintains 'that is why it depends on faith, in order that the promise may rest on grace and be guaranteed to all his descendants – *not only* to the adherents of the law *but also* to those who share the faith of Abraham, for he is the father of us all'. As I have argued elsewhere,[11] the fact that 'οἱ τοῦ νόμου' is used in this verse in a neutral rather than a pejorative sense underlines the fact that Paul specifically stresses the national or ethnic sense[12] – the inclusion of Jews *per se* and not simply Christ-following gentiles or even nondescript individuals.[13] Paul's thesis is that God's intention revealed in the Christ-event is to offer to two peoples an inclusive salvation that includes *Jews as Jews and gentiles as gentiles,* and that the grace of God is fully revealed when Israel and the nations share in the nurture of the one olive tree.[14] Significantly, when Paul in 9.24 defines the 'vessels of mercy' (σκεύη ἐλέους), although he tends to use the more favourable term 'Israel' in most places in Romans 9–11, here he specifically notes Jews as being included and in such a way as to demonstrate the supplementary status of believing gentiles, 'not from the Jews only but also from the gentiles'.

8.2 The Remnant in Paul: a Saving Remnant and a Sign of Hope

It is impossible that Paul would have envisaged the obliteration of Judaism as such or the rejection of all Jews. This can be illustrated in two ways. Paul did not equate Christ-following Jews with the entirety of the people of Israel. He argues

---

9. Contra Cosgrove who claims that Paul's own teaching on impartiality contradicts his stance in Ch. 11 (1997: 191), cf. Barth 1959: 143.
10. Cf. Ehrensperger 2004a: 53–6.
11. Cf. Campbell 2000: 194.
12. See Dunn 1988: 216.
13. Cf. Harink (2003: 180–4). Harink severely criticizes Wright's individualism 'Perhaps Wright hardly intends it, but in his hands the biblical understanding of the chosen people of Israel is reduced to Jews (with gentiles) as individual seekers and choosers of Christianity, who participate in the new movement primarily through self-moved individual faith rather than through election into a specific corporate body' (182). See also Campbell 2004: 53–6.
14. Campbell 2000: 194–6.

for a faithful remnant maintained by divine grace. Whilst there is a remnant there is hope for all Israel because in Paul's thinking a remnant, though a sign of severe judgement is proof of God's future purposes for Israel. A remnant in Paul's thought is not merely negative, reflecting failed plans or hardening of hearts. It is rather a forward-looking token of grace for the future, a saving remnant rather than a saved remnant. This is because in Pauline eschatology, the future is still open. Unlike some New Testament scholars with an over-realized eschatology, he holds neither salvation nor judgement as already totally realized.

Thus however severe God's judgement on Israel may be, it is not yet final, but is provisional upon his future plans for Israel and the response given to them. The fact of a remnant correlates with the fact of the rest i.e those not included in the remnant. In Romans 9–11, Paul presumes the existence of both the remnant (τὸ ὑπόλειμμα) and the rest (οἱ λοίποι). Already in Romans 4, Paul has specifically designated the seed of Abraham as comprising both Jewish and gentile Christ-followers. This indicates that Paul presupposes a distinct Christ-following Jewish remnant will exist in parallel to a similar group of gentiles (4.11–16). This shows how foreign to his hopes is a view of Israel as rejected. Similarly it is likewise entirely un-Pauline to view the faithful remnant of Christ-following Jews as equivalent to or as a substitute for 'all Israel'. The remnant represent all Israel in terms of a hopeful future, but to represent is not to be identical, it actually implies differentiation. The 'church' of Jewish and gentile Christ-followers is not Israel, nor is the believing remnant of faithful Jews to be regarded as the whole of Israel. In Paul's theology, he rejoices with his fellow-Jews in Christ, but he never gives up on his hope for those who as yet do not respond in faith.

Some commentators have suggested that Paul's patriotism or his emotional attachment to Israel is the reason why he finds it difficult to envisage the total rejection of Israel.[15] But such is far from the case. Paul's hope is not based either on familial or emotional but rather on theological factors. It is his understanding of God that is at issue. Hence the depth of his concerns whether emotional or otherwise. The covenant represented for Paul the divine faithfulness and the Christ-event was an affirmation of this rather than a replacement. Hence his view of God's faithfulness is reinforced rather than diminished or displaced. What Paul is attempting in his discussion of Israel is to hold together two apparently conflicting realities, first that God is faithful to Israel and, second, that Israel is by and large not responding to the gospel. This conflict could have been resolved if Paul had not held firm to the distinction between Jew and gentile in Christ. A 'new Israel' mainly gentile in composition can, according to some interpretations, overcome Paul's problem because a redefined Israel still exists and a remnant of Jews is included. But this would not have been an adequate solution for Paul. In 9.27 where the remnant (ὑπόλειμμα) is first introduced in Romans

---

15. Especially Dodd, '...the special importance here assigned to the Jews and their conversion in the forecast of the destiny of mankind appears artificial... We can well understand that his emotional interest in his own people, rather than strict logic, has determined his forecast' (1932: 183). From differing perspectives on this cf. also Cosgrove 1997: 36–7 and Meeks 1990: 111–18.

9–11, it plays only a preliminary role as an indication that God has not rejected his people.¹⁶ In 11.5 Paul presents himself as an example of the remnant. Significantly his argument stresses his descent from the seed (σπέρμα) of Abraham.¹⁷ In addition he elaborates on his fleshly descent (of the tribe of Benjamin) and by acknowledging that he himself is an Israelite.

Remnant theology re-emerges in 11.13–24 where the wild gentile shoots are grafted into the olive tree amongst ἐν αὐτοῖς (but not 'in place of' as the RSV and even more surprisingly, the NRSV translates) the natural branches. Thus a Jewish believing remnant is a presupposition, branches amongst which gentiles can be grafted. These gentiles do not displace the natural branches but are called to *share* (συγκοινωνός) the richness of the olive tree. 'The thrust of the verse is that gentiles join the Jews who believe, not that they replace the Jews who do not'.¹⁸ Even in Rom. 15.25–27 the sharing of gentile Christ-followers in the spiritual blessings of the Christ-followers in Jerusalem is again stressed indicating Paul's basic conception that gentile Christ-followers are dependent on Jewish Christ-followers for their transmission of the gospel to gentiles and in this as in other ways they are 'indebted to them' (ὀφείλεται εἰσιν αὐτῶν).¹⁹

The remnant is basic to Paul's argument in that, at the present time (11.5), they represent God's continuing faithfulness to Israel. But they are not a substitute for Israel since in Paul's argument they function as a promise and a sign that 'all Israel' will be saved. But, prior to the salvation of all Israel, the Jewish remnant also functions as evidence that the Christ-movement is not one undifferentiated reality but encompasses people of differing ethnic backgrounds in their distinctiveness and particularity.

8.3 *The Church is not Israel (or New Israel)*

We have already noted in Chapter 7 that in Romans 9 the church is not equated with Israel. We need, however, to give the detailed reasons for this assertion. There are a number of issues that need to be addressed in this respect. Because gentile Christ-followers, as likewise their Jewish siblings in Christ, are designated as 'called' many scholars hold that this is sufficient evidence that Paul regards gentiles in Christ not only as equal with Jews but in some sense identical in that all the 'called' whether Jew or gentile not only share the promises but must also share the covenant, and are therefore part of Israel. This is in fact to claim that

---

16. That this remnant is small may be inferred from the contrast to 'the sand of the sea' but the 'only a remnant' of the RSV is gratuitous.

17. Käsemann argues against 'a category of a salvation history running its course in chronological continuity' on the grounds that this is 'inappropriate as a hermeneutical principle for the illumination of Paul's picture of Abraham'. He notes that the idea of a holy remnant (which was so important to Jewish Christianity, providing a verifiable transition from Israel according to the flesh to Christianity) plays no part in Paul's writings except for Rom. 9.27-29, 11.4-5, 13-16 (1971: 87).

18. Donaldson 1997: 179.

19. Cf. also Gal. 3.13-14 where Paul states 'Christ redeemed us from the curse of the law…in order that in Christ Jesus the blessing of Abraham might come to the gentiles'. Here the 'us' implies that the gospel is transmitted to the gentiles via the believing remnant of Jews.

the 'called' and Israel are identical which is not necessarily the case. Likewise the question needs to be asked, are 'Israel' and 'covenant' identical? Is it in fact possible for gentiles legitimately to share in the title 'Israel' and yet not to be part of the covenant? Or vice versa, are they part of the covenant but should not be designated as 'Israel'? Alternately should there be two separate covenants in order to safeguard the distinctiveness of Jew and gentile?

There seems to be good reasons why Paul should regard gentile Christ-followers as part of Israel. As we noted above, he makes a strong case that, through Christ, gentiles can become children of Abraham and share in the inheritance of Israel (Rom. 4.13–16). Should all the seed of Abraham, Jewish or gentile, not be identical since they share the same inheritance? This might appear perfectly reasonable but it is not the way Paul argues. Again in Rom. 9.22-24 he seems to combine Jews and gentiles into one people 'οὕς... ἐκάλεσεν ἡμᾶς'. Whilst there is no doubt that Paul does here, for the first time in this chapter, refer to the salvation of the gentiles nevertheless it should be noted that it is no more than a passing reference and that the focus of the argument is still on historic Israel. The citation from Hosea following in 9.25 has its primary reference to the restoration of Israel and only in a secondary sense by analogy can include the gentiles.[20] Thus the reference to gentiles is, as we have argued, at this point of secondary rather than primary significance. This means we must be careful not to read more into this verse at this point than seems to have been intended. Whilst everyone can readily agree that Paul does acknowledge the inclusion of gentiles, precisely how this happens is not explicit. We have to recognize that in Paul's scriptural citation καλεῖν does figure (9.7 and also 9.26), so there can be no dispute that gentile Christ-followers are 'called' the same as Jews. If we follow the logic of traditional Paulinism this could be seen as another argument for one common identity for all Christ-followers whether Jewish or gentile. But as we have already maintained, Paul expected gentiles in Christ to continue to live in accordance with their status at the receipt of call and likewise Jews in Christ (1 Cor. 7.17-24). On this reading of Paul which we think is more appropriate, then even the shared identity of those in Christ comprises differing sub-group identities, oneness despite differences, rather than sameness. Another option in this respect would be to hold that both Jews and gentiles in Christ share one and the same new identity in a new entity, new Israel. As we will note later, we regard this as un-Pauline and as having no basis in his letters. Our position is that since Paul never explicitly calls gentile Christ-followers Israel and since new Israel is not an option, then although gentiles share 'calling' with Israel they do so as gentiles in association with Israel and remain gentiles.

---

20. It would be surprising for Paul to use the Hosea citation with reference to gentiles when this was not its original purpose and since it is followed by two other citations that clearly apply to Israel. Paul takes the Hosea citation to apply *primarily* to Israel and thus the three citations have all the same point of reference, Israel. Rejected Israel, like the northern tribes, will be restored. This is Paul's primary thesis, but in and with the restoration, another 'non-people', the gentiles, will also be blessed, thus applying the Hosea citation to gentiles in a secondary sense, typologically, to gentiles also, cf. Campbell 2000: 198-200.

8. Self-Understanding in Christ and the People of God

Some scholars have sought to safeguard the distinctiveness of Jew and gentile, which most interpreters recognize as a legitimate aspect of Paul's theology, by positing the existence of two separate covenants, one for Israel and another for the gentiles.[21] This option does take seriously, as we do, the abiding difference between Jew and gentile in Paul. The apostle to the gentile nations who was deeply aware of the differing roles of Jew and gentile in the divine economy, is rightly deemed not to easily confuse their differing identities even with the advent of Christ. But we do not see this two-covenant hypothesis as Paul's solution to the relation of Jew and gentile in Christ. In our reading the distinctiveness of Jew and gentile in Christ is safeguarded and abides but in a common transformation in Christ. Whilst a new covenant is offered in Christ, we do not see this as a second covenant, but more as a renewal so that continuity in the divine purpose is thereby ensured.[22] We do appreciate however the serious concern of such scholars who have posited two covenants recognizing with them that Paul maintained the distinction between Jew and gentile even after the advent of Christ. We also recognize the seriousness with which they interpret Paul in such a way as to safeguard the integrity and future of Israel, something we also seek to do.

Thus whilst it must be affirmed that gentiles are called and thus in this respect cannot be differentiated from Israel, our reading of Romans 9 indicates that Paul is both consistent and clear that Israel refers only to the historic people of God; gentiles though sharing with these in the promises remain gentiles even in Christ. The most that can be claimed from Romans 9–11 is that the ἡμᾶς of Rom. 9.24 refers to a mixed group of people, Jews and gentiles, who together share one calling in Christ. But Paul goes on to differentiate between branches on a common olive tree and also to make reference to a part of Israel which already has responded positively to the gospel and to 'the rest' who have not yet done so. Neither of these groups include gentiles in Paul's further discussion throughout Romans 11 and it is unlikely that the passing reference in 9.24 should be viewed as the basis for the reconstitution of Israel. Paul's argument concerning this is that though 'not all Israel are Israel' (9.6), this implies only a selection within the people of Israel but not the inclusion of gentiles in the covenant which is dealt with by Paul elsewhere.

One question however remains. Though gentiles are not Israel, are they nevertheless part of the covenant ? We have opposed the option of a two-covenant reading of Paul. If there is not a separate covenant for gentiles, do they in fact

---

21. On this see Gager 2000: 59–66.
22. As W.D. Davies has noted, 'the adjective "ḥᵃdasah" in Jer. 31.33, translated *kaine* by Paul, can be applied to the new moon, which is simply the old moon in a new light. The new covenant of Paul, as of Jeremiah, finally offers re-interpretation of the old' (1978: 11). Käsemann fiercely opposes any posited continuity in earthly history; this is due partly to his own experience of and opposition to the ideology of the Third Reich and a resultant scepticism regarding earthly continuity of any kind especially theories of salvation history. But in this respect, he tends to be unduly negative, especially in his tendency firstly to demolish arguments about earthly continuity entirely, but then to proceed to allow them a limited significance within his own perspective.

need to be part of any covenant? If they are associate members of Israel as Wyschogrod suggests,[23] is it not sufficient for them through Christ to be satellites of Israel? Our view on this is no doubt influenced by the traditional view of Paul's theology as widening the covenant, extending it to include gentiles also. Our reading of Paul is that this extension of the covenant to gentiles does not pose any serious problems though it could be argued that if gentiles are through Christ members of the covenant, this is essentially equivalent to incorporating them into Israel and that therefore there can be no objection to their being regarded as part of a redefined Israel. The alternative to the latter, which appears to give real status to gentiles in Christ is to refuse to regard gentiles in Christ as within the covenant. This might seem to reduce their standing compared with Jews in Christ, but it would on the other hand safeguard their identity as gentiles which we maintain Paul also sought to do.

This is why as we already argued, Paul does not equate the 'church' of Christ-following Jews and gentiles with Israel. To do so would imply a disregard of the 'rest' and a disregard for the differentiation still remaining between Jew and gentile even in Christ. The 'new Israel' is both a post-Pauline and an un-Pauline concept.[24] To claim therefore that the 'Christian' is the true or real Jew is not only usurping another's name and inheritance, but flies in the face of all proper ethnic, religious and moral understanding. To claim the 'church' is the new Israel is now easily recognized as imperialistic displacement theology. But it is even more astounding to claim that Christ-followers are the true Jews – this is to go further in the same direction.[25] In the contemporary world, one of the increasingly common crimes is to gain access to a person's credit card and thus to usurp their good name, to take over the identity and credit of another person. It is quite similar for Christ-following Jews or gentiles to take over the name of the Jew, claiming there is no one else who truly answers to this description, name and identity better than they.

Of course this fraudulently 'solves' the Jewish problem. All real Jews would or should have become Christ-followers and since there are no real Jews other than those in Christ (and their fellow gentile Christ-followers), then Judaism has effectively been displaced, taken over and dismantled. Those Jews of New Testament times who were not convinced about the 'Christian' message and all their descendants of similar conviction are then not really part of the historic people of God. This 'theology' solves the problem of those people whom Paul bore witness to as having a zeal but not according to knowledge. In real life and history, real Jews have coexisted alongside Christ-followers across the centuries. Some theolo-

23. See Chapter 4.1.
24. On 'people of God' see Campbell 1997 part I.
25. It was quite different for Paul to speak of one who is a Jew inwardly or circumcised in the heart rather than outwardly. The Christ-movement was then still part of Israel and not yet a new religion in any sense, so whatever Paul said, was related only to differentiation *within Israel*, but to claim Christians are the true Jews when the two religions have been separate for centuries is a very different claim and one that can only be counter-productive for both Christian self-understanding and relations with people of other faiths.

gians have sought to theologize on this (perhaps unexpected) phenomenon.²⁶ However biased or creative their theological conceptions may have been, at least they have recognized what is plain for all to see – that the Jews did not disappear with the advent of Christ, the Fall of Jerusalem, the Bar Kochba revolt, or even the Holocaust. To theologize concerning ongoing Jewish existence is one thing, but to theologize Jews *out of existence* is quite another. It is to claim a knowledge Paul asserted to be quite beyond him as he says in one of his crowning benedictions in Romans 'Who has known the mind of the Lord?' (11.34–5).

8.4 Paul's Eschatology is Based on Confirmation of the Promises rather than Fulfilment

For Paul it sufficed to acknowledge the remnant and to hope for the salvation of all the rest, of all Israel whilst acknowledging that the future is known only to the mind of God. Not all Christ-followers are content to follow Paul or to leave the future of Jews to God. They want a more realized positive as well as negative eschatology; the future of both Christ-followers and non-Christ-followers has to be assured or fully realized in the here and now. Somehow the existence of Jewish people who do not acknowledge Christ is a threat rather than a challenge to Christian evangelism. It somehow seems to raise doubts about the power of the gospel or the claimed superiority of Christianity. Are we not as confident as Paul was that 'God is able to graft them in again?' (11.23).

Such a (fearful) kind of eschatology is radically at odds with the Pauline perspective. In any case, fulfilment of the promises is not the dominant Pauline approach in Romans but rather *confirmation* of the promises in Christ. That there are verses in Paul's letters which could be taken as evidence of full realization in the present, such as e.g. 'all God's promises find their "yes" in him' (2 Cor. 1.20), we cannot bypass those passages where there is clear witness to the contrary. In Romans references to 'confirm' or 'to be firm' occur at significant stages in the argument in relation to the promises. In Ch.4.16, faith is stressed as the means by which the promise may rest on grace and be firm (βεβαίαν) for all the descendants of Abraham, both those who adhere to the Law and those who as gentiles follow in the faith of Abraham. But the clearest enunciation comes in 15.8 , 'For I tell you that Christ became a servant to the circumcised to show God's truthfulness, in order to *confirm* (εἰς τὸ βεβαιῶσαι) the promises given to the patriarchs and in order that the gentiles might glorify God for his mercy'. This verse with justice could be taken to be a summary of Romans as a whole. Confirmation of the promises does not preclude a waiting, looking and longing for a coming final victory of God as Beker has alerted us.²⁷

It is at this point that some Christian theologians take leave of this difficult aspect of Paul's theology, preferring some view which gives more significance

---

26. As e.g. Augustine. As Paula Fredriksen notes, 'Augustine imputes an abidingly revelatory function to carnal Israel, precisely because of the dogged Jewish loyalty to the traditional observance of the law'. Fredriksen 2002: 100–1.

27. Cf. Beker 1980: 351–66. Cf. also Chapter 10.5.

to the church as replacing Israel. But how could someone such as Paul, who had confidence that God was faithful, regard the Jewish people as finally rejected, and that even before the final victory of God? If the kingdom has been fully inaugurated in and with the coming of Christ, but not yet fully realized, how can a final verdict on Judaism have already been delivered, even prior to the judgement of those in Christ and the rest of humanity? Realized judgement for Jews is often the reverse side of a coin that posits over-realized grace for Christians.[28] Thus *fulfilment* seems to elicit a more ready hearing than confirmation, and this contributes to the arrogant and boastful ecclesiology of a church claiming to have arrived but still exposing all the dominant signs of human sinfulness. We can hear Paul's ironic words to the Corinthians, 'Already you are filled! Already you have become rich! Without us you have become kings!' (1 Cor. 4.8). If for 'filled' we substitute a related term, the outcome is clear, 'Already you are fulfilled'. Paul's irony at the boastful claims of the Corinthians demonstrates how alien is an over-realized eschatology to his way of thinking. The fact that Paul concentrated his energies on the mission to the gentiles does not warrant the thesis that he had no longer any place for a mission to the Jews. Nor does the fact that he is depicted in Acts as symbolically shaking the dust off his feet mean that he is finished with the Jews, but only that he is moving on to another town or region.[29]

For Paul, his planned visit to Spain is yet to take place – the work of preaching the gospel to the ends of the Empire is still in process.[30] And since in his understanding, there seems to be some form of correlation between the incoming of 'the full number of the gentiles' and the final destiny of the Jewish people, it is unlikely that the one can take precedence over the other.[31] Thus Paul is never pessimistic about what God can yet achieve with Jews or gentiles. In this he is a true prophet. He hopes against hope, he hopes all things, believes all things because only God knows the future. What Paul does know with absolute certainty is that he who did not spare his own Son, but gave him up for us all, will with him freely give us all things (Rom. 8.32). Paul's future vision was not dependent on the actual response of the Jews to his gospel, nor upon the good response from gentile converts – it had a much more secure foundation offering a more certain hope – it was based upon what God had achieved already in Christ Jesus, and what that achievement would yet mean for the future of the world.

8.5 God's Covenant is Irrevocable:
The Identity of Israel is not Transferable

E.P. Sanders, surprisingly to some,[32] considering his general stance towards Paul and Judaism, claimed that covenant no longer functions as a central category in

---

28. Cf. Dodd's statement, 'according to 1 Thess. 2.16, "the wrath" had fallen on the Jews – εἰς τέλος – implying that this sentence of reprobation cannot ever be reversed' (1954: 120–1).
29. J.B. Tyson 1999 on whether mission to Jews continued despite Paul's gesture.
30. Cf. Jewett 1988: 142–61; but note πεπληρωκέναι in 15.19.
31. On this see Donaldson 1997: 215–26.
32. Cf. e.g. Hooker 1982.

Paul's thought. Paul's 'pattern of religion' differs from the 'covenantal nomism' of Palestinian Judaism in crucial ways mainly as a result of his christology of 'participation in Christ'. This aspect of Sanders' work has attracted much criticism.

Nils Dahl, in an early review of Sanders' *Paul and Palestinian Judaism*, stated that:

> Sanders would have sharpened, rather than weakened, his argument if he had more fully realised that the identity of the risen Lord with the crucified Messiah, Jesus, is at the centre of Paul's theology; that we cannot fully understand Paul without paying serious attention to his interpretation of scripture; and that Paul meant what he said about righteousness by faith and about the sanctity of the law and the remaining validity of God's promises to Israel.[33]

Whilst recognizing the enormous contribution of Sanders to the study of Christian origins, I must recognize the deficiencies noted above, particularly concerning the election of Israel. That the election of Israel is fundamental to Paul is the only adequate reason for his terrible dilemma at their limited response to the gospel. In our opinion, the acknowledgement of Jesus as Lord, stands clearly in opposition to the lordship of Caesar[34] and is perfectly in keeping with his identity as Messiah of Israel. It seems to us that Romans as a letter is particularly designed to demonstrate the faithfulness of God in his commitments to Israel. This is clearer if we hold together, and do not separate, two distinguishable aspects of the letter united in Paul, i.e. to demonstrate God's righteousness, (1) 'to prove at the present time, that he himself is righteous', and (2) 'that he justifies him who has faith in Jesus' (Rom. 3.25b–26).

The affirmation of God's commitment to Israel does not mean that Paul minimizes in any way the seriousness of Israel's failure to respond to the gospel. As noted above, his grief expressed vividly in Rom. 9.1–5, makes this plain. But Israel's lack of response, though a fact not to be ignored, is not to be misinterpreted. Both Paul and all his interpreters agree on the lack of response but it is in the interpretation of the meaning of this that scholars often part company with the apostle. For Paul, Israel remains Israel and is not redefined as the 'church' of Jews and gentiles.[35] Israel's election remains and is not transferred to another.[36] This is because the covenant was made with Israel, and the whole complex of ideas which has been termed 'Jewish Restoration Eschatology', is based entirely on the conviction that God has established an eternal covenant with Israel.[37] Where gentile Christianity has erred is in its assumption that because the covenant promise was that in and through Abraham they would be blessed, this assures

---

33. Dahl 1978: 157. Cf. also W.D. Davies' criticism of Sanders' claim that the category of the Lordship of Christ in Paul supersedes that of Messiahship, reduces the significance of apocalyptic for the apostle, consigns Paul to a vacuum, and underestimates the messianic dimension of his thinking which was not submerged by Paul's use of the term 'lordship of Christ'. Davies (1980: 31-4).

34. Georgi 1991, Horsley 2000a, Elliott 2005b.

35. Contra Wright; on this see Harink 2003: 156.

36. Contra Dodd's claim, 'Therefore, even if the entire Israelite nation is rejected, the promise has not been broken. It has been fulfilled by God in his own way…' (1932: 154-5).

37. On this see E.P. Sanders 1985: 77–119 and Wagner 2002: 29-31 and 286-8.

Christ-following gentiles that they have covenant participation with or without Israel. But this is actually by no means the case.[38]

The covenant is essentially a covenant with Israel which in addition and from its inception also offers blessings to gentiles. To assert this is not to minimize the role of gentiles in the divine plan for the world. But to ignore the fact that the covenant was first and foremost a covenant with Israel is to misunderstand its nature and scope. Israel's divinely given destiny is to be a light to the nations and that remains an inalienable part of Israelite identity and calling which cannot be taken away or transferred to another. We disagree with Käsemann's claim that '…when the apostle thinks of the covenant he no longer thinks of Moses and Sinai, but in a transferred sense of the creation of the world'.[39] This leads him to the startling conclusion that 'The Christian church with its members is the eschatological charter which *replaces* (emphasis mine) the Mosaic Torah' and that 'The phenomenon of the true Jew…is eschatologically realised in the Christian who has freed himself from Judaism…'[40]

Despite this negative view of continuity in the covenant, Käsemann recognizes that at a later date than Paul '…what Paul considered in Rom. 11.17–24 as a threatening possibility has already happened', 'the gentile-Christians were pushing the Jewish-Christians aside'. Thus in Ephesians 2.11–22 '…the continuity with Israel as the people of God is energetically stressed'. He explains this as '…further confirmation of the fact that every definition of the church relates to a concrete situation and must be interpreted in that light'. But by viewing the faithfulness of God to Israel as '…a special instance of his faithfulness to all creation',[41] Käsemann generalizes in opposition to his own insights in relation to Ephesians where he recognizes that '…every definition also contains its own particular danger if it is transferred into absolute terms, i.e. if it is removed from its historical situation and used in a timeless sense'.[42]

We have already argued above that divine freedom with regard to Israel is limited by divine commitment, and God is not free of all obligation to Israel. We may illustrate this further by a modern example from my own experience. When my father died, his will stated that I should inherit his farm for my lifetime only and that then it should be inherited by my son. When my son was sadly killed in an accident, it would have appeared to a casual observer that I was now the sole inheritor and that I could simply take over the full ownership of the property. But this was not so. Legally the farm still belonged to the estate of my son, and despite the closest family link, it did not belong to me. Only two years later after much legal discussion in the law courts was I able to alter the will and transfer

---

38. According to Käsemann, 'For Paul there can be no church of gentile Christians alone…the concept of the people of God growing out of the root of Israel has, therefore, an indispensable function in Paul's ecclesiology, even though it is only one of its aspects and not even the centre'. 1980: 309.
39. Käsemann 1980: 80.
40. Käsemann 1971: 149; 146.
41. Käsemann.1971: 109–10.
42. Käsemann.1971: 109–10.

legally to me the full ownership of the farm. Thus Christ-following gentiles cannot by right claim the inheritance of Israel in and by themselves, the covenant is not their covenant but the promises are mediated via Israel and shared through Christ and Israel.

What is open to gentile Christ-followers is through Christ to be enabled gratuitously to share with faithful Israel the blessings provided through the covenant. But this inheritance comes only in and through Abraham and his descendants, not through any inherent rights accruing to gentile Christ-followers. Only *with Israel* can gentiles *share* the richness of the olive-tree (Rom. 11.17–18). To claim that Israel failed in her destiny and that therefore her election is annulled or lost is to misunderstand both law and grace. It has been asserted that the Jews, despite being given the covenant through which God intended to redeem the world, have failed in their task and that Christ as the representative of Israel achieved what God had intended for Israel.[43] As Harink notes, this means that Israel's election is purely functional,[44] and if that purpose can be otherwise achieved, then Israel is rendered redundant. To regard Christ as representative of Israel, is not to solve the problem. At best this representative represents only the faithful in Israel, and his vindication in the resurrection does not change Paul's post-resurrection statements that there exists still a body of people, 'beloved for the sake of the fathers, but as regards the gospel, enemies for your sake' nor his added affirmation that 'the gifts and call of God are irrevocable' (Rom. 11.28–29). We note Paul's exact wording and qualification – he does not say 'enemies' as a bare statement of fact but rather, 'enemies for your sake' with all that this implies concerning the interrelationship of Jew and gentile in the gospel and in the divine economy.[45] Nor does he say 'enemies of God' as the RSV and NRSV amazingly translate without a shred of support in the text.

Continuity in salvation history is not to be limited to Jesus Christ and his history, but must include also the wider community of those who with him represent Israel.[46] What we are considering here is not just a theological concept, as if Israel were an idea or a flexible concept whose meaning could be simply transposed to its opposite. As Käsemann notes, 'There can be no question of "ideal Israel" '.[47] What Paul did in his driving a wedge into Judaism in Romans 9 was effectively to demonstrate that there had always been divine selection within

---

43. Wright 1997: 106. Wright also argues that this means that those Jews failing to recognize this are no longer truly Jews or part of God's elective purpose.

44. Harink 2003: 156.

45. Cf. Cosgrove's translation, 'From the standpoint of the gospel, they are enemies for your sake; but from the standpoint of election they are beloved for the sake of the fathers, for the gifts and call of God are irrevocable', 1997: 29.

46. Cf. Jervell 1972: 53.

47. Käsemann 1980: 263. Käsemann in citing here from Jülicher, goes on to ask, 'Is there in fact a continuity of the promise in earthly Israel which, however, is not sustained or guaranteed by the people as such but solely by the acting God?' He concludes, 'If so, then God is in truth this continuity and Israel is simply the earthly sphere chosen by him'. Despite his reservations, we do not see that Käsemann has entirely escaped the problem of earthly continuity so long as God, by his own choice, is tied in some sense to this particular earthly sphere.

Israel. In this he was limiting the membership of Israel to a certain group rather than to the totality of the people. But this limitation or reduction differs radically from a complete redefinition of Israel as possibly including gentiles[48] or even more surprisingly, including gentiles only. It is also different from maintaining that any one individual, even if he be the Messiah, can completely take the place of Israel. To loosen the correlation between Jews and Israel is to negate a simplistic nationalism, but to loosen is not the same as to completely detach.

We are dealing here with real people, not with a generalized concept of 'the Jew' or of Israel. Nor is Paul a post-Enlightenment philosopher for whom ideas may be the ultimate reality. We are not discussing universals but dealing with the particularity of a historic people.[49] Theological or philosophical fiat can appear to free us from the obligation to take seriously a people whose existence is difficult to reconcile with some forms of Christian theology. But this will not do. A naïve theological escapism that hides from inconvenient historical realities is of no real benefit to anyone, and conversely leads to a dangerous arrogance. Jesus Christ as God's elect can represent all those who trust in him and we must deal with this later. But Jews have still to be acknowledged and taken as seriously as Paul viewed them, rather than being dismissed by a theological fiat that too readily crosses the dividing line between idealism and historical reality.

Much of this theological construction arises from a failure to distinguish Jew and gentile and their respective roles in the history of salvation. As we argue in Chapter 6 above, in Pauline thought Jews remain Jews and gentiles remain gentiles even though ethnic significance like all other human interests is thereby somewhat relativized.

Gentile Christ-followers form satellite communities related to Israel but they are not actually Israel. If gentiles are not Israel and Christ himself is not Israel, then both Christ-following Jews remain Jews and Christ-following gentiles remain gentiles, and we are not at liberty to speak of the church as the New Israel. 'In Christ' Jews and gentiles do form one real association in which they are indissolubly connected because they all belong to him. Their unity emerges not from an ethnic transfer on either part but from their being reconciled to one another in their abiding difference to form one new body in him. By itself, the fact of the existence of the church does not solve the problem of Israel.

In real history real Jews remain Jews. One cannot simply take over the good name and identity of another without fraudulent activity taking place. Thus gentiles are not the New Israel but remain gentiles, even in Christ. To regard ethnicity as something that can be easily discarded or left behind is rather naive. An individual may break away from their historic social community, but that does not mean they have not been, and are not still being, influenced by it and its mores.[50] To speak of 'the Jew first' is not a sign of unjustified residual judaizing

---

48. We disagree with Dunn that in order for gentiles to share the blessings and Scriptures of Israel they need in some sense to see themselves as Israel. They need only to see themselves in some positive relationship to Israel. Contra Dunn 1998: 506–10.

49. On this see Harink. 2005: 12 n. 17 and Chapter 10.2.

50. Contra Zetterholm despite his useful discussion of Antiochus the Apostate (2002: 75–80).

8. Self-Understanding in Christ and the People of God

on Paul's part, but rather a recognition that Jews were a chosen vehicle in the transmission of the gospel from the Messiah to the gentiles.

To claim therefore that Christians, especially gentile Christians, are the real Jews is to seek to attain a laudable goal by the wrong means. In making this claim Christians are acknowledging gentile indebtedness to Israel. They are acknowledging their dependence on Jewish roots, their need for a proper identity. But the way to achieve this identity is to allow Paul's paradigm of the relation of Jew and gentile in the light of the Christ-event to guide our reflection. In this pattern or blueprint of identity, gentiles do have status as gentiles by virtue of their relation to Christ as Messiah and of his and their relation to the historic people of God.

Chapter 9

CHRIST-DEFINED IDENTITY

One of the most cited verses in Paul's letters is 2 Cor. 5.17, 'If anyone is in Christ, he is a new creation'. Since being 'in Christ' is here clearly associated with a new creation, there is thus a strong tendency to regard Christianity itself as a totally new creation, either in antithesis to, or to the detriment of, Judaism. Such a Christianity is in danger of developing a self-understanding as a new religious movement originating in the first century, a Jesus cult lacking any significant pre-history. In this chapter we will consider two aspects of identity in Christ. Firstly, to what degree is Christian identity in real continuity with Israelite identity and the narrative of Israel? Secondly, in what sense is Christ identity an aspect of the new creation ? We will also consider the individual and corporal aspect of Christ identity and the extent to which this identity is determined by the identity of Jesus as the Messiah of Israel.

9.1 Christ-Defined Identity and Continuity with the Narrative of Israel

One of the difficult issues for those wishing to stress continuity within the Bible is that of defining the Christ-event so as to stress its radical otherness whilst still maintaining a positive relation to what preceded it, that is, God's action and activity as witnessed to by the scriptures of Israel. The perception of divine activity is troubled by differing approaches and perspectives. A covenantal or *heilsgeschichtlich* approach may be open to the charge of limiting the significance of the Christ by viewing him as meeting a preconceived or already prescribed need. In this scenario the Christ is seen as determined to some extent by the need he meets rather than by the nature of his own mission and function. E.P.Sanders argues that since the conventions of apocalypticism had so little influence upon Paul, the hypothesis might be put forward that before his conversion and call Paul was not especially apocalyptically oriented. He continues, 'This is one more reason for not supposing that Paul began with a set apocalyptic view and fitted Christ into it'.[1] If we start from a preconceived framework then

---

1. Sanders 1977: 543. We disagree with Sanders that Paul was little influenced by apocalyptic, cf. Nickelsburg, 'Most of the wide spectrum of eschatological belief in the NT can be attested in contemporary Jewish writings, and conversely, the NT attests most forms of eschatological belief found in these writings. The defining characteristic of Christian eschatology was its connection with Jesus of Nazareth' (2003: 146). Cf. also Beker's comment: 'It is curious that Paul, so conscious of

there is apparently so much continuity that this impinges strongly on the image of the Messiah so as to determine his identity, rather than the opposite way around. The Messiah is determined rather than determining. He is not the focus or activator of the process.

The advent of Jesus as Messiah is, moreover, not an entirely new or even unexpected occurrence – he comes to a people already familiar with varying conceptions about how God will radically intervene for the deliverance of Israel, the defeat of her enemies etc. In short, a framework of interpretation already exists to enable comprehension of this new occurrence that is happening. Thus the Christ-event is the outcome of a story that stretches back into the dim recesses of Israel's troubled history.

This story did not have a precise formulation, having been created out of the twin convictions that God is the supreme ruler of this world and that he has called his people Israel. But both this world and this chosen people seem to be so beset by evil and contradiction that confident faith is rendered difficult and confused. These convictions were generative of particular beliefs that are visible in theologizing about the Messiah and the significance of his advent. To this extent, if not the event itself, at least the interpretation of the Christ-event, was directly influenced by the convictional world of the variegated Judaism of the first century,[2] itself a product of a long history of scriptural interpretation and reinterpretation.[3] The recognition of this factor is both necessary and foundational for any understanding of Jesus as the Christ. Its pervasive importance for emergent Christianity is clearly demonstrable in the frequency with which biblical texts are used to explain or develop the significance and identity of the Christ. As Harink has pointed out, 'Apart from the testimony of Israel's law and prophets, Jesus Christ would be a mere cipher, unrecognizable as the *apokalypsis* of the God of Israel'.[4]

9.2 Christ-Followers as New Creation?

The messianic movement that was eventually to become early Christianity was heir to the traditions that informed the diverse body of opinions in the varied Judaism of that era. Although the coming of the Christ radically altered previous hopes and expectations, it did not constitute for Christ-followers a complete disjuncture with all that preceded it. There was continuity in the convictional world it occupied and the story of God's dealings with Israel still predominated albeit with the major difference that now the focus of this was centred around the saving events of the life, death and resurrection of Jesus Christ. These events were not seen as just more events of a similar kind in a series of interactions

---

his universal call to be "the apostle to the gentiles" (Rom.11.13), insists on a particularist Jewish apocalyptic ideology to communicate the truth of the gospel in 1 Corinthians 15' (1980: 170–1).

2. Whilst we are aware of the plurality of Jewish groups in the first century, we have refrained from describing these as 'Judaisms'. In this we are guided by Nickelsburg's book noted above.
3. See Campbell 1993a: 234–54.
4. Harink 2005: 23.

between God and his people – they were viewed as radically altering the perspective of faith in which past and present were inevitably intertwined. As Karl Barth asserts, 'We are concerned with the new creation, and not with the sequence of cause and effect'.[5]

Paul, more than any other New Testament writer, is aware of this as e.g. Rom. 3.21 illustrates, 'But now the righteousness of God has been manifested…'. For a Jew nothing could ever devalue or detract from the patriarchal narratives and the giving of the Law, foundational to Israel's self-understanding and identity. But if Jesus is Messiah, then the narrative of God's dealings with Israel cannot be adequately developed by a simple addition to Judaism of a narrative of the advent of the Messiah.

It was Paul's distinction that he inherited the narrative and convictions of his Pharisaic background, but he was destined to have to radically revise these to take full account of the recognition that Jesus was the Christ. We think the apostle is best understood as seeking to apply and to express in his letters, in relation to problems within his communities, his revised convictions in the light of the Messiah concerning the people of Israel and the incoming of the gentiles. These convictions are what lie behind the theologizing in his letters concerning real community issues. The story of Israel, recounted in his Pharisaic community and reflected in its communal practices and especially his vision of the risen Christ[6] when applied to the concrete problems faced by his communities provided Paul with the raw material for his theologizing.[7] Whilst he could claim the advent of a new era, even of a new creation in Christ, this does not necessarily involve a complete denial of the convictions that preceded this. As I have previously argued in an earlier article, it was his 'tradition (that) gave Paul the language for expressing a theophany, and his vision of Christ provided a new point of departure within a traditional web of ideas'.[8]

His new theology of life lived 'in Christ' is certainly very different from Jewish halakhah in many respects,[9] but even this is not so much a denial of his Pharisaic past as a radical reformulation of this in the light of a new perspective. It represents not so much a complete departure from, as a reinterpretation of, a previous way of life. We need to recognize that Paul did not inherit the concept of the Messiah from Hellenism. Even if some Hellenistic influence is allowed, the content of the term is Jewish. Nor does a claim to allow gentiles some place in the divine economy involve a complete repudiation of the election of Israel. The issue for Paul is not one of Jew versus gentile, but of Jew and gentile within the one divine economy. Paul still moves within the traditions he inherited and is only adequately understood in the light of such traditions. Suffice to say that in his case, it is not just that scripture and tradition helped him to interpret the significance of the Christ, as if this were a separate distinguishable entity capable

5. Barth 1968: 364.
6. Cf. Burrowes 2004: 19–20.
7. On Paul's theologizing see Chapter 10.
8. Campbell 1993a: 234–54 (254).
9. But cf. Tomson 1990, and B. Rosner 1994: 181.

9. Christ-Defined Identity

of being viewed dispassionately on its own terms, but rather that even the significance of the Christ was largely influenced by the language and thought of his ancestral faith. That Paul had to extend his vocabulary and introduce new theological formulations is entirely in keeping with the recognition that though these may look very different from Pharisaic expressions, they are not necessarily inconsistent with them. Paul, like Jesus, still operated within a Jewish symbolic universe.[10] Even the term 'new creation', itself a Jewish concept, implies the existence of a previous creation, otherwise it has no real content, and the newness is only conceivable in relation to that which it claims to have surpassed.[11] To claim to be a new creation in some absolute sense is no longer convincing. We now recognize that imported knowledge requires a social base – a plausibility structure otherwise the knowledge becomes meaningless because it has been separated from the authenticating community.[12]

9.3 Divergent Interpretations of Divine Action in History

We find problems with the concept of new creation when used within a distinctly existentialist approach which so stresses the radical newness of the Christ-event that it leaves little room for an adequate recognition of previous divine activity in the world or, more precisely, in relation to the people of Israel.[13] Recent emphasis upon apparently unpredictable divine incursions into the human scene, what we might term, punctiliar revelation, leaves no real place for the influence of the church as a divinely appointed community of witness and the effect of this witness in influencing towards faith. Although via Ernst Käsemann the earlier existentialist approach of Rudolf Bultmann was strongly modified, if not corrected, mainly by his stress on apocalyptic, there remains a heavy influence of this approach in Käsemann's own work. The resultant legacy of Käsemann's excellent use of apocalyptic is that, in my opinion, an existentialist dimension is sometimes perceived as an inalienable element of the apocalyptic approach, a perception that would be difficult to defend.[14]

Käsemann's reaction to Stendahl's innovative approach to Paul led to his claim that 'the basic question today is still that of the relation between the doctrine of justification and salvation history'.[15] Whilst there may be some reason to suggest

---

10. Cf. K. Ehrensperger 2004b; cf. also W. Stegemann 2002: 45–61 (53).

11. E. Käsemann and P. Stuhlmacher were criticized by K. Kertelge for overstressing God's creative action thus diminishing God's covenant faithfulness (1967: 308). Similarly see M.T. Brauch's Appendix to Sanders (1977: 523–6) where he challenges the supposed Pauline transfer of God's faithfulness from the covenant-people to the entire creation (541–5).

12. Cf. Berger 1969: 46.

13. One of the strengths of Käsemann's theology is that he sought to modify Bultmann's excessive individualism with its consequent neglect of the 'extra nos' of salvation and of Rom. 9–11, as well as of Paul's Jewish heritage. The existentialist view of authentic human encounter and decision failed to pay proper attention to temporal continuity, cf. H. Anderson 1964: 37.

14. I have felt this to be the case in my reading of some of J.L. Martyn's work, e.g. his 1997a and 1997b.

15. 1980: 255. Most recently, D.A. Campbell has taken up this theme, and criticized both 'justi-

that Käsemann somewhat overreacted to Stendahl's theses, the issue of how to describe divine activity in the world in the history of Israel and through the gospel, remains a subject of great unclarity. If a continuous activity demonstrable in history is posited, this is rightly challenged as limiting the divine by a covenant people who failed to be faithful and thus to be a light to the gentiles as they were called to be. This challenge itself, however, very readily lends itself to being somewhat anti-Jewish in that Christians tend to look back on Israel's history from the (superior) vantage point of hindsight and of messianic fulfilment. The undoubted attraction of the term 'new creation' would seem to suggest that an apocalyptic perspective[16] is inherently more fitting than a covenantal historical approach, but this needs to be carefully assessed, rather than merely regarded as obvious. My own concern is not whether a scholar's stance is apocalyptic or otherwise, but rather on the effect of this stance on interpretation, whether explicit or implicit. If, to caricature opposing stances, it were to be claimed that covenantal approaches tend to overemphasize continuity in the divine purposes, and thus to favour a less critical stance towards Judaism and to a Jewish understanding of Paul, the alternative complaint would be that New Creation emphases tend to be implicitly anti-Jewish and to frequently result in an over-realized eschatology. One of the best discussions of some of these issues has recently been offered by Douglas Harink whose views we will consider at some length in order to see how one scholar seeks to give a coherent overview of divine action in history.[17]

Following J.L. Martyn, Harink argues that 'the "*apokalypsis theou*" is not one more event (perhaps even the greatest one) in a sequence of God's saving deeds within the history of creation and Israel. It is, rather, that God invades the cosmos, and inaugurates a fundamental change in cosmic regimes'.[18] But then Harink goes on to ask 'what remains if God invades the world in this way?'

> So thoroughly is the old world demolished by the cross for Paul, that we might ask if anything at all remains. If κόσμος οὗτος as the pre-apocalyptic world order and the σάρξ as our form of knowing and participating in it are both destroyed on the cross ('the world has been crucified to me and I to the world') does anything at all survive the destruction?[19]

Surprisingly, Harink then admits that relations between κόσμος οὗτος and

---

fication by faith' and 'salvation history' interpretations of Paul, arguing instead for his own version of apocalyptic eschatology which he terms as 'pneumatological participatory martyrological eschatology', 2005: 56–68. Harink, whilst appreciating the specificity of D.A. Campbell's stance, holds that it 'loses by shifting away from God's decisive action, and the cosmic dimension of that action vis-à-vis the powers opposing God and enslaving humankind…in Campbell's label, the emphasis seems to make a turn toward anthropocentrism, even granted the pneumatological component' (2005: 3).

16. The strength of the apocalyptic approach to Paul is reflected in the work of scholars in addition to those mentioned above (Käsemann, Martyn, Harink, and D. A.Campbell) see de Boers 1989, and especially, Matlock 1996.

17. In his book, 2003, and in his paper presented at SBL Annual Meeting 2005.

18. Harink 2005: 3.

19. Harink 2005: 6.

9. Christ-Defined Identity

κτίσις, between σάρξ and σῶμα, are more complex[20] than, on this scenario, we might have anticipated. 'What binds the stories of creation, Christ and the church together is not a linear historical causality or progression, but God's creating and recreating action... For Paul there is a singular recreative act of God – to which Israel's scriptures bear witness, and which they prefigure and eagerly anticipate, but which they do not lead up to'. For Harink God's act in Christ is a 'direct and original act of God, ...comparable only to God's act of creation in the beginning'.[21]

Harink then asks 'where is Israel in this dramatic divine invasion?' Israel is indeed there, 'not as a bit-player in Paul's account of the gospel in Romans, but as the original and irreplaceable, yet most difficult, witness to the truth of the gospel... *Israel herself is nothing less than a creation by the word of God*'.[22] In this important insight, Harink is in accord with Soulen's argument that Israel is not brought into being as a 'solution' to the fall, i.e., for a primary redemptive purpose. Rather Israel has its origin in a specific creative act of God...and so must not be seen as an interim and finally superseded stage in 'the history of salvation'.[23] Thus Israel is created not out of its own natural resources ('children of flesh' – Rom. 9.8) or decisions or works, but by God's word of promise, election call and grace (9.6–15) and God cannot fail to remain true to this word, and to the creature created by it, without rendering himself unfaithful, untrue, and unjust (Rom. 3.3–7).

Harink thus proceeds to the conclusion that Israel cannot be superseded in the divine purpose for this would pit the God of creation and Israel's election against the God of apocalyptic deliverance – God would supersede himself; but this cannot be, because God is not in conflict with himself, or with his prior creating/electing deeds. God's act of new creation in the apocalyptic event of Jesus Christ is God's utter faithfulness to his own act of creation and election – it is his very own *dikaiosune*'. Indeed the messianic community, though created through the gospel, despite its crucial role as witness will itself finally be superseded by the full redemption of Israel, and all creation.[24]

We are indebted to Harink for his comprehensive and coherent expression of divine action in history. We see it as a potential solution to problems arising from Käsemann's resistance to the recognition of any kind of earthly continuity in divine action in history. Käsemann has argued that though 'there is no immanent continuity in salvation history' (in so far as faith or denial results from confrontation with God's word), 'the faithfulness of God, who never leaves creation without his address and promise, is its true continuum, to which there corresponds on earth the experience that there always has been and is a band of hearers...'.[25] It might seem according to this scenario as if the Almighty has finally given up on

---

20. Harink 2005: 7.
21. Harink 2005: 11.
22. Harink 2005: 11–12.
23. Cf. Soulen 1996: 109–40, also Harink 2003: 160–8.
24. Harink 2005: 17–19.
25. Käsemann 1980: 256.

human agency and taken the whole matter into his own hands thereby ruling out any subsequent need for human mediation. According to Käsemann, God never leaves creation without his address and promise, and thus there always has been and is a band of hearers. But where are these hearers to be found and how are they to be recognized? God can truly maintain continuity on his side, but is there no apparent pattern of life within history common to those moments when God's word is (sporadically) active? Are there any particular groups of people more likely than any others to illustrate the continuity of the divine word operative in history? It seems to me that the emphasis upon continuity only on God's side leaves gaps in the understanding of the mediation of the gospel through the 'hearers' of the word. The role of the church seems not to be adequately and theologically recognized and accounted for. True it always has been and continues to be a body of sinful people liable to sin and corruption, but apart from miraculous intervention or invasion, how is the gospel to be mediated and proclaimed to a sinful world except by those confessing and attempting to obey the name of and person of Christ? The Spirit acts to make the gospel effective, but this is done in and through the witness of the church as a body of Christ-followers and not through stones or visions. So my contention is that though with Käsemann, Harink and others, we cannot maintain a linear and unbroken earthly continuity, we should despite this not minimize the role of the church which through the Spirit makes the word of God effective generation after generation. 'The promise is to you and to your children', cannot be diluted as if there should be no recognition that the church does have real historical continuity in its historical proclamation of the word, even though all its activity is still subject to the judgement of God.

Another most significant factor emerging from our discussion above is that the new creation cannot be depicted as simply in opposition to and total discontinuity with the first act of creation. There may be no earthly continuity in the full sense of that term, but there is continuity in that God does not reject, displace or supersede all that he has previously created through his word. He is faithful to Israel and faithful to his created world.[26] He will not destroy it again as in the time of Noah. Thus new creation so understood becomes an affirmation of God's continuing creative activity and that especially where his people witness faithfully to the truth of the gospel. New creation is both an affirmation of newness and of continuity within the ongoing purposes of God. We should beware therefore of setting up simplistic contrasts between old and new covenants, or between God's past and present activity in the world. One of the more frequently noted of these is where some scholars suggest that whereas in the past, God operated through a chosen people, since the Christ-event, he operates through individual response and salvation, 'the world simply becomes the theatre of individual decisions, the Creator no longer reaches out for his world...'[27]

If on the other hand 'new creation' is understood as involving both newness

---

26. As D. Harink stresses, 'God in His apocalyptic action cannot be unfaithful to His creative and elective action' (2003: 179 n. 34).

27. Käsemann 1980: 255–6.

9. Christ-Defined Identity

and continuity in the divine activity, then the role and identity of Christ-followers must reflect both of these emphases and not overemphasize either of these to the detriment of the other. Such an understanding guards against simplistic views of continuity or exaggerated claims of newness.

9.4 Individualism and Faith in Christ

In relation to the issue of corporate or individual emphasis it would appear to be the case that the less emphasis one lays on continuity with previous divine activity in human society as reflected in Israel or in the church, correspondingly more significance tends to be concentrated around the individual and their response to revelation.[28] There can be no doubt that the people of God as a religious community, through the Spirit of God, mediates the faith to the individual whether in Judaism or Christianity. On some rare occasions, there seems to be little evidence for the human mediation of faith, but in most instances the influence of communally transmitted religious life is clear for all to observe. Though the person as an individual makes their own unique response, in so doing they follow a pattern of revelation and response common to the transmission of faith. A very important factor in this transmission is contact with believing family members or significant others who positively (and also negatively) influence the individual to participate in the communal faith to which the significant others belong. In this aspect, Saul, later to become Paul, was no more an isolated individual than other humans.[29]

It is possible, dependent on which aspect one stresses, to regard Paul's conversion/call as a supreme example of God taking the initiative to reveal himself to an unwilling and resistant Saul in 'an event that owes absolutely nothing to upbringing, human development, or cultural tradition'.[30] But this is to overlook the religious nurture and upbringing Paul experienced as a Pharisee. It is likewise to overlook the influence of the close contact Paul had with those early Christ-followers whom he severely persecuted. Nor should we fail to take into account the influence of the Christ-followers at Damascus who initiated him into the new faith. Even within Paul's Jewish background there were clear models of human and divine interaction and encounter in the records of the calls of Isaiah, Jeremiah and Ezekiel.[31] These were part of his previous religious experience so that when

---

28. Cf. J.D.G. Dunn's comment that 'It is only by limiting his discussion to (Romans) 9.1–23 that Piper (in his) *Justification,* is able to maintain his thesis that election in that passage concerns individuals and their eternal destinies' (1998: 509 n. 46).

29. On this see Richard L. Rohrbaugh's claim that 'It is important to recognize that no society is one way or the other, either completely individualistic or collectivist… Individualistic behaviour did exist in the vertical, collectivist societies of the ancient Mediterranean world. That said, however, we must point out that these 'individualistic' persons in collectivist societies are not the equivalent of the introspective, psychologically minded, self-reliant individuals familiar to modern Americans' (2002: 27–44, 32). Cf. also his views on 'The Identity of Jesus' (2002: 36).

30. Barclay 2003: 133–56 (139).

31. Cf. A.F. Segal 1990. Segal views the distinction between apocalypticism and mysticism as being artificial and theoretical, not warranted by the realities of first-century experience, cf. 1990:

Paul himself experienced a radical divine presence, he had some experience to which to relate it and categories of understanding through which to interpret it. Even if, as is claimed, Judaism merely provided the language in which to express the meaning of the revelation Paul experienced,[32] we must still recognize the power of language which as a vehicle is far from neutral but always culturally laden and identity forming in the most basic sense.[33] It is totally unwarranted therefore to claim (with Barclay) that Paul's reference to being 'set apart from his mother's womb' whilst echoing prophetic call narratives, 'also expresses in the most dramatic form possible, the conviction that God's fashioning of history is independent of the normal channels of human causation' or that 'this "setting apart" happens before birth, before human nurturing, before cultural socialisation, and before Paul himself became a human agent' or that 'the only agency here can be that of God'.[34] The implied absolute contrast here between human activity and divine revelation represents a radical cynicism about what God through the Spirit can actually do through co-operative and trusting human activity whether in the pre-Christ or post-Christ era. Although God's fashioning of history may be described as independent of the normal channels of human causation this is not to deny that he has created humans in his own image or that he may still choose to use these as and when he wills, as in the supreme example of the Incarnation. To think otherwise is to assume a dualism that negates any possibility of co-operation between the Lord of history and the normal channels of human causation.[35]

However, we must not fail to take into account the fact that when Paul himself, with the aid of subsequent reflection, spoke of this experience it was always Christ-orientated and Christ-defined. There is nothing more apparent or more unquestionable than this unique feature of Paul's theologizing. We might sum it up in the phrase, 'For me to live is Christ'. This Christological focus is most visible in the 'in Christ' formula, often repeated in varying forms. Paul and his co-believers live in Christ, die in Christ, their entire life has a Christ focus. But it can legitimately be claimed that, properly understood, this is not in contradiction to continuity with Jewish expressions and records of revelation and response, divine initiative and human co-operation typical of biblical narratives.

---

39 and 69–71.

32. Barclay 2003: 140.

33. Cf. D.G. Horrell's critique of Barclay's view on this matter: 'It is somewhat one-sided to say that Paul's theological categories have been changed at the most fundamental level…without at the same time pointing out how thoroughly Paul's scriptural tradition continues to provide him with the categories in which he thinks' (2003: 161).

34. 2003: 139. Cf. Francis Watson's comments on the links between biblical texts and their environment: 'To abstract the biblical texts from their environment would be to treat them docetically, as originating directly from above without the mediation of historically and culturally located human agency', 'The Scope of Hermeneutics', Watson 1997: 65–80 (77).

35. Cf. E. Käsemann, 'He (Paul) holds fast to the identity of the God who reveals himself in history, because to do otherwise would be to lose the creator, as was the case with Marcion' (1971: 94), see also 96.

9.5 Continuity and Discontinuity in Personal Identity in Christ

Our discussion of this section of our topic up to this point has been designed to show how ill-advised it is to speak of Paul's conversion/call as if it entails a complete repudiation of all his previous life and its norms, as Barclay maintains. He asserts,

> Paul makes it as clear as possible that he no longer regards himself as living within 'Judaism'. But this is not because he has entered some other cultural medium, with its own rules of human traditioning, but because he now sees with utterly different eyes, from a perspective that radically relativizes, if it does not wholly obliterate, all social and historical categories (cf. Gal. 3.28; 6.15).[36]

It is beyond debate that Paul confesses to a complete re-evaluation of everything 'in Christ' as Phil. 3.7–9 illustrates. But what this actually entails is that elements or motifs of his theological thinking are being reorganized or reconfigured within a revised value-system. This cannot possibly represent the entire replacement of one way of life by another, as if every element in Paul's Pharisaic background stood in complete opposition to Christ. E.P. Sanders' summary of this issue suggests that Paul took over some motifs from Judaism while rejecting others, and that Christianity achieved its own identity by pursuing a course which 'involved the simultaneous appropriation and rejection of Judaism'.[37] Whilst Sanders is not purely negative on this issue we would wish to give a more differentiated account of the formation of Christian identity. Though Paul may assert that he died with Christ claiming that 'I live and yet not I but Christ lives in me', we still have no real difficulty in recognizing the individual and personal continuity evidenced in this 'new man in Christ'. This is not to deny or to seek to devalue the significance of the change in even a devout Jew such as Paul. Paul's life was changed for ever after his Damascus road experience. We are merely putting this in context so as to prevent unrealistic and unfounded exaggeration between personal and communal past and present.[38]

More importantly, this claimed reorientation ought not to be perceived or explained as incompatible with a Jewish identity, as if there were an inherent opposition between everything genuinely Jewish and all that is distinctly Christian. If identity in Christ is perceived or explained as a repudiation of Jewishness, then it would follow according to Tom Wright's thesis that the only solution to the 'exilic plight' of Jews is for individuals as individuals no different from gentiles to *abandon their ethnic covenant status*, embrace or grasp in faith Jesus Christ and so regain their covenant status. According to Wright, after the Christ-event God in Jesus Christ eradicates any theologically relevant difference between Israel and the nations and establishes a *universal* relationship with the individual members of Israel and the nations in terms of their common humanity as crea-

---

36. Barclay 2003: 139–40.
37. Sanders 1983: 210.
38. Cf. L. Keck's comment, 'As Paul sees it, gentiles abandon their religion when they accept the gospel (1 Thess. 1.9–10), but observant Jews who accept it do not change religions but reconfigure the religion they already have' (2005: 286). Cf. also Segal 1990: 75.

tures of God who have fallen into sin and stand in need of the redemption offered by Christ.[39]

On this view of the radical changes wrought by the advent of the Christ, Israel as a historical and theological entity is dissolved, only to be replaced by a modern liberal form of individualism. Ethnic identity is to be negated and even obliterated so that a universal relationship to individuals as individuals may be established. On this view ethnic and other historical particularities are relativized or obliterated.[40] In contrast to Paul's vocabulary we are no longer dealing with Israel and the nations but with the concept of a universal undifferentiated humanity.[41] As Harink maintains, this has wide-reaching effects, for not only is corporeal Israel thus cancelled as an historical entity, but the same result applies to the corporeal body of Christ.[42] The problem of 'Israel according to the flesh' has been solved, but at what cost? To be 'in Christ' has lost something of its corporate dimension and a Christ-defined identity applies in the first instance to an individual Christ-follower's identity, rather than being the corporate identity of those who together coexist united as one body. (Wright does speak of regaining covenant status through faith in Christ, but it cannot be the same covenant status as that of Israel, and those members of historical Israel who do not exercise faith in Christ suffer theological annihilation.)[43] What emerges here is that a modern concept of change through conversion is being anachronistically applied to the apostle. It is claiming to know what conversion involves and arguing backwards to Paul, who as one who is claimed to have been converted must then be seen to exhibit all the (already) known characteristics of a modern conversion experience. So instead of Paul becoming the paradigm for (one form of) 'conversion' experience, he becomes the vehicle of later conceptions to which he is obligated to conform.

But as we have sought to demonstrate above, there is no absolute discontinuity either in Paul's relation to his Pharisaic background in his interpretation of the Christ-event nor in the continuity between past and present in his own personal life. In both of these there is both continuity and discontinuity and neither of these elements can be disregarded. The continuity functions to negate any alleged claim

---

39. Cf. D. Harink's detailed critique of Wright's theology of Israel in Ch. 4 of his book (2003: 151–207, esp. 182–3). On this see also E. Käsemann's critique of G. Klein 1969: 145–79 (148) 'The view that the history of Israel is "radically profaned and paganized" demonstrates precisely the arrogance against which we are warned in (Romans) 11.20. No one can be forbidden to go beyond the apostle if his own theology forces him to do so. But to do this in the name of the apostle and of our chapter is simply unjustifiable, because that is to do violence to both', Käsemann (1971: 87).

40. Neither Paul nor Jesus could step outside the moral world of their culture. Hence the attempt to obliterate either ethnic or other forms of cultural identity is not viable. As Wolfgang Stegemann asserts 'It is a false presumption to think that Jesus had a reflexive or distanced relationship to the symbolic world of his people, similar to the one we can adopt as historical observers' (2002: 45–61, 53).

41. Whereas, as Malina notes, 'There is no evidence of universalism of any sort in antiquity' 2002: 3–26 (9).

42. See Harink 2003: 184.

43. See Wright 2000: 176. Cf. Harink's devastating critique of Wright's supersessionist interpretation of Paul (2003: 180–5 and 198–207).

that to be in Christ means necessarily to be in opposition to Jews and Judaism. To be anti-Jewish is certainly not a legitimate or essential aspect of Christian identity, though it is often represented as such and functions thus in terms of negative self-definition. We have moved a long way from the roots of our faith when a Christ-defined identity can be conceived as somehow inherently anti-Jewish.

9.6 *Christ-Defined Identity and Antagonism to Judaism*

What is surprising is that some decades later than Paul we are faced with the extreme example of Ignatius who not only claims 'it is monstrous to confess Christ and to practise Judaism',[44] but he even proceeds to set grace in contrast and opposition to Judaism (rather than to sin), as if there were an inalienable and insurmountable opposition between them.[45] In this he is diverging from the Pauline pattern and perspective. Although the practice of the law as a way of life is normative within Judaism, Paul, despite his transformation to become a Christ-follower, is still able to refer to adherents of the law in a neutral rather than a pejorative sense as we have noted in relation to Rom. 4.16. Yet, in the instance of Ignatius, the surprising development emerges that the actual practice of Judaism has itself become a negative identity marker for those in Christ, a development foreign to Paul's perspective. It is our contention that when Paul's interpreters are unable to follow him in this particular (neutral) reference to Judaism, they exhibit characteristics of subsequent developments in interpretation that are hostile and inimical to a fruitful understanding of the apostle, however well intentioned their motives.

The problem of stressing continuity between Pauline Christianity and Judaism is that it involves our perception of *progression* and development. If Jesus Christ is truly the Messiah, and focus of divine activity, then how can he be viewed simply as a development of a Jewish faith whose glory in Pauline terms he surpasses? Alternatively, if we claim absolute discontinuity, we are left with a Messiah who is totally inexplicable in human terms, a Melchizidek, the result of an arbitrary incursion of an unpredictable deity. But since there is general agreement in Christian theology on the fact that the Christ must radically relativize everything that preceded him, we should perhaps take this as our starting point. This means that with the recognition of Jesus as the Messiah, a radical re-evaluation of the tradition takes place. Thus some form of break in continuity seems inevitable though, as already noted, we should also recognize that what is 'new' is not necessarily inconsistent with Judaism.

This element of discontinuity, as we have already argued, must not be exag-

---

44. *Magnesians* 10: 3, cf. *Philadelphians* 6.1 where Ignatius maintains 'it is better to hear Christianity from the uncircumcised than Judaism from the uncircumcised', indicating that his strongest opposition is towards gentile Christians whom he regards as judaizing. Cf. Zetterholm 2002: 203–8.

45. As Dunn notes, 'It is precisely as a differentiating term that "Christianity" first emerges in Ignatius...that is, Christianity as different from Judaism, Christianity defined as not Judaism' (1998: 531 n. 154).

gerated since there can be no doubt that for Paul Jesus is not only Lord, but the promised Messiah of Israel. It becomes clear that in the post-Pauline era, whilst still retaining its Jewish roots, a distinctively Christian self-understanding was rapidly developed. It is the adequate recognition of this christologically generated dichotomy as well as its proper theological expression that lies at the heart of many differences between contemporary scholars. The thorny question remains, 'How may scholars affirm simultaneously the integrity of Judaism on its own terms and likewise the radical newness of Christianity?' It does not make good sense to describe the latter as 'the essentially Jewish story now redrawn around Jesus ?'[46] David Horrell (following T. Donaldson) offers a better explanation of the theological processes involved here. 'The fundamental story of God's gracious dealings with humanity reach their zenith in the Christ event, itself the generative centre of this story, which *then* provides the paradigmatic story with which Paul shapes his telling of any other stories, including those about himself'.[47]

We are in close agreement with Horrell that the Christ-event becomes the centre of the story of salvation and the paradigm which shapes the whole of Pauline thought about the world as well as about himself. But caution must be exercised lest the use of terms such as 'centre' should seem to negate the Pauline hope of the coming victory of God, the consummation of the activity inaugurated by the Christ-event.[48] However central the Christ-event might be for Paul, it did not negate a forward-looking expectation of a final victory of God over enemies and evil. As Beker asserts, 'Paul knows himself to be the eschatological apostle who spans the times between the resurrection of Christ and the final resurrection of the dead'[49] and that 'the resurrection of Christ ...marks the appearance of the end in history and not simply the end of history'[50] This 'not yet' of salvation means that premature condemnation of Israel as already rejected must be ruled out and likewise premature boasting in salvation as having been already achieved.[51] In the interim, the church of Christ is subject to suffering and tribula-

---

46. Contra Wright 1992: 79.
47. Horrell 2003: 168. Horrell regards 'reconfigure' as a helpful term in this discussion – 'Paul may consider himself to have had an experience that renders him dead to everything in his past and that causes him to see all things from an entirely new perspective, but the fact that he narrates the experience in terms drawn precisely from that past, and describes the new things precisely in the language and categories of Judaism and its scriptures, means that there is a much more complex interrelationship between "old" and "new" than Barclay's essay (and Paul's rhetoric) seems to imply. Paul's new epistemology, in other words, represents, as it must in all such human experience, a reconfiguring of his language and tradition rather than a creation *ex nihilo* – which would be meaningless to Paul and his contemporaries' (2003: 160–1).
48. Cf. Beker, 'Paul's gospel does seem welded to the apocalyptic world view... Paul connects the coherent centre of the gospel with the particularity of an apocalyptic idiom' (1990: 171). Cf. also n. 1 above.
49. Beker 1980: 145.
50. Beker 1980: 149.
51. As Beker maintains, 'A theology of the cross that is unrelated to the resurrection as 'first fruits' of the kingdom of God and the future resurrection of the dead is in danger of neglecting the created order and the hope for God's final cosmic victory over his rebellious creation, which he

9. Christ-Defined Identity

tion, and thus sees through a glass darkly, not having complete knowledge either about its own or Israel's salvation, even though it is now armed with the paradigm of God's activity in Christ in the world. Setting the Christ-event in the wider context of divine activity in the world,[52] helps to diminish Christian triumphalism and to prevent a naive critique of Judaism from a supposed platform of Christian superiority. But this in no wise reduces the significance in Paul of a Christ-defined identity as the model and goal of those whom he describes as being in Christ.

9.7 Corporate Identity in Christ

When we begin to consider more precisely what Paul intends by this description of Christ-followers, we are led to the realization that there is much more continuity implied within this than might have been anticipated. In particular, Paul reinforces the identity of his communities by referring to them in terms of a people called, echoing as I have noted elsewhere, the election of Israel.[53] This drawing upon Jewish conceptions such as family or children of God is typical of Paul's strategy with his new communities.[54] Wayne Meeks has amply illustrated how this corporate emphasis on the language of belonging, especially the intensity of kinship language, creates a sense of group identity distinct from outsiders.[55] In solidarity with Christ they form one body, one family of which they are all a part and to which they all owe obligation. They are not simply isolated individuals linked individualistically to Christ but together they now share one corporate life in him. They become joint-heirs with Christ and through him become neither proselytes nor Jews but children of Abraham.[56] There is here a possibility of another dimension of single importance for gentile identity in Christ which has not been sufficiently realized or acknowledged. This is what we might term the inclusive nature of the Messiah. What we wish to note here is that Christological language though it can of course be exclusive, is actually used in a corporate and inclusive way.

When Paul in Romans 6 uses many συν compounds to accentuate the changed

---

promised in the resurrection of Christ' (1980: 180).

52. In a recent lecture, as yet unpublished, Professor George Newlands emphasized that a Christomorphic view of the world is not narrowly exclusive, focused only on the church but one that encompasses the divine plan of creation as well as that of redemption, and that these must not be viewed in a mutually exclusive fashion.

53. Campbell 1993a: 249–54. As J.D.G. Dunn rightly stresses, 'the identity of Israel is determined by God's call', 1998: 510.

54. See M. Tellbe 2001: 134–5.

55. Meeks 1983: 85–7. Cf. also B.J. Malina's claim '…we know that persons in antiquity were inculturated in collectivistic societies; hence, they were collectivistic personalities. They were not individualistic', 2002: 3–26 (5).

56. Nor are they designated as Israel, despite sharing a common calling with Christ-following Jews, contra J.D.G. Dunn (1998: 525–6). Dunn gives a very thoughtful and fair discussion of the textual evidence but fails to recognize that differentiation in Christ still remains, though relativized, so that the 'called' are not all identical.

allegiance of Christ-followers, his argument hinges on the fact that they literally share in the death of Christ.[57] Just as he died to sin so too must those who follow him. Christ's death to sin has a sharing possibility of 'dying with' because he died as the anointed Davidic king when he won a victory over sin and death by being raised from the dead.[58] Those who belong to the anointed King of God share in his victory in that if the king is victorious, the people are free. It is from this known identity of Jesus as the victorious king – first indicated in Rom. 1.4 (cf. stem of Jesse Rom. 15.12) – that Paul develops his 'συν' language (coalesced with the likeness of his death, crucified with him, buried with him). Sin is viewed as a slave-master exercising dominion (6.12,14,16,18,20,22). Paul claims he was crucified with Christ so that by this death his body would be released from the slave-master sin and its dominion. Christ, having died is no longer vulnerable to the power of sin and believers can share in his victory by being buried with him and thus obtaining release from sin.

This is not just to emphasize the finality or reality of (Jesus') death, but rather that followers in Christ become part of his family and as such are buried together with him. Paul's point in the metaphor of death is not simply of someone who died but about someone who is buried with someone else. This idea of being buried with someone also points to the fact that they are part of the same family or dynasty.[59] The emphasis is not so much on something that truly arrives at an end (burial as the seal of death) but on something that starts because of the reality of belonging to the same family. In Jewish texts the reference to being 'buried with' is almost always to those who were part of the royal families as being buried with their fathers/ancestors. Thus Christ-followers are buried with their king, the anointed Davidic king who is the first-born of a large family (Rom. 8.29). The action of God in baptism in burying the follower with Christ makes him a member of the family. As a dead member of the family, he can be buried in the family tomb, and the outcome of this death has as its result the start of walking in newness of life made possible by Christ's resurrection.[60] The study of the with (συν) terminology in relation to Christ, taken along with the frequent use of the 'in Christ' formula demonstrates convincingly the corporate aspect of Christ-following. In 1 Cor. 6.20 Paul can assert that 'You are not your own, you are bought with a price' but this is just another way of affirming the corporeality of those in Christ. We should not think in terms of isolated individuals individually adhering to Christ but of a corporate entity in which individuals together grow and develop in one body.[61] In this way, whether it is life in Christ or life with Christ, the emphasis is the same, the totality of this life is defined and deter-

---

57. Though they do not yet share in Christ's resurrection, Cf. Beker 1980: 163.
58. I am indebted here to S.V. Sabou's 2005: 94–116.
59. Cf. Sabou 2005: 143–4.
60. Sabou 2005: 90–101.
61. Contra Wright, as Harink has critiqued the issue 'Perhaps Wright hardly intends it, but in his hands the biblical understanding of the people of Israel is reduced to Jews (with gentiles) as individual seekers and choosers of Christianity, who participate in the new movement primarily through self-moved individual faith rather than through election into a specific corporate body' (2003: 182).

mined by the identity of Jesus as Messiah.

9.8 The Identity of Jesus as Messiah of Israel

Moreover we must be quite clear that the Messiah does actually have a very particular identity – he is the promised Messiah of Israel. When we wish to stress the historical origins of Christianity, it is important to speak of the Jesus-movement, or of the historical Jesus. It is also important to stress that Jesus was a Jew, a real person in a first century Jewish context. But care needs to be exercised lest we speak only of Jesus – since this is not an adequate description of his identity in as much as he is not merely Jesus but rather Jesus the Christ. There were other men with the name 'Jesus' in the first century but the one of central significance for Christian faith is Jesus the Christ, who was crucified but vindicated by God in the resurrection, not just any Jesus. Christianity is not so much a Jesus-movement as a Christ-movement – it should not be a Jesus cult but rather a Christ-centred movement as its title indicates. We cannot therefore simply use the words 'Jesus' and 'Christ' interchangeably as if they meant exactly the same.

When we check Paul's use of terms in this respect it is very illuminating. He uses 'in Christ' very frequently but never 'in Jesus'.[62] Although it is debated whether in Paul's time Jesus Christ had already become just the common name for Jesus, it is most likely that Paul deliberately and self-consciously uses terms that tell his mainly gentile communities that this Jesus whom they proclaim is the Messiah of Israel. Paul feels no necessity to argue that Jesus is the Messiah but he does not speak of Lord Messiah which probably indicates that he regards both of these as titles which should not therefore be simultaneously applied. Thus Paul sees the whole of the believer's life as being conjoined with Christ (σύμφυτοι) but not with Jesus. What needs to be recognized is that for Christians the Christ of faith is no less real than the Jesus of history and these two aspects of identity are in this instance inseparable.

By not stressing Jesus as the Christ, it is easier to remove him from his Jewish context as if he were entirely without historical antecedents. Granted, Paul modified traditional messianic concepts, but this constitutes only a realignment and adjustment of already existing expectations. The frequent use of scripture and even novel uses of texts had as its central function to emphasize the connection between this Jesus as the Christ and Israel's scripture-based hope. Thus the Pauline gospel presupposes a positive link with Israel rather than the rejection of Israel. As Beker asserts, 'a rejection of Israel by God would simply cut the connection of the gospel to its foundation in the Hebrew scriptures and degrade the God of Jesus Christ into the God of Marcion – a new God who has no relation to creation or to Israel's salvation history'.[63] The character and the faithfulness of God are determined to a great extent by how the identity of Jesus Christ is

---

62. The references to Jesus in 2 Corinthians are not representative of Paul's letters generally.
63. Beker 1986: 10–16 (14).

understood. If Jesus Christ bears no particular relation to the revelation of God as received in the scriptures of Israel, and to the people of Israel then it is difficult to discover how it would be possible to speak meaningfully of God's redemptive activity as faithfulness.[64]

This particular identity of Jesus as the Messiah of Israel also means, as we have already noted, that the life in Christ is further defined – it is not individualistic but corporate, and the Jesus-movement is not a new religious movement without any prehistory but linked via Christ and the earliest Christ-followers to its origins as a messianic sect of Judaism.[65]

We can agree with Wright that human beings approach Christ as particular human beings from a specific context in time and place.[66] Moreover we must also recognize that Paul can only be the paradigm for all Christians if we assume one common undifferentiated identity for all. We must think in terms of Christian identities rather than identity. Thus although Paul is in one sense the model for Christian existence in Christ, he cannot be the prototype of all Christians. We have argued that such universalization is foreign to Paul's thinking. Paul therefore is the paradigm for Jewish Christ-identity but not for gentile. In this sense the particularity if not the individuality is emphasized.[67] This is again to insist that life in Christ is not a Christ-mysticism where the identity of the believer is fused with the identity of the Christ in such a way that their particularity is lost. Nor are we claiming that being in Christ and participating in the body of Christ necessitates the loss of particular identities, to allow the creation of some new entity, a 'third race' that rises above the particularity of culture and social relatedness in almost magical fashion.[68] Rather, in Christ there is no fusion of identity. To be united with Christ is not to be fused with Christ – particularity is retained but transformed through the relationship, yet only as a transformation of particular identity rather than as a replacement of it. Thus despite the fact that Christian identity is a Christ-defined identity, to be in Christ is to retain one's particularity whether as a Jew or as a gentile, and diversity is thereby demonstrated as normative for the body of Christ.

9.9 Multiple Identities in Christ

The retention of one's particularity in Christ, whether as Jew or gentile, is a fundamental plank in our understanding of the process of identity-construction as Christ-followers. This basic claim to particularity is of great importance because we wish to stress in the light of our recent and increasing awareness of the

---

64. Beker 1986: 15. To speak only of faithfulness to the creation is not adequate, see n. 11 above.

65. Cf. Beker '…the Gentiles must hear that the gentile church has no authenticity or identity unless it realizes that it "is grafted" contrary to nature, into a cultivated olive tree' (1986: 16).

66. Though we would wish to qualify this by stressing the work of the Spirit in the people of God and the effect of this upon the individual in drawing them through the Spirit to Christ rather than by the agency of self-moved individual faith.

67. See Campbell 2004.

68. On socialization and enculturation see Malina 2002: 3–26 (5–6).

9. Christ-Defined Identity

'constructedness' of claimed identities,[69] that despite our enormous potential for identity construction, not all structures are feasible or available to us as potential builders.[70] We are forced to start from where we are and, in the world of Paul's day, that meant as either Jews or gentiles, accepting these components to a great extent as part of the given.[71] So we construct from where we are and this limits the constructions open to us. In one sense we do create ourselves and our identities, but from the perspective of recognizing the given and its undeniable influence on our options,[72] we can no longer boast that we are entirely self-made individuals. At best we can claim with Sinatra, 'I did it my way'. Significantly, at the conclusion of a long discussion of the nature of ethnicity, Esler asserts, 'In any particular case, therefore, we need to be open to the possible stubbornness of ethnic affiliation, while not underestimating the power of individuals and groups to modify ethnic identity for particular social, political or religious ends'.[73] In agreeing with Esler our perception of this issue is that, whilst culture may be socially constructed, the fact of birth within a culture limits the possible varieties of constructional options available to individuals.

If we take Paul and his self-description as an exemplar of the construction of identity in Christ we discover that within the larger Jewish/Judean descriptor are several sub-identities that are also significant for him. In times of great stress or focal points of arguments he resorts to a catalogue of self-ascriptions such as circumcised, of the seed of Abraham, of the tribe of Benjamin, a Hebrew born of Hebrews, according to the Law a Pharisee, blameless before the Law (cf. Rom. 11.1; Phil. 3.5–6). Our view of this is that whilst all of these self-ascriptions are important to Paul they are not all equally so. Rather than regarding these as each comprising distinct identities, such components could be described as sub-identities in a nested hierarchy of identity of which being in Christ is the primary.

Paul shares with gentiles in Christ the primary identity-marker[74] which is faith in Christ. He shares with gentiles a special bond as apostle to the gentiles but he differs from them in that he is both Jewish and, by divine commission, apostle to

---

69. On this see J.A. Nagata, 1974: 332 and also her book 1984. I am indebted to my research student Kar Wong Lim for directing me to these references.

70. To recognize the cultural constructedness of identity does not imply that we can escape completely from our social and cultural locatedness, cf. J. Derrida's stance that everyone is born into a specific social, cultural and geographical context, into a specific language at a specific moment in time, 'Everything is drawn for me from the...experience of this "preference" *that I have at the same time to affirm and sacrifice*' (1995: 363).

71. Cf. P.F. Esler 2003a esp. Chs. 2 and 3, 19–39 and 40–76.

72. On this see Clifford Geertz on 'primordial attachments' by which is meant , 'one that stems from the "givens" – or, more precisely as culture is inevitably involved in such matters, the assumed "givens" – of social existence: immediate contiguity and kin connection mainly, but beyond them the givenness that stems from being born in a particular religious community, speaking a particular language, or even a dialect of that language, and following particular social practices...' Esler (2003a: 45).

73. Esler 2003a: 48.

74. Contra Dunn 1990: 129–82. Dunn claims that faith in Christ in becoming the primary identity marker, 'renders the other superfluous' (161–2).

the gentiles. So whilst Paul shares the primary identification of being in Christ, this is accompanied by a differentiation in terms of ethnic and cultural affiliation. He is an Israelite but they are not Israelites despite being in Christ.

To be in Christ is not universal and the same for all peoples. Paul's converts from the nations are clearly designated by him as gentiles throughout his letters. His strong insistence on their not becoming Jews underlines the fact that for Paul Jew and gentile are fundamental categories and that however much Jews and gentiles share in Christ this in no wise makes them the same. Gentiles, though sharing in Christ, are not designated as Israelites. In Christ ethnic difference is not transcended but the hostility that accompanies this should be.[75] This by no means overlooks the fact that a pure ethnic origin is a dangerous fantasy similar in kind to the concept of a Christianity that is without ethnic dimensions (a church that is neither Jewish nor gentile). Neither does the modern concept of 'hybrid' identity offer a solution to the problem of Jew and gentile in Christ. To be in Christ does not represent a fusion of identities so that Christ-followers are a fusion of Jewish and gentile identities. However useful such concepts may be, they are foreign to Paul's understanding.

Paul's theologizing is dynamic and he by no means views his converts as continuing in an unchanged existence. They are continually changed by being in Christ but this involves their transformation as Jews or as gentiles, not into some third entity. It is their sinful nature that is transformed not their ethnicity. Thus Paul permits, even supports, Jewish Christ-followers living a different life-style from gentiles in Christ. For some theologians such asymmetry smacks of inequality and therefore seems un-Pauline.[76] But Paul's struggle was for gentile equality in Christ, not to make gentiles and Jews the same in Christ. Thus properly understood, there can be no dispute concerning gentiles as equal to Jews in Christ though following a different life-style.

The thrust of our argument has been that Jewish identity in Christ is maintained and, to a different extent, that of gentiles also. Such reasoning should not be viewed as relating only to a minor element of Paul's thinking. It is in fact central to his entire pattern of theologizing. To view Paul thus is to advocate a new paradigm. It involves a reassessment of his entire theological thought, that is, of themes such as the Torah, grace, sin and salvation. In Paul there can be no separation between theology and social reality. It is on the basis of the latter and in ongoing conversation with it that he makes his theological statements concerning the new life in Christ. Therefore we now need to consider Paul's method of theologizing and his conception of transformation in Christ.

---

75. Campbell 2008.
76. See Ehrensperger 2007.

Chapter 10

PAUL'S 'THEOLOGY' OF TRANSFORMATION

10.1 *Theology or Theologizing?*

It is difficult to avoid speaking of Paul's theology, and yet the terminology itself may imply a misleading image of the apostle, leading to wrong assumptions and expectations in relation to a theological system or framework. The same issue arises when Paul is described as a 'theologian', hence Munck's refusal to locate him in this category.[1] This is not to suggest that Paul is not coherent and consistent, nor in any way to seek to diminish his unassailable status as one of the greatest thinkers and teachers of all time. It is rather that the term 'theology' carries with it traditional associations that are not fitting to describe the apostle to the gentiles. Paul's thought cannot be adequately perceived as a systematic or static set of concepts or propositions of universal validity. This is a major factor in his being frequently misinterpreted or misunderstood. To speak of Paul's theologizing is a better way to conceive his teaching of his communities in the way of Christ. Theology suggests something concrete, something already achieved and fully formulated that can be reapplied in a similar manner to successive differing situations, thus maintaining continuity and conformity. But this view of theology is anachronistic if applied to Paul who thought and wrote without the presence of what we understand as Christian theological tradition. We prefer to speak of Paul's theologizing since for the apostle this is an activity rather than simply an acquired mode of thought.[2] It is moreover in Paul never a finished product, but an ever ongoing and dynamic process. As some interpreters have recognized, we do not really possess Paul's theology as such. We have numerous examples of his theologizing in various and disparate contexts, but no one example can legitimately be claimed to represent Paul's theology as such,

---

1. Munck accordingly and interestingly regards Romans 'as a missionary's contribution to a discussion' (1959: 200). In his view, 'we misunderstand Paul much more fatally if, as has been usual, we regard him as a theologian' (65). His theology 'arises from his work as an apostle and directly serves that work' (67). This is why Munck, in quite a large book, has no chapter on the theology of Paul. But he points out that he does deal with Paul's call and his conception of that call, with Paul's relations to Jesus' disciples, and to his own churches, with the missions to the Jews and gentiles, with his journeys and their destinations. His claim is that 'all this is in the deepest sense Paul's theology' (67).
2. Cf. Wagner's comment, 'If Paul's theology is best conceptualized as an *activity* rather than as a relatively static set of convictions, then Paul's use of scripture should be understood along similar lines' (2003: 3 n. 11).

not even Romans.³ Yet despite the decade-long discussions at the Pauline Theology Consultation at the SBL annual meetings (beginning in 1985) where this issue was continuously debated, probably because no easy or clear solution to the problem of the occasional nature of Paul's writings was arrived at, the insights thus gained have not been sufficiently recognized or acted upon. Thus older and less relevant views of Paul are perpetuated because of a failure to take note of serious problems inherent within them.

This is partly due to a scholarly preoccupation with arriving at theology or information rather than the more important question of what Paul is actually trying to achieve by means of his rhetoric. The outcome of this is a tendency to universalize the Pauline letters and to abstract them away from their immediacy into a set of propositions or doctrinal centres.⁴ Thus Victor Furnish has drawn attention to the fact that the vast majority of works devoted to Pauline thought have sought to find its centre in some particular *theological doctrine*.⁵ As James A. Smith asserts, 'There has been a fundamental hermeneutical failure to recognize the difference between function and information in the writings of Paul'.⁶ Our emphasis is therefore upon Paul's theologizing as an activity, upon his *strategy* as well as his convictions,⁷ upon what he was doing by means of his theological thinking, rather than seeking to identify in his letters a fully worked out set of ideas. This means that we focus on Paul's theologizing as part of his apostolic activity rather than the outcome, or deposit resulting from this.⁸ Hence Paul's goals are not secondary to the meaning of his rhetoric but must be considered as part of the meaning of these statements when viewed as an interactive process of communication between particular people.⁹ As a number of scholars have stressed, this is Paul's own particular hermeneutical approach,¹⁰ an understanding of which is indispensable to the interpretation of his letters. By taking into account what Paul was trying to do to his readers, what actions he was trying to promote by writing what he wrote, we can aim to locate the letters within the overarching purposes of his life and mission in which the letters serve as means to realize these purposes.¹¹

---

3. Cf. James A. Smith's critique of Dunn's Pauline theology (2005: 14ff.). This dogmatic interest was rightly deplored by F.C. Baur 1876: 313.
4. Cf. Beker 1980: 35.
5. 1989: 321–50 (335).
6. 2005: 19.
7. Cf. my chapter 'Paul's Strategy in Writing Romans', in 1992: 132–60.
8. Cf. Chapter 1.4 above, also Tomson 1990: 49 and Roetzel 1999: 93–99.
9. Engberg-Pedersen draws attention to the indirect functions of Paul's statements as no less important than the more manifest (1994a: 258–9). Smith goes further and claims that 'it is only *after* we discern the *function* of Paul's texts that we can even begin to consider issues of significance or theology' (2005: 21).
10. E.g. P. Meyer 1995: 697, C. Roetzel 1999 and J.A. Smith 2005: 19–21. Roetzel sees Paul's theologizing as 'an interactive process, dynamic and flexible' (1999: 93). Smith regards Paul as a 'theologizer' rather than as a theologian (2005: 20).
11. Smith argues that 'the panoptical privileging of Romans as the Pauline point of reference is plagued by a disproportionate focus on significance over function'. He holds that 'we can attain a

10.2 The Catalyst: Social Factors in the Concrete Context of Paul's Communities

In a recent illuminating essay, Bengt Holmberg notes that ethical and theological factors in Paul's writing may not turn out to be as significant as first perceived.

> To put it briefly, the rich and socially powerful Christians were the leaders in the Corinthian congregation, and they created most of the problems that the apostle addresses in his Corinthian correspondence. *Thus what may look at first like theological and ethical problems and discussions were actually caused more by social factors like stratum-specific behaviour patterns operative in the everyday life of these Christians than by differing religious perspectives on theological traditions.*[12]

As Holmberg insightfully recognizes, Paul's concerns here are with everyday life and reality rather than theology *per se*. Thus we may affirm that whilst the problems in Paul's communities are primarily social, his responses to these are both theological and social. If this insight is carefully observed, it may prevent us from reading everything in Paul's letters too theologically, thereby distancing the apostle from the concrete political and social realities of everyday life in the Roman Empire. Whilst Paul endeavours as much as possible to build up his converts in the faith, this is not necessarily only a development of their theological thinking but more a growth in their life in all its aspects. Theologizing in Paul is designed to change people, to transform communal life and to create a Christ-like pattern of life within his communities. Thus it is with the social realities of their life that Paul begins to theologize rather than with an already developed creedal form of theology, even if such were to consist of 'sound doctrine'.[13]

One example of how this observation might influence interpretation is in relation to Rom. 14–15. As Kathy Ehrensperger has pointed out, although 'weak' and 'in faith' occur in conjunction in Rom. 14.1, in faith (τῇ πίστει) is not repeated in the reference to the strong or the weak in 15.1. Thus a legitimate reading, despite the parallels in relation to Abraham's strengthening or weakening faith in Romans 4, might be that Paul is advising on *how* the strong (οἱ δυνατοί) are to welcome (προσλαμβάνεσθε) the weak one (τὸν ἀσθενοῦντα) rather than assessing the quality of his/her faith.[14] This would support Mark Reasoner's stress on weakness and strength as elements in the hierarchical value system of Roman society where the elite equated 'strength' or 'power' with honour and wealth and 'weakness' with the shamefulness of the lower classes.[15] On this reading of

---

far greater sense of coherence in Paul's texts, and greater social product, if we think in terms of function and performance over significance' (2005: 34).

12. Holmberg 2005: 255–71 (261). Cf. also Tellbe 'Paul's theology should thus be perceived as an outcome of the complex interplay between ideas and social structures, theological concepts and socio-historical phenomena' (2001: 296).

13. We will return to this later to deal with the theological resources which Paul uses in his interaction with his communities' problems.

14. Ehrensperger, 2004a: 182–3.

15. Reasoner 1999.

Romans 14.1–15.13 Paul's concern is not then primarily with the weakness or strength of an individual's faith (which in any case is a psychological perspective atypical both of Paul and his era) but with the divisive influence which Roman imperial values are effecting within the Christ-communities.[16]

Aasgaard has similarly drawn attention to Paul's use of the sibling metaphor in his theologizing. The varied rhetorical use of the metaphor and the fact that it is Paul's most frequent way of speaking of his co-'Christians' and almost his only way of addressing them directly, shows that it plays a central role in Paul's understanding of 'Christian' relations. Aasgaard points out that whilst most often presentations of Paul's ecclesiology take their point of departure in other elements of his theological thinking, such as his eschatology, christology or soteriology which are thought to govern his strategies towards his environment, and to affirm his strategies for community building or for handling community conflicts:

> ...with Paul's use of the sibling metaphor, however, the direction appears to be the opposite: here, a well-established social role, the sibling relationship, serves as a model for Christian relations. That is, a central part of Paul's thinking on the church has been informed by his social context, namely by the ideas and ideals generally associated with the sibling role. More than in other elements of his ecclesiology, Paul here enters into an active interplay with the social context: he develops his ecclesiology on the basis of it, and to an extent even on the premises given by that context. By this social dynamics are – in a sense – turned into theology![17]

In maintaining that Paul theologizes on the basis of social realities, we may be able to avoid the tendency to transform social realities such as historic Israel into idealistic concepts such as election and predestination.[18] Even the Jew as a figure of history has sometimes been transformed into a negative, anti-type within each individual, 'the Jew in every man'. I have argued in some detail that many of the misunderstandings of Paul's statements in Romans 9–11, in particular, derive from a misconception of his language and mindset which is focused on the concrete reality of historic Israel, and is not primarily concerned with abstract philosophical issues that have tended to typify post-Reformation theological thought. That there are indications of an interest on the part of Paul in abstract concepts such as e.g. grace need not be denied, but a careful regard to context will often indicate that what passes for abstraction, is simply Paul's repetition in another form of statements about historic entities whether Israel or Christ-followers.

A clear example can be found in Rom. 11.5–6. Paul asserts 'So too at the present time, there is a remnant' but he adds 'chosen by grace' and continues, 'But if it is by grace, it is no longer on the basis of works; otherwise grace would

---

16. This reading would also help to avoid the equating of 'weakness' with Jewish identity, since according to this perspective, both Jews and other ethnic groups were being despised by the Roman elite. On the assumed superiority of the Roman people see N. Elliott 2005b: 17–23.

17. Aasgaard 2004: 309–10.

18. D. Harink cites from an unpublished paper on 'The Tenacity of Anti-Judaism' by Walter Lowe where it is argued that Christian theology has transformed the idea of a 'chosen people' into the idea of 'election', which in turn is transformed into the idea of 'predestination' (2005: 12 n. 17).

10. Paul's 'Theology' of Transformation

no longer be grace'. It is essential to note here that the immediate topic is the remnant of faithful Israelites at 'the present time'. Paul is emphasizing that despite the apparent hardening of Israel, there still exists a body of faithful people in his own time. Thus despite the threefold repetition of the term χάρις and the accompanying contrast with ἔργα it is clear that Paul's primary purpose here is not to offer a theological discussion of grace and works, but rather to point to the historical evidence that a believing remnant offers proof that God has not cast off Israel.

What we are asserting in the examples noted above is that Pauline interpretation has an inherent tendency which frequently results in Paul's statements being misunderstood. The tendency to generalize and thus to universalize enables the reference to be released from the referent in its context and thus to facilitate an abstract discussion unhampered by historical and contextual limitations. By this device the Jew is not necessarily a real Jew,[19] nor Israel historic Israel, but possibly the Christian church.

In contrast to this tendency we wish to stress Paul's deep involvement in the actual social realities of life in his communities and with one factor in particular which has not been given the prominence it deserves. This is, as argued earlier, that Paul's principle of remaining in the situation in which converts were at the point of receipt of their call to Christ is a supreme example of how social factors can constitute a significant element in Paul's theologizing. We will develop the significance of this aspect of Paul later in the present chapter, but prior to this we need to consider what may with confidence be affirmed as a fundamental aspect of his theologizing, his relation to Jesus as the Christ.

10.3 The Basis: Belonging to Christ

Paul uses a variety of expressions to describe the new life in Christ. His soteriological terms include being 'in Christ', baptism into Christ, putting on Christ, being crucified with Christ etc. Our specific interest here is in how this new relationship leads to transformation into the desired pattern of life of those 'in Christ'.[20] Our concern is not to differentiate between the diverse terms but rather to consider what they have in common, i.e participation in Christ and individual and corporate transformation of life as a result of that relationship. The imagery of redressing after baptism most likely lies behind the image of putting on Christ and putting off the old life or the old man. Being in Christ emphasizes the corporate nature of belonging as do the συν compounds used as e.g. in Romans 6. Here Paul interprets baptism as a death to sin and as a raising to walk in newness of life (οὕτος... περιπατήσωμεν). Belonging to Christ has ethical consequences; because the follower of Christ has died to his old way of life, the old person has

---

19. Contra E. Käsemann, 'the apostle's real adversary is the devout Jew, not only as the mirror-image of his own past – though that too – but as the reality of the religious man' (1969: 184).

20. Paul 's formulaic expression 'in Christ' occurs no less that 52 times in his letters. Cf. Peerbolte 2003: 213. n. 36. This highlights particularly the corporate dimension of Paul's theologizing rather than the individualistic, as we have already argued.

been put to death. This might suggest a complete death to all aspects of previous existence if we take the imagery literally. Paul states, 'It is no longer I who live, but Christ who lives in me' (Gal.2.20). By putting on Christ, it might appear that Paul's old self has been replaced by a new Christ-self, making him literally a new creation.

But this is not the best way to interpret this transformation. Paul asserts, 'I live' an indication that it is only aspects of his old self that have died. In Col. 3.9–10 and Eph. 4.24, the emphasis lies on putting off the old person with its practices, not casting off the body itself but rather 'putting off the old sinful nature that results in sinful practices, to allow new ethical living in the same body. As Paul's exhortation in Romans 13.14 ἀλλὰ ἐνδύσασθε τὸν κύριον Ἰησοῦν Χριστὸν καὶ τῆς σαρκὸς πρόνοιαν μὴ ποιεῖσθε εἰς ἐπιθυμίας demonstrates, putting on the Lord Jesus Christ refers to ethical renewal and not the erasure of all bodily differences to produce a new person. As Judith Gundry-Volf asserts,

> Only the *sinful self* has died – the self that stands under the condemnation of the Law, as implied in 'I died to the Law'... and been raised to live in the same 'bodily environment' – ἐν σαρκὶ – as before its death. Whatever other continuity there may be between the life that is 'no longer' (οὐκέτι) and the life that is 'now' (νῦν), there is clearly a continuity of the gendered and ethnically or culturally differentiated 'flesh'.[21]

The fact that his followers dwell in one and the same Christ or that he dwells in them, does not remove their distinguishing features; as Gundry-Volf concludes, 'Though believers "put on" the *one* Christ, he "puts on" their *differentiated* "flesh"...and "lives in me", that is, in each individually differentiated "me".'

The new creation, therefore, takes place not by simple annihilation of the old creation, but by the death of the enfleshed self and the indwelling of Christ in the same flesh; the particular identity of this flesh can be Jew or Greek, slave or free, male or female.[22] For Paul, the transformation involves the entire person, both body and mind. His command in Rom. 12.2, 'Do not be conformed to this world' is preceded by the appeal to present their bodies as a living sacrifice to God in everyday living. It is succeeded by a powerful appeal for transformed perspectives resulting from 'the renewal of your mind' (12.2) and several word plays on attitude of mind particularly the verb φρονεῖν which link back to the arrogant attitude of group cultural superiority on the part of the gentile Christ-followers in 11.17–24. Rather than being conformed to the arrogant mindset of Roman imperialism, the Christ-followers are commanded to 'be transformed (μεταμορφοῦσθε) by the renewal of your mind'. Paul's command is preceded by the appeal to present your bodies as a living sacrifice in worship of God. It is apparent that the renewal here includes both the everyday use of, and life in, the body as well as a renewing of the mind. The emphasis on sober and humble self-image and pattern of thinking pervades these verses at the beginning of Romans 12. The goal of

---

21. 2003: 8–36 (30).
22. This is because 'if we trace the line of Paul's thought from the problem to the solution, it does not run from "difference" to "undifferentiated unity", but from "sameness in sin despite outward differences" to "unity with outward differences in Christ"', Gundry-Volf 2003: 35–6, cf. also 30.

Paul at this point appears to be to resocialize the gentile Christ-followers into a world view which involves transformation of identity and increasing social distance from a non-Israelite heritage and culture.[23] More specifically, it is now easier in the light of recent studies to read in Romans Paul's anti-imperial rhetoric, a contrasting of the reign of Christ with the promised peace and benevolence of the Caesars. Not even the mighty power of Rome can separate the elect from their Lord (8.31–39). He would allow the nations and their leaders to discipline his people, but his wrath has now been openly revealed against them. From this we can see that Paul's goals include not only a new spiritual outlook but a transformed use of the body and resocializing with a view to a transformed social existence.

10.4 The Process:
The Interaction Between Relativization and Transformation

The new creation presupposes the old and transforms it. In Paul's theologizing we encounter the renewal of creation rather than its obliteration. Thus whether we speak of 'call' or 'conversion' in relation to Paul's Damascus road encounter, we are still dealing here with issues of continuity as well as of discontinuity. As Alan Segal notes, 'The one expression that Paul uses most comprehensively in his own writing to describe this experience is *transformation*'.[24] According to Segal,

> No convert forgets everything previously known. Rather, the convert changes a few key concepts, revaluing everything else accordingly. Old doctrines often remain intact but are completely changed in significance through the imposition of a new structure.[25]

Thus despite the required 'biographical reconstruction' and the 'change in universe of discourse',[26] there is real continuity between past and present in the life of the believer. Because there is real continuity, those who are in Christ cannot be presumed to become all the same. This means that all differentiation does not disappear in Christ. Being in Christ can be likened to being one body or one universal family. But as Paul maintains, 'there are many parts yet one body' (1 Cor. 12.20). Again, a family, however close, is not a group of identical members, but by definition presupposes diversity of various kinds. Being one in Christ rather demands difference since, if all were identical, there would be no need to seek for oneness or unity.

This means that unity in Christ also allows for differentiation between Jews and the gentile nations, and likewise also differentiation amongst differing ethnic identities. As Segal argues, 'the degree of socialization depends on the distance the convert must travel between the old and new communities and the strength of the new commitment. Conversion can take place within a single religion, where

---

23. Thus Minna Shkul describes the aim of the author of Ephesians 2005: 1–10 (1).
24. Segal 1990: 73. A tradition of liberation as transformation is common to Paul and early rabbinic Judaism, cf. Plietzsch 2005: 35.
25. Segal 1990: 75.
26. Segal 1990: 78–9.

less socialization is needed'.[27] Thus Jews in Christ can retain a Jewish identity and gentiles must not be forced to become Jews. This is due to the fact that though everything is relativized at the point of entering the body of Christ, since there cannot be complete obliteration, transformation is still possible. The creation in Paul is not so corrupt in a dualistic sense that only its complete obliteration and destruction will be adequate – thus care must be taken with phrases such as dying and rising with Christ – Paul does not hold that we are already resurrected to new life. Nor, as we have argued above, does he hold that in conversion, all the past is left behind as totally corrupt. Instead one's previous life, its culture and its social context are viewed by Paul as the raw material of a transformed existence.

Thus the previous life with its commitments, whilst undergoing a radical testing by the encounter with Christ, nevertheless abides as a formative and defining element in the new existence. Culture and life are transformed by the Christ-encounter but not obliterated or displaced by some new culture descending from heaven, or otherwise mystically achieved. In this we see the life in Christ as confirming much in the previous life of converts, but at the same time transforming it. The past is not completely obliterated but 'baptized' into Christ at a given point which can neither be ignored nor eliminated, because one enters the community of Christ once and for all. The outcome is that Jews remain Jews in Christ, as likewise gentiles. Each retains their identity in Christ and both are transformed but not, as we have already argued,[28] into some super-Christian identity that is neither Jewish nor gentile. They do not become the same nor need their cultures be identical. In fact there can be no identical universal Christian culture, but only differing cultures more or less transformed by the presence of people transformed by the presence of Christ living in them.

This is not to overlook the fact that the resocialization of Israelites is not identical with that of gentiles. Radical change is demanded of both, but the degree of resocialization is much greater in the case of gentiles (and also in the case of very Hellenized Jews). Thus, in relation to gentiles, it may be legitimate to speak at points of a reversal of values as part of the process of transformation. The Corinthian context offers us a good example of this process especially where 'new creation' terminology is operative. A striking example of paradoxical reversal appears in the Corinthian letters when Paul asserts, 'I am content with weaknesses, insults, hardships, persecutions and calamities for the sake of Christ; for when I am weak, then I am strong' (2 Cor. 12.10). Earlier, in 1 Cor. 4.10, Paul had contrasted the Corinthians' self-perception with his own, 'We are weak but you are strong! You are held in honour, but we in disrepute!' Paul's linking of being regarded as 'strong' and worthy of 'honour' would make good sense in this context where young men were taught from infancy to strive for honour and high social status, where lessons in competing and dominating began at home, and were intensified in adolescence.[29] Paul's problems possibly

27. Segal 1990: 74.
28. See Chapter 6.3 above.
29. I am indebted here to an excellent essay by S.S. Bartchy 2005: 49–60.

resulted from his first visit to the city, 'I was with you in weakness and in much fear and trembling' (1 Cor. 2.3). He had not appeared to offer a good model of leadership because he appealed to them 'by the meekness and gentleness of Christ' (2 Cor. 10.1). But the effect of this counter-cultural leader image[30] was exaggerated beyond measure because Paul when criticized, instead of fighting for more honour and repute, embraced his 'dishonourable' situation with a perverse satisfaction (2 Cor. 6.10; 12.10). Not only did Paul happily accept such shameful circumstances for himself, 'we go hungry and thirsty, we are in rags, we are brutally beaten, we are homeless. We work hard with our hands... We have become the scum of the earth, the garbage of the world – right up to this moment' (1 Cor. 4.11 NRSV); but Paul apparently wishes all Christ-followers to imitate his example in embracing enthusiastically this 'shameful' way of life (4.8–21 and 11.1).[31]

The outcome was that when so-called 'super-apostles' arrived in Corinth, Paul had to embark on a fierce struggle in defence of his brand of leadership and its basis in the example of Christ. But Paul perceived these as false apostles who would undo the 'new creation' values he had been trying to exemplify and teach to the Corinthians.

Bartchy concludes that:

> The sharply counter-cultural perception of power that Jesus taught and demonstrated, with his execution on a Roman cross as the central symbol, had created a profound upheaval in Paul's own sense of honourable behaviour. As one who had been liberated by the Spirit of Jesus from the need to dominate and control others, Paul became motivated to use his power, training, and gifts to empower, to build up, to reconcile, to befriend the socially inferior and to encourage the weak...[32]

From this discussion of Paul's reversal of Corinthian values, it is clear that in such societies, resocialization represents a major transition to the values of the new creation, and the reconfiguration which life in Christ entails. But it is interesting that for Bartchy, though he does not deny that such 'theological' issues as 'divine enthusiasm', or the performing of 'signs and wonders', or the legitimation of 'judaizing' missionaries, played a role, his interest is to test how far foregrounding the dominant cultural values and social codes of Paul's world can take us in clarifying what was at stake in his competition for leadership with the 'super-apostles' of 2 Corinthians 10–13.[33] Here we have another example of Paul's use of social factors as the catalyst of his theology. It also illustrates the

---

30. As Bartchy reminds us, it was Edwin Judge who in his 1972 article, 'St Paul and Classical Culture' first called attention to Paul's 'pursuit of radical self-humiliation' which Judge finds running through all Paul's work 'in theology and ethics alike, and on into his practical relations with both followers and rivals' an attitude that was 'in violent reaction to much that was central to the classical way of life', Bartchy 2005: 56.
31. As Bartchy notes, 'In each case he was challenging behaviour that he regarded as spiritually arrogant and divisive, behaviour characterized by competitive honour seeking and lack of concern for the loss others might suffer thereby', 2005: 56.
32. Bartchy 2005: 56–7.
33. Cf. Bartchy 2005: 51.

extent of the resocialization required of a mainly gentile community living in an environment hostile to the gospel.

Somewhat in contrast to the above example, the relativization of all things in Christ and the resulting transformation of those in Christ, need not imply an abandonment of Israel-centred convictions, but as with all other convictions, these must be revised in the light of the Christ-event. It should of course be recognized that deeply held convictions represent a continuity of character which should not be ignored, and it is quite clear that in many respects, Paul's convictions, though radically revised in Christ, were by no means completely abandoned.[34] But in this respect also, Jews differ from gentiles, or at least from those gentiles not well inducted into the narrative of God's covenant with Israel and its binding obligations. As L. Keck asserts, 'As Paul sees it, Gentiles abandon their religion when they accept the gospel (1 Thess. 1.9–10), but observant Jews who accept it do not change religions but reconfigure the religion they already have'.[35] Whether we should then speak of conversion within a single religion, as Segal does,[36] or use another term for gentiles converting to an entirely new faith is open to much debate. For me it is more important, whilst recognizing the differing backgrounds of Christ-followers, to stress the fact of being committed to Christ which is of primary importance whatever the prehistory, significant though this may be. But since we have recognized a major difference in Jews' and gentiles' respective initiation into Christ, we must follow out the significance of this and consider how this affects our view of Israelite identity and culture. Is the culture and identity of Israel relativized, rejected, or in some sense retained? We can state the issue in this way: if Israel is obliterated with the coming of Christ and the gospel, then there can be no continuity within the people of God. On the other hand, if Israel remains the same, then the Christ-event is apparently denied any significance.

At first glance, Paul's insistence in Rom. 3.31 that he maintains the law, when taken in conjunction with his support for the right of the weak to observe Mosaic food and Sabbath laws, appears to offer clear evidence for Paul's unequivocal recognition of an abiding Israelite identity. However, John Barclay has argued that Paul actually 'subverts the basis on which Jewish law-observance is founded and thus precipitates a crisis of cultural integrity among the very believers whose law-observance he is careful to protect'.[37] By demanding of the weak 'Chris-

---

34. On this see also our discussion of 'Christ-Followers as New Creation' in Chapter 9.2 above. On Paul's convictions and their revision in Christ see also the useful discussion by Terence Donaldson (1997, especially 17–27). An important aspect of using the terminology of convictions and taking these into account is that this draws attention to deeply held beliefs *and attitudes* from which people cannot easily be dissuaded, thus hindering a simplistic perspective on conversion or transfer to a new belief system. Contra cf. Wagner who speaks of 'a relatively static set of convictions' (2003: 3 n. 11). But see also P. Bourdieu's emphasis that people are initially influenced by the world they inhabit, and that their actions cannot escape this particular history, since we all learn through the body in a permanent interaction with our social context which 'inhabits us' (2000: 141).

35. 2005: 286.
36. Segal 1990: 63–71.
37. Barclay 1996b: 308.

tians', commitment to a church in which the Jewish mode of life is tolerated but not required, Paul threatens what he appears to support, thus undermining the theological and intellectual foundation of their tradition. But there is no evidence in Romans that Paul intended or that he deliberately planned to subvert Jewish traditions and thus to seek to eliminate the difference between the ethnic groups. At best it may be claimed that this in the long term may have been the effect of Paul's strategy, but certainly it cannot be seen as his intention.[38] Esler notes the pro-Israelite dimension to Paul's thought evident in Romans 11 and 14.1–15.13, and claims it is 'inaccurate to attribute to him the positive aim of destroying the differences between Judeans and non-Judeans'. Rather,

> Paul does not tell the Judean members of the Christ-movement to stop being Judeans. He does not ask them to sever any ties they may have with the Roman synagogues, and he is tolerant of their continued practice of the Mosaic law, at least in regard to provisions relating to food, wine and holy days.[39]

Again, should Israel not then be transformed into 'New Israel'? It seems as if it cannot be otherwise since, if Israel does not continue in some form, then Israel the bearer of the promise disappears and thus also the promise she carried. Yet it must be firmly asserted that Israel remains despite all things being relativized in Christ. This seems at first as special pleading, an inconsistency of argument, but it is more complicated than such consistency would appear to allow. Israel remains because Israel is part of the given social reality which is the starting point for Paul's theologizing. Even if she is part of a sinful social reality, this does not disqualify Israel. As Harink insists, Israel is the creation of God's word – as such she can and must remain despite as yet imperfectly realizing her own destiny. Harink opposes the view of Wright who gives Israel only *functional* significance[40] so that God can easily dispense with her due to a failure to achieve her given destiny. Because of God's unchanging faithfulness to his word by which Israel was created and is sustained, Israel remains, despite all odds, as an abiding witness to God's activity in history. Also because of the mighty power of God, not only to create, but also providentially to exercise responsible sovereignty over his creation, there can be no question of ultimate failure or a dualistic partial failure as if evil were greater than righteousness. After Noah God neither destroys nor gives up on his creation, but continues to work with it to achieve his own purposes,[41] and Israel has a positive and central role in these activities. Her identity is not transferred to another, not even to her Messiah. We can accept

---

38. On this see Esler's clear distinction, 2003: 354–6. Esler affirms that the new Pauline groups require a distinct identity, one that will be lodged as social identity in the minds and hearts of the members – meaning that sense of who they are that derives from belonging to this group, but concludes 'yet such identity will need to co-exist with whatever remains of the member's original Judean and Greek identities' (140).
39. Esler 2003: 364–5.
40. Cf. Harink 2003: 161–8.
41. Cf. Susanne Plietzsch, 'Die Verantwortlichkeit des Menschen vor dem einen Gott wird hier gleichsam umgekehrt gelesen und es wird gesagt, dass selbst Gott die Relation, in die er sich mit der Schöpfung begeben hat, nicht auflösen oder negieren kann' (2005: 80–2).

that Jesus may rightly be described as the true Israelite who alone fulfilled the divine destiny. But that does not allow us to displace an historic people by even the most righteous of her sons in whom the promises of Israel's restoration have allegedly been fulfilled.[42] Representation is one thing, but displacement is quite another.[43]

In Paul's imagery, the gentile branches are joined to the stem of Israel, but the Jewish branches are regrafted into their own olive tree (rather than being joined to some other entity) thus reaffirming their historic identity.[44] It is very difficult for Christians today to recover Paul's perspective on Israel at this point. Centuries of Christian theologians have failed to read Romans 9–11 from Paul's perspective rather than their own. As Keck maintains,

> Understanding what Paul is saying in this paragraph (Rom. 11.25–32) requires most Christian Gentiles to flush out of their minds what they assume Paul is talking about, namely the conversion of Jews to 'Christianity'...and their entry into the predominantly Gentile church. From Paul's angle, it is not Jews who do the 'entering' but Gentiles, the wild olive shoots grafted into Israel, yet without becoming converts (proselytes to Judaism).[45]

We must continue then to stress that the 'church' in Paul's perspective is inseparably related to Israel – through Christ as Israel's Messiah and through the righteous remnant of Israelites, that nucleus of Christ-followers through and from whom, the church grew and developed. But however related to Israel, the church is not Israel; Israel's identity is unique and cannot be taken over by gentile Christ-followers, or even completely shared by them. But together the two differing groups share one new common experience as Christ-followers with Christ as their focus and point of unity.[46] Thus Christ-following Israelites are the link between the church and Israel. In parallel with Jews who do not follow Christ, they also remain Israelites but in common with gentile Christ-followers, they follow the same Christ. All Christ-followers have a shared identity in that all of them are together one in Christ, but oneness is not sameness and they differ in that some are and remain Israelites and some are of gentile extraction.

---

42. See Wagner's thorough and critical discussion of Wright's view that the fullness of the gentiles will *complete* rather than lead to the salvation of 'all Israel', and that the completion of the gentile mission is the salvation of 'all Israel' without remainder, 2003: 278 n. 193 and 194.

43. Contra Wright 1995: 34. For a more detailed critique of this aspect of Wright's thesis, see Harink 2003: 153–207. Harink gives a combined criticism of John H. Yoder and Wright as follows 'Wright holds that Israel's election bears fruit and is sustained, finally, in the Jewishness of the story and worldview that Paul brings to the gentile world. Yoder emphasizes the Jewishness of the Diaspora form of life as the peculiar gift of the Jews to the world. In both cases the biblical and Pauline doctrine of God's election of a specific, nonsubstitutable, fleshly historical people tends to disappear behind a set of "Jewish" ideas or practices' (202).

44. Wagner criticizes Bell's view that 'Israel comes *to the church* through jealousy' (1994: 275 n. 323). 'However this completely inverts Paul's figure, in which it is gentiles who join Israel ("the root"). The "rest" of Israel are still "natural branches" who will be regrafted to their own root, not joined to another entity. In Romans 11, the Church does not supersede Israel: rather, gentiles have been joined *to Israel*, who remain *God's one people*', Wagner 2003: 275 n. 182.

45. Keck 2005: 286.

46. Cf. Esler 2003: 153–4.

10. Paul's 'Theology' of Transformation

Thus Israel remains as a given in Paul's theologizing. Paul theologizes in relation to the narrative of God's purposes for Israel in the light of the Christ-event, and the relation of his gentile communities to this history. However, Israel is not left untouched by the Christ event, but according to Paul is now divided into the faithful remnant who have recognized in Jesus Christ their Messiah, and 'the rest' who have not done so. Whilst at the same time in the early centuries of the church, continuing to share in a common history with other Israelites, the remnant now share with gentile Christ-followers a common concern that eventually 'all Israel' will be saved. Together Christ-following Jews and gentiles participate in one new and common aspect of their identities as both being in Christ and thus sharing common experiences of spiritual life and its diverse expression.

10.5 Transformation in Paul: An Ongoing Process with an Inalienable Eschatological Dimension

The crucial aspect of Paul's understanding of transformation is that it is an ongoing and as yet an incomplete process. The Christian church has always been tempted to an over-realized eschatology, in contrast to Jews who, in Christian perspective, are too futuristic in their understanding of the messianic dimension. The problem with a realized eschatology is not just that it misrepresents the status of Christ-followers, but that it likewise tends to posit already realized judgement for Jews. What is distinctive about Paul's conclusion to Romans 11 is that it is open-ended. Any other conclusion would not have assisted in discouraging the pride and incipient anti-Judaism of the Roman gentile Christ-followers. Nor is it any different in the church of today. Over-inflated self-estimates often accompany an over-realized eschatology to the detriment of the church and its relation to other faiths, especially Judaism. It frequently exemplifies itself in an unwarranted Christian triumphalism that discourages realism and humility in relation to the church's failings and isolation from society.

Part of the problem is that there has been a tendency to emphasize only fulfilment in relation to the promises. Paul's emphasis on confirmation has been overlooked.[47] This is surprising since it occurs in a climactic section of Rom. 15.8-9, which epitomizes the significance of Christ's ministry for both Jews and gentiles. Its place at the concluding section of the letter and the parallels with earlier sections, most notably Chs. 9-11,[48] and its careful structure reveal that this passage is intended by Paul to have a significant effect. The first half of a

---

47. As already emphasized in Chapter 8.4.
48. The parallels are striking; patriarchs –   15.8   9.5; 11.28
                              promises –   15.8   9.4, 8–9
mercy (linked with glory) ἐλεέω 6 times in 9–11   15.9   9.23; 11.23
the inclusion of gentiles ἔθνη 9× in Rom. 15 and   15.8–12 9–11
9× in Rom. 9–11 (out of 28 occurences in Romans).

'That the climax of the letter bears such striking thematic and verbal affinities to Romans 9–11 is an argument for the centrality of 9–11 to the concerns and purposes of the letter as a whole', cf. Wagner 2003: 308 n. 5.

carefully balanced declaration is modified by two prepositional phrases, the second of which 'εἰς τὸ βεβαιῶσαι τὰς ἐππαγγελίας τῶν πατέρων' reveals that the purpose of Christ's service to the Jews was 'to confirm the promises made to the patriarchs'. This not only sets Paul's gospel within the larger narrative of God's election of Abraham and his descendants[49] to be God's own people, but it stresses the reaffirming of the promises to the Jews by Christ's ministry as God's commissioned servant as the Messiah (ὁ Χριστός).[50] This declaration represents one of the strongest positive affirmations of Israel in the New Testament. The benefit of the term 'confirmation' is that it offers a measure of achievement – something has been confirmed in Christ. It also prevents a negative view of the Hebrew scriptures and of Israel's faith. But most of all this emphasis reminds us that what is confirmed is not yet completely fulfilled and must therefore be hoped for rather than boasted in. As Beker claims, 'Indeed, the Christ-event ratifies the Old Testament promises, but it is not a closure event, because it reactivates the hope of his Parousia in glory (1 Cor. 1.7–8). And it seems that the hope entails the expectation of new revelation and new acts of God'.[51]

In contrast, Paul admits that he does not know the mind of the Lord on the future (Rom. 11.33–36). He hopes that the coming to faith in Christ of gentiles would somehow effect a positive influence on his as yet unconvinced brethren. Yet even this hope is not a prediction but a prophetic expectation based on what the Christ-event has already achieved, 'For if their hardening means the reconciliation of the gentile world, what will their acceptance mean but life from the dead?' (Rom. 11.15, my translation). Paul is not a pessimist about the gospel or about the Jews or the future of the world. He is convinced that God has both the will and the power to achieve what men despair of and in ways they cannot begin to conceive. In his view, 'God has the power to graft them in again' (Rom. 11.23). This open-ended view of the future, whether for Jews or Christ-followers is indicative of how Paul's expectations were fundamentally inspired by the coming of Christ, so that in the famous Corinthian passage on the resurrection, there is real confidence for those in Christ because 'death is swallowed up in victory' (15.24) and therefore labour is not in vain in the Lord (15.58). Thus Christians are called to live with imperfection and incompletion which humans and especially theologians do not relish. As Wagner comments in relation to Wright's reading of Israel in Romans 11,

> The strongest objection to Wright's reading, however, is that by denying that the solution Paul offers to the problem of Israel's rejection of the gospel, is essentially a *temporal* one – partial hardening now, fullness later – Wright leaves out 'the rest' of Israel who have been temporarily rendered insensible: once 'the fullness of the gentiles comes in', the show is over; those who have been hardened can expect only judgement...[52]

---

49. Wagner notes the parallels between Paul's statements in Romans 4 concerning Abraham and those concerning Christ in 15.8–9 and holds that this use of similar language to depict Christ and Abraham suggests that he saw a typological relationship between their faithfulness. 2005: 309 n. 11.

50. Cf. Dunn 1998: 197–9, also Wagner 2003: 308.

51. Beker 1980: 148. Cf. also W. Krauss 2004: 343–4.

52. Cf. Wagner 2003: 279 n. 194.

10. Paul's 'Theology' of Transformation

Here all that is important has already been realized and, outside of the Christian church, there is nothing else to look forward to. When the salvation of the church becomes an end in itself rather than leading to the salvation of the world, we have lost Paul's confident open-ended hope, and selfishly condemn already those whom God has reserved for future purposes which exclude neither judgement nor salvation.[53] As Bockmuehl argues,

> If, then, revelation for Paul is not complete until its consummation in the future, the most appropriate description of the two dimensions of revelation currently accessible must surely be that these revelations (both past and present) are indeed partial incursions of the new age into this age… But the consummation of God's promises of salvation and vindication (and thereby the conclusive answer to the promise of historical theodicy) still awaits its revelation.[54]

As this new age impacts on present historical reality, the vision it supplies guides the pattern of life of the Christ-community,[55] thus preventing it from becoming totally conformed to this world, and its value-systems.

---

53. 'The tensions inherent in Paul's use of the term "Israel" can be resolved only by recognizing the eschatological substructure of his thought… For Paul Israel will be a complete entity only when " the fullness of the gentiles" comes in and "the Redeemer" comes from Zion to take away their sins', Wagner (2003: 279 n. 193). In this sense, it may be correct with Engberg–Pedersen to regard Paul's theologizing as dynamic and open-ended, a symbolic universe *in the making*, not fully worked out or final (and therefore static), 1993: 106.

54. Bockmuehl, 1990: 147.

55. Thus Paul's halakhah for gentiles in Christ is also subject to the impact of the coming consummation of this new age.

Epilogue

> Oneness in Christ is not the same as collapsing differences into sameness. It implies equality of righteousness for Jews and gentiles in Christ – no more, no less. Jews remain Jews, gentiles may remain gentiles. Together but distinct, Jews and gentiles constitute the people of God (Mitternacht 2002: 410).

In establishing that Jews and gentiles could and should retain distinct identities in Christ, we have been dealing with what is in the first instance a first century issue. But this is still of major significance for contemporary church and society. To fail to acknowledge diversity in the Pauline communities has an inevitable consequence for the acknowledgement of diversity within church and society today. On the other hand, to acknowledge diversity between Jew and gentile in the church of the first century has foundational significance, and puts obligation upon contemporary Christians to give a similar recognition by no means limited to the area of ethnicity alone.

This recognition of diversity in Christ has its primary reference within the Church but its significance extends far beyond this. The obligation to acknowledge and accept the other who is and remains different is an inner-Christian stance that is determined by Christ and life in Christ. It does not depend on the identity of the other, since it is a stance that originates from acknowledging the inherent diversity of God's creation. There is therefore no limit to its extent. A healthy society is not produced by seeking to replicate our own image in the other who is different. Such a tendency to assimilation has the effect, for example, of producing a generation of young people of minority culture who assimilate with the majority culture and may thus live in tension with their roots in their immediate family. Some of these may become victims of powerful ideologies because they are lacking any real sense of personal and communal identity. Alternatively, because they are not accepted and recognized for what they are in their diversity, some may react strongly and become a source of conflict with the dominant society.

Despite its problems, there is no real substitute for recognizing the identity of those who are and remain different and the Christian Church in particular could play a significant role for the peace and well-being of contemporary society. In its earliest days the Church had to learn to accommodate and to live with the 'other' who is and remains different. This 'primary other' constituted much 'soul-searching' for Paul and others who wished the Jewish people all to have the same view of Christ as they did. But Paul in his theologizing had to work out what it meant to be committed to Christ, to the point of martyrdom, and yet relate hopefully to those Jews who were and who remained different. His letters and the attitude revealed in them in the multi-ethnic context of the first century Roman Empire offer a viable blueprint for Christian citizenship in the diverse world of today. This means that Christians must define themselves positively in relation to Christ rather than negatively in relation to fellow-Christians or fellow-citizens who retain their difference. Negative self-definition, whether against Jews or other groups has always, whether in the past or the present, deplorable, even horrific consequences particularly for such minorities (though its malicious influence also has a destructive power in those who discriminate against others). The message of Paul's gospel is that through Christ the hostility against those who are different is overcome, enabling difference to be accepted and celebrated in anticipation of the coming kingdom of God.

BIBLIOGRAPHY

Aasgaard, R.
   2004   *'My Beloved Brothers and Sisters!': Christian Siblingship in Paul* (London, New York: T&T Clark).

Adams, E., and D.G. Horrell (eds.)
   2004   *Christianity at Corinth: The Quest for the Pauline Church* (Louisville, KY: Westminster/John Knox Press).

Alexander, P.
   1992   '"The Parting of the Ways" from the Perspective of Rabbinic Judaism', in J.D.G. Dunn (ed.), *Jews and Christians: The Parting of the Ways A.D. 70 to 135* (Tübingen: Mohr): 1–25.

Anderson, H.
   1964   *Jesus and Christian Origins* (Oxford: Oxford University Press).

Anderson, R.D. Jr.
   1998   *Ancient Rhetorical Theory and Paul*. Revised Edition (Leuven: Peeters).

Avemarie, F.
   1996   *Tora und Leben: Untersuchungen zur Heilsbedeutung der Tora in der frühen rabbinischen Literatur* (Tübingen: Mohr Siebeck).
   1999   'Erwählung und Vergeltung: Zur optionalen Struktur rabbinischer Soteriologie', *NTS* 45: 108–26.

Bachmann, M. (ed.)
   2005   *Lutherische und Neue Paulusperspektive* WUNT 182 (Tübingen: Mohr Siebeck).

Badenas, R.
   1985   *Christ the End of the Law: Romans 10.4 in Pauline Perspective* (Sheffield: JSOT Press).

Baird, W.
   1992   *History of New Testament Research*, Vol.1 From Deism to Tübingen (Minneapolis: Fortress Press).

Banks, R.
   1994   *Paul's Idea of Community* (Peabody, MA: Hendrickson, rev. edn).

Barclay, J.M.G.
   1996a   *Jews in the Mediterranean Diaspora: From Alexander to Trajan (323 BCE–117 CE)* (Edinburgh: T&T Clark).
   1996b   '"Do we Undermine the Law?" A Study of Romans 14.1–15.6', in J.D.G. Dunn (ed.), *Paul and the Mosaic Law* (Tübingen: Mohr): 287–308.
   1996c   'Neither Jew Nor Greek: Multiculturalism and the New Perspective', in M.G. Brett (ed.), *Ethnicity and the Bible* (Leiden: E.J. Brill): 171–96.
   2002   'Paul's Story: Theology as Testimony', in B.W. Longenecker (ed.), *Narrative Dynamics in Paul: A Critical Assessment* (Louisville, KY: Westminster/John Knox Press): 133–56.

Bartchy, S.S.
   2005   '"When I'm Weak, I'm Strong": A Pauline Paradox in Cultural Context', in Ch. Strecker (ed.), *Kontexte der Schrift Band II: Kultur, Politik, Religion, Sprache, Text Wolfgang Stegemann zum 60.Geburtstag* (Stuttgart: Kohlhammer): 49–60.

Barth, F.
1997   *Rethinking Ethnicity: Arguments and Explorations* (London: Sage).
Barth, K.
1951   *Kirchliche Dogmatik 3/4* (Zollikon-Zürich: Evangelischer Verlag 1951, 4th edn).
1968   'The Epistle to the Romans' (trans. E.C. Hoskyns Oxford: Oxford University Press).
Barth, M.
1968   'Jews and Gentiles: The Social Character of Justification in Paul', *JES* 5.
1983   *The People of God* (Sheffield: University of Sheffield).
Barton, S.C.
1993   'Early Christianity and the Sociology of the Sect', in F.W. Watson (ed.), *The Open Book* (London, SCM Press): 140–62.
1998   'Paul and the Limits of Tolerance', in G.N. Stanton and G.G. Strousma (eds.), *Tolerance and Intolerance in Early Judaism and Christianity* (Cambridge: Cambridge University Press): 121–34.
Bassler, J.M.
1984   'Divine Impartiality in Paul's Letter to the Romans', *NT* 26.
Bassler, J.M. (ed.)
1991   *Pauline Theology Volume I: Thessalonians, Philippians, Galatians, Philemon* (Minneapolis: Fortress Press).
Baur, F.C.
1831   'Die Christuspartei in der korinthischen Gemeinde, der Gegensatz des petrinischen und paulinischen Christenthums in der aeltesten Kirche, der Apostel Petrus in Rom', Tübingen Zeitschrift für Theologie 5:61–206. Reprinted in F.C. Baur, *Historisch-kritische Untersuchungen zum Neuen Testament* (Ausgewählte Werke 1: Stuttgart-Bad Cannstatt: Friedrich Frommann 1963): 1–146.
1864   *Vorlesungen über neutestamentliche Theologie* (ed. F.F. Baur; Leipzig: LF Fues).
1876   *Paul, His Life and Works.* ET A. Menzies (Edinburgh: Theological Translation Fund Library).
1878   *The Church History of the First Three Centuries*, ET Allan Menzies (London: Williams and Norgate).
Beker, J.C.
1980   *Paul, the Apostle: The Triumph of God in Life and Thought* (Edinburgh: T&T Clark).
1986   'The Faithfulness of God and the Priority of Israel in Paul's Letter to the Romans', in G.W.E. Nickelsburg, G.W. MacRae (eds.), *Christians Among Jews and Gentiles. Essays in Honor of Krister Stendahl on His Sixty-fifth Birthday* (Philadelphia: Fortress Press): 10–16.
1991   'Recasting Pauline Theology: The Coherence-Contingency Scheme as Interpretive Model', in J.M. Bassler (ed.), *Pauline Theology Vol I* (Minneapolis: Fortress Press): 15–24.
Bell, R.H.
1994   *Provoked to Jealousy: The Origin and Purpose of the Jealousy Motif in Romans 9–11* (WUNT 2.63; Tübingen: Mohr Siebeck).
Berger, P.
1969   *The Sacred Canopy: Elements of a Sociological Theory of Religion* (Garden City, NY: Doubleday).

Bockmuehl, M.N.A.
1990 *Revelation and Mystery in Ancient Judaism and Pauline Christianity* (Grand Rapids: Eerdmans).
1995 '"The Noachide Commandments" and New Testament Ethics: With Special Reference to Acts 15 and Pauline Halakah', *RB* 102: 72–101.
2003a *Jewish Law in Gentile Churches: Halakhah and the Beginnings of Christian Public Ethics* (Grand Rapids: Baker Academic, pb edition).
2003b 'Syrian Memories of Peter: Ignatius, Justin, and Serapion', in P.J. Tomson and D. Lambers-Petry (eds.), *The Image of the Judaeo-Christians in Ancient Jewish and Christian Literature* (WUNT, 158; Tübingen: Mohr Siebeck): 124–42.

de Boer, M.C.
1989 *The Defeat of Death: Apocalyptic Eschatology in 1 Corinthians 15 and Romans 5* (JSNTSup, 24; Sheffield: Sheffield Academic Press).
1998 'The Nazoreans: Living at the Boundary of Judaism and Christianity', in G.N. Stanton and G.G. Strousma (eds.), *Tolerance and Intolerance in Early Judaism and Christianity* (Cambridge: Cambridge University Press): 239–63.

Bornkamm, G.
1963 'The Letter to the Romans as Paul's Last Will and Testament', in *Australian Biblical Review 1963*, 2–14. GT 'Der Römerbrief als Testament des Paulus', in *Geschichte und Glaube 2, Gesammelte Aufsätze IV* (München: Christian Kaiser Verlag, 1971).

Bourdieu, P.
2000 *Pascalian Meditations.* ET R. Nice (Oxford: Blackwell).

Boyarin, D.
1994 *A Radical Jew: Paul and the Politics of Identity* (Berkley: University of California Press).
1999 *Dying for God: Martyrdom and the Making of Christianity and Judaism* (Stanford: Stanford University Press).
2004 *Borderlines: The Partition of Judaeo-Christianity* (Philadelphia: University of Pennsylvania Press).

Brawley, R.L.
2005 'Meta-Ethics and the Role of Works of Law in Galatians', in Bachmann 2005: 135–59.

Brett, M.G. (ed.)
1996 *Ethnicity and the Bible* (Leiden: E.J. Brill)
2003 'Israel's Indigenous Origins: Cultural Hybridity and the Formation of Israelite Ethnicity', *BibInt* xi/3-4: 400–12.

Brooke, G.J.
2005 *The Dead Sea Scrolls and the New Testament* (Minneapolis: Fortress Press).

Brown, R.E., and J.P. Meier
1983 *Antioch and Rome: New Testament Cradles of Catholic Christianity* (New York: Paulist Press).

Buell, D.K.
2005 *Why This New Race: Ethnic Reasoning in Early Christianity* (New York: Columbia University Press).

Bultmann, R.
1952 *The Theology of the New Testament* (London: SCM Press).

Burnett, G.W.
2001 *Paul and the Salvation of the Individual* (Leiden: E.J. Brill).

Burrowes, B.
 2004 *From Letter to Spirit: the Transformation of Torah in Paul's Symbolic World as Reflected in His Letter to the Romans* (PhD thesis submitted to the University of Durham).

Calvert-Koyzis, N.
 2004 *Paul, Monotheism and the People of God: The Significance of Abraham Traditions for Early Judaism and Christianity* (London/New York: T&T Clark).

Campbell, D.A.
 1996 'Unravelling Gal 3.11b', *NTS* 42: 20–32.
 2002 'Apostolic Competition at Corinth', review of M. Goulder, *Paul and the Competing Mission in Corinth* in *JBV*, Vol. 23/2, 2002.
 2005 *The Quest for Paul's Gospel: A Suggested Strategy* (London and New York: T&T Clark International).

Campbell, D.A (ed.)
 2003 *Gospel and Gender: A Trinitarian Engagement with Being Male and Female in Christ* (London, New York: T&T Clark).

Campbell, W.S.
 1982 'The Place of Romans ix–xi within the Structure and Thought of the Letter', paper presented to the 5th International Congress on Biblical Studies, Oxford 1973, published in E.A. Livingstone (ed.), *SE* VII (Berlin: Akademie Verlag): 121–31.
 1988 'Paul's Application of Scripture to Contemporary Events', paper given at the British New Testament Studies Seminar on the Use of the Old Testament in the New, Hawarden.
 1990 'Did Paul Advocate Separation from the Synagogue?', *SJT* 42: 457–67 (reprinted in Campbell 1992: 122–33).
 1992 *Paul's Gospel in an Intercultural Context: Jew and Gentile in The Letter to the Romans* (Berlin, Bern, Frankfurt am Main: Peter Lang).
 1993a 'The Contribution of Traditions to Paul's Theology', in D.M. Hay (ed.), *Pauline Theology, Vol II, 1 & 2 Corinthians* (Minneapolis: Fortress Press): 234-54.
 1993b 'Israel', in G.F. Hawthorne, R.P. Martin and D.G. Reid (eds.), *The Dictionary of Paul and his Letters* (Downer's Grove, IL: InterVarsity Press): 441–6.
 1995 'The Rule of Faith in Romans 12:1–15:13: The Obligation of Humble Obedience as the Only Adequate Response to the Mercies of God', in D.M. Hay and E.E. Johnson (eds.), *Pauline Theology Vol III Romans* (Minneapolis: Fortress Press): 259–86.
 1997 'The Church as Israel/People of God', in D.G. Reid (ed.), *Dictionary of the Later New Testament and its Developments* (Downers Grove, IL: IVP): 204–19.
 1999 'Divergent Images of Paul and His Mission', in C. Grenholm and D. Patte (eds.), *Reading Israel in Romans: Legitimacy and Plausibility of Divergent Interpretations* (Romans Through History and Cultures Series; Harrisburg, PA: Trinity Press International): 187–211.
 2000 'Martin Luther and Paul's Epistle to the Romans', in O. O'Sullivan (ed.), *The Bible as Book: The Reformation* (London: British Library): 103–114.
 2001 'The Interpretation of Paul: Beyond the New Perspective' (Paper given at the British New Testament Conference Manchester).
 2004a 'All God's Beloved in Rome: Jewish Roots and Christian Identity', in S. McGinn (ed.), *Celebrating Romans: A Template for Pauline Theology* (Grand Rapids: Eerdmans): 67–82.

2004b   'Review of G. Burnett, *Paul and the Salvation of the Individual* in *IBS* 26.1: 53–56.
2005   'Perceptions of Compatibility between Christianity and Judaism in Pauline Interpretation', *BibInt* XIII/3 Special Issue *Paul between Jews and Christians* (ed. M.D. Nanos): 298–316.
2006   'Reading Romans in Conversation with Medieval Interpreters: The Challenge of Cross-Fertilization', in W.S. Campbell, P. Hawkins and B. Schildgen (eds.), *Medieval Readings of Romans* (London and New York: T&T Clark).
2008   'Unity and Diversity in the Church: Transformed Identities and the Peace of Christ in Ephesians', in *Transformation: An International Journal of Holistic Mission Studies* Vol. 25 No. 1 (January).

Carroll, J.T., C.H. Cosgrove, E.E. Johnson (eds.)
1990   *Faith and History: Essays in Honor of Paul W. Meyer* (Atlanta, GA: Scholars Press).

Cartlidge, D.R.
1975   '1 Cor. 7 as a Foundation for a Christian Sex Ethic', *JR* 55 (1975): 220–34.

Castelli, E.A.
1991   *Imitating Paul. A Discourse of Power* (Louisville, KY: Westminster/Knox Press).

Ciampa, R.E.
1998   *The Presence and the Function of Scripture in Galatians 1 and 2* (WUNT 2/102; Tübingen: Mohr Siebeck).

Clarke, A.D.
2000   *Serve the Community of the Church: Christians as Leaders and Ministers* (Grand Rapids: Eerdmans).
2004   'Equality or Mutuality? Paul's Use of "Brother" Language', in P.J. Williams, A.D. Clarke, P.M. Head and D. Instone-Brewer (eds.), *The New Testament in Its First Century Setting: Essays on Context and Background in Honour of B.W. Winter on His 65th Birthday* (Grand Rapids, MI: Eerdmans): 151–64.

Cohen, S.D.
1989   'Crossing the Boundary and Becoming a Jew', *HTR* 1: 13–33.
1993   ' "Those Who Say They Are Jews and Are Not": How Do You Know A Jew in Antiquity When You See One?', in S.J.D. Cohen and E.S. Frerichs (eds.), *Diasporas in Antiquity* (Atlanta: Scholars Press): 1–45.
1999   *The Beginnings of Jewishness: Boundaries, Varieties, Uncertainties* (Berkeley, CA: University of California Press).

Collins, J.J.
2000   *Between Athens and Jerusalem: Jewish Identity in the Hellenistic Diaspora* (Grand Rapids, Mich.: Eerdmans, 2nd edn).

Cornell, S., and D. Hartmann
1997   *Ethnicity and Race: Making Identities in a Changing World* (Thousand Oaks, London: Pine Forge Press).

Cosgrove, C.
1997   *Elusive Israel: The Puzzle of Election in Romans* (Louisville, KY: Westminster/John Knox Press).

Cranfield, C.E.B.
1979   *The Epistle to the Romans* Vols I and II (Edinburgh: T&T Clark).

Crüsemann, F.
2003   *Kanon und Sozialgeschichte. Beiträge zum Alten Testament* (Gütersloh: Ch.Kaiser/Gütersloher Verlagshaus).

Dabourne, W.
1999　　*Purpose and Cause in Pauline Exegesis: Romans 1.16–4.25 and a New Approach to the Letters* (SNTSMS, 104; Cambridge: Cambridge University Press).

Dahl, N.A.
1963　　'The Particularity of Paul as a Problem in the Ancient Church', *Neotestamentica et Patristica: Eine Freundesgabe, O.Cullmann zu seinem 60. Geburtstag überreicht* (Leiden, Suppl.NovT. 60): 260–71.
1977　　*Studies in Paul: Theology for the Early Christian Mission* (Minneapolis: Augsburg Publishing House).
1978　　'Review of E.P. Sanders' *Paul and Palestinian Judaism*, *RSR* 4: 153–8.

Davies, W.D.
1978　　'Paul and the People of Israel', *NTS* 24: 4–39.
1984　　*Jewish and Pauline Studies* (Philadelphia: Fortress Press).
1998　　*Paul and Rabbinic Judaism: Some Elements in Pauline Theology*. Fiftieth Anniversary Edition (Mifflintown, PA: Sigler Press).

Dawson, J.D.
2002　　*Christian Figural Reading and the Fashioning of Identity* (Berkeley, CA: University of California Press).

Deming, W.
2003　　'Paul and Indifferent Things', in Sampley 2003.

Derrida, J.
1995　　*Points: Interviews, 1974–1994* (Stanford.CA: Stanford University Press).

Dodd, C.H.
1932　　*The Epistle to the Romans* (London: Hodder & Stoughton).
1954　　*New Testament Studies* (New York: Scribner).

Donaldson, T.L.
1997　　*Paul and the Gentiles: Remapping the Apostle's Convictional World* (Minneapolis: Fortress Press).

Donfried, K.P. (ed.)
1991　　*The Romans Debate* (Peabody, MA: Hendrickson, rev. and exp.edn of the 1977 edn).

Donfried, K.P., and P. Richardson (eds.)
1998　　*Judaism and Christianity in First Century Rome* (Grand Rapids: William B. Eerdmans).

Dunn, J.D.G.
1982　　'The Relationship between Paul and Jerusalem according to Galatians 1 and 2', *NTS* 28: 461–78.
1988　　*Romans 1&2* (WBC 38A, 38B; Dallas: Word Books).
1990a　 *Jesus, Paul and the Law: Studies in Mark and Galatians* (London: SPCK).
1990b　 'Judaizers', in R.J. Coggins and J.L. Houlden (eds.), *A Dictionary of Biblical Interpretation* (London: SCM Press): 369–71.
1990c　 'The New Perspective on Paul', in Dunn 1990a: 183–206.
1991　　*The Partings of the Ways Between Christianity and Judaism and Their Significance for the Character of Christianity* (Philadelphia, PA: Trinity Press International).
1998　　*The Theology of Paul, the Apostle* (Grand Rapids: Eerdmans).
1999　　'Who Did Paul Think He Was? A Study of Jewish-Christian Identity', *NTS* 45/2: 174–93.

Ehrensperger, K.
2002 '"…Let everyone be convinced in his/her own mind": Derrida and the Deconstruction of Paulinism', in *SBLSP*: 53–73.
2003 '"Be Imitators of Me as I am of Christ": A Hidden Discourse of Power and Domination in Paul?', *LTQ* Vol 38/4: 241–61.
2004a *That We May Be Mutually Encouraged: Feminism and the New Perspective in Pauline Studies* (New York/London: T&T Clark International).
2004b 'Scriptural Reasoning – the Dynamic that Informed Paul's Theologizing', *IBS* (26.1): 32–52 now also in *JSR* 5/2 2005 http: //etext.lib.virginia.edu/journals/ssr.
2005 'Paulus und die Gnade. Zu Fragen von Macht, Dominanz und Ermächtigung', in G. Gelardini (ed.), *Kontexte der Schrift Bd.1: Text, Ethik, Judentum und Christentum, Gesellschaft.Ekkehard W.Stegemann zum 60. Geburtstag* (Stuttgart: Kohlhammer Verlag): 60–73.
2006 'Levinas, the Jewish Philosopher meets Paul, the Jewish Apostle: Reading Romans in the Face of the Other', in D. Odell-Scott and D. Patte (eds.), *Reading Romans with Philosophers and Theologians* (Romans Through History and Cultures Series; London, New York: T&T Clark).
2007 *Paul and the Dynamics of Power: Communication and Interaction in the Early Christ-Movement* (London, New York: T&T Clark).
Eisenbaum, P.
2000a 'Paul as the New Abraham', in R.A. Horsley (ed.), *Paul and Politics: Ekklesia, Israel, Imperium, Interpretation* (Harrisburg, PA: Trinity Press International): 130–45.
2000b 'Is Paul the Father of Misogyny and Anti-Semitism?', in *Crosscurrents* 50.4: 506–24.
2005 'Paul, Polemics and the Problem of Essentialism', *BibInt* xiii/3: 236–7.
Elliott, N.
1990 *The Rhetoric of Romans: Argumentative Constraint and Strategy and Paul's Dialogue with Judaism* (Sheffield: Sheffield Academic Press).
1995 *Liberating Paul: The Justice of God and the Politics of the Apostle* (Sheffield Academic Press).
2000 'Paul and the Politics of the Empire', in R.A. Horsley (ed.), *Paul and Politics: Ekklesia, Israel, Imperium, Interpretation, Essays in Honor of Krister Stendahl* (Harrisburg, PA: Trinity Press International): 17–39.
2005a 'An American "Myth of Innocence"', in *Bib Int* xiii/3: 239–49.
2005b 'Political Formation in the Letter to the Romans', a paper presented at the SBL Annual Meeting, Philadelphia.
Engberg-Pedersen, T.
1994a 'Stoicism in Philippians', in T. Engberg-Pedersen (ed.), *Paul in His Hellenistic Context* (Edinburgh: T&T Clark).
2000 *Paul and the Stoics* (Louisville, KY: Westminster/John Knox Press).
Engberg-Pedersen, T. (ed.)
1994b *Paul in His Hellenistic Context* (Edinburgh: T&T Clark).
2001 *Paul Beyond the Judaism/Hellenism Divide* (Louisville KY: John Knox Press).
Epp, E.J.
2005 *Junia: The First Woman Apostle* (Minneapolis: Fortress Press).
Eskola, T.
1997 'Paul, Predestination, and Covenantal Nomism', *JST* 28 (390–412).

Esler, P.F.
1994 *The First Christians in their Social Worlds: Social-Scientific Approaches to New Testament Interpretation* (London New York: Routledge).
2001 'Ancient Oleiculture and Ethnic Differentiation: The Meaning of the Olive-Tree Metaphor in Romans 11', a paper presented at the Social-Scientific Criticism of the New Testament Section, SBL Annual Conference, Denver.
2003a *Conflict and Identity in Romans: The Social Setting of Paul's Letter* (Minneapolis: Fortress Press).
2003b 'Social Identity, Virtue Ethics and the Good Life: A New Approach to Romans 12:1–15:13', *BTB* 33: 51–63.
2003c 'Sodom Tradition in Romans 1:18–32', *BTB* 34: 2–16.
Esler, P.F. (ed.)
1995 *Modelling Early Christianity: Social-Scientific Studies to the New Testament* (London: Routledge)
Feldman, L.
1998 *Josephus's Interpretation of the Bible* (Berkeley, CA: University of California Press).
Fitzmyer, J.A.
1993 *Romans* (AB, 33; New York: Doubleday).
2000 *The Dead Sea Scrolls and Christian Origins* (Grand Rapids: Eerdmans).
Fredriksen, P.
1991 'Judaism, Circumcision of Gentiles, and Apocalyptic Hope: Another Look at Galatians 1 and 2', *JTS* 42, .2: 532–64 now also in Nanos 2002e: 235–60.
2002 'Augustine and Israel: *Interpretatio ad litteram*, Jews, and Judaism in Augustine's Theology of History', in D. Patte and E. TeSelle (eds.), *Engaging Augustine in Romans: Self, Context, and Theology in Interpretation* (Romans Through History and Cultures Series; Harrisburg, PA: Trinity Press International): 91–110.
Furnish, V.
1968 *Theology and Ethics in Paul* (Nashville: Abingdon Press).
1989 'Pauline Studies', in E.J. Epp and G.W. MacRae (eds.), *The New Testament and its Modern Interpreters* (Atlanta: Scholars Press).
Gager, J.G.
2000 *Reinventing Paul* (Oxford: Oxford University Press).
Garlington, D.
2005 'The New Perspective on Paul: An Appraisal Two Decades Later', *Criswell Theological Review*, N.S. 2.2: 17–38.
Gathercole, S.J.
2004 *Where is Boasting? Early Jewish Soteriology and Paul's Response in Romans 1–5* (Grand Rapids: Eerdmans).
2005 'The Petrine and Pauline *Sola fide* in Galatians 2', in M. Bachmann (2005).
Gaston, L.
1987 *Paul and the Torah* (Vancouver: University of British Columbia Press).
1998 'Faith in Romans 12 in the Light of the Common Life of the Roman Church', in Julian V. Hills *et al.* (eds.), *Common Life in the Early Church Essays honoring Graydon F. Snyder* (Harrisburg, PA.: Trinity Press International): 258–64.
Georgi, D.
1991 *Theocracy in Paul's Praxis and Theology*, ET (Minneapolis: Fortress Press).
1997 'God Turned Upside Down', in Richard Horsley (ed.), *Paul and Empire: Religion and Power in Roman Imperial Society* (Harrisburg, PA: Trinity Press International): 148–57.

Geertz, C.
  1963 *Old Societies and New States* (New York: Free Press).
Gorday, P.
  1983 *Principles of Patristic Exegesis: Romans 9–11 in Origen, John Chrysostom and Augustine* (New York: Edwin Mellen Press).
Gorman, M.
  2001 *Cruciformity: Paul's Narrative Spirituality of the Cross* (Grand Rapids, Mich.: Eerdmans).
Goulder, M.
  1994 *A Tale of Two Missions* (London: SCM Press).
  2001 *Paul and the Competing Mission in Corinth* (Peabody, MA: Hendrickson).
Grenholm, C., and D. Patte (eds.)
  2000 *Reading Israel in Romans: Legitimacy and Plausibility of Divergent Interpretations* (Romans Through History and Cultures Series; Harrisburg, PA: Trinity Press International).
Gruen, E.S.
  1998 *Heritage and Hellenism: The Reinvention of Jewish Tradition* (Berkeley, Los Angeles, London: University of California Press).
Gundry, R.H.
  1985 'Grace, Works and Staying Saved in Paul', *Bib* 66 (1–38).
Gundry-Volf, J.
  2000 '"The One" and "the Two", Jews, Gentiles, and the Church in Ephesians', paper read at the SBL Annual Conference, Nashville.
  2003 'Beyond Difference? Paul's Vision of a New Humanity in Galatians 3:28', in D.A. Campbell (ed.), *Gospel and Gender: A Trinitarian Engagement with Being Male and Female in Christ* (London & New York: T&T Clark International): 8–36.
Gunton, C. (ed.)
  1997 *The Cambridge Companion to Christian Doctrine* (Cambridge: Cambridge University Press).
Haacker, K.
  2003 *The Theology of Paul's Letter to the Romans* (Cambridge: Cambridge University Press).
Hall, J.M.
  1997 *Ethnic Identity in Greek Antiquity* (Berkeley, CA: University of California Press).
Hanson, G.W.
  1989 *Abraham in Galatians: Epistolary and Rhetorical Contexts* (Sheffield: Sheffield Academic Press).
Harink, D.
  2003 *Paul Among the Postliberals: Pauline Theology Beyond Christendom and Modernity* (Grand Rapids: Brazos Press).
  2005 'Paul and Israel: An Apocalyptic Reading', paper delivered at the Pauline Soteriology Group at the SBL Annual Meeting Philadelphia.
Harvey, A.E.
  1985 'Forty Strokes Save One: Social Aspects of Judaizing and Apostasy', in A.E. Harvey (ed.), *Alternative Approaches to New Testament Study* (London: SPCK): 79–96.
Hawthorne, F., and O. Betz (eds.)
  1987 *Tradition and Interpretation in the New Testament: Essays in Honor of E. Earle Ellis* (Grand Rapids: Eerdmans, Tübingen: J.C.B. Mohr): 290–300.

Hay, D.M. (ed.)
  1993   *Pauline Theology Volume II: 1&2 Corinthians* (Minneapolis: Fortress Press).
Hay, D.M., and E.E. Johnson (eds.)
  1995   *Pauline Theology Volume III: Romans* (Minneapolis: Fortress Press).
Hays, R.
  1989   *Echoes of Scripture in the Letters of Paul* (New Haven and London: Yale University Press).
  1996   'The Role of Scripture in Paul's Ethics', in E.H. Lovering and J.L. Sumney (eds.), *Theology and Ethics in Paul and His Interpreters: Essays in Honour of Victor Paul Furnish* (Nashville: Abingdon Press).
Hellholm D., H. Moxnes and T. Karlsen Seim (eds.)
  1995   *Mighty Minorities? Minorities in Early Christianity – Positions and Strategies* (Oslo: Skandinavian University Press).
Heschel, S.
  1998   *Abraham Geiger and the Jewish Jesus* (Chicago and London: The University of Chicago Press).
Holmberg, B.
  1998   'Jewish versus Christian Identity in the Church', *RB* 105.3: 397–425.
  2004   'The Methods of Historical Reconstruction in the Scholarly "Recovery" of Corinthian Christianity', in E. Adams and D. Horrell, *Christianity at Corinth: The Quest for the Pauline Church* (Louisville, KY: Westminster/John Knox Press): 255–71.
Hooker, M.D.
  1982b   'Paul and Paulinism', in *Paul and Paulinism: Essays in Honour of C.K. Barrett* (London: SPCK): 102–114.
  1986   *Continuity and Discontinuity: Early Christianity in its Jewish Setting* (London: Epworth Press)
  2002   '"Heirs of Abraham": The Gentiles' Role in Israel's Story – a Response to Bruce W. Longenecker', in B.W. Longenecker (ed.), *Narrative Dynamics in Paul: A Critical Assessment* (Louisville, KY: Westminster/John Knox Press): 85–96.
Hooker, M.D., and S.D. Wilson (eds.)
  1982a   *Paul and Paulinism: Essays in Honour of C.K. Barrett* (London: SPCK).
Horbury, W.
  1998   *Jews and Christians in Contact and Controversy* (Edinburgh: T&T Clark).
  2003   'The depiction of the Judaeo-Christians in the Toledot Yeshu', in P.J. Tomson and D. Lambers-Petry (eds.), *The Image of the Judaeo-Christians in Ancient Jewish and Christian Literature* (WUNT, 158; Tübingen: Mohr Siebeck): 280–6.
Horn, F.W.
  2005   'Juden und Heiden. Aspekte der Verhältnisbestimmung in den paulinischen Briefen. Ein Gespräch mit Krister Stendahl', in M. Bachmann.
Horowitz, D.L.
  1985   *Ethnic Groups in Conflict* (Berkley: University of California Press).
Horrell, D.G.
  2000   '"No Longer Jew or Greek", Paul's Corporate Christology and the Construction of Christianity', in D.G. Horrell and Ch. M. Tuckett (eds.), *Christology, Controversy and Community: New Testament Essays in Honour of David R. Catchpole* (Leiden: E.J. Brill): 320–44.
  2002   'Paul's Narratives or Narrative Substructure? The Significance of Paul's Story',

in B.W. Longenecker (ed.), *Narrative Dynamics in Paul: A Critical Assessment* (Louisville, KY: Westminster/John Knox Press): 157–71.
2005 *Solidarity and Difference: A Contemporary Reading of Paul's Ethics* (London, New York: T&T Clark).

Horsley, R.A. (ed.)
1997 *Paul and Empire: Religion and Power in Roman Imperial Society* (Harrisburg, PA: Trinity Press International).
2000a *Paul and Politics: Ekklesia, Israel, Imperium, Interpretation. Essays in Honour of Krister Stendahl* (Harrisburg, PA: Trinity Press International).

Horsley, R.A.
2000b 'Rhetoric and Empire – and 1 Corinthians', in R.A. Horsley (ed.), *Paul and Politics: Ekklesia, Israel, Imperium, Interpretation* (Harrisburg, PA: Trinity Press International).
2004 '1 Corinthians: A Case Study of Paul's Assembly as an Alternative Society' (1997), in E. Adams and D.G. Horrell, *Christianity at Corinth: The Quest for the Pauline Church* (Louisville, KY: Westminster/John Knox Press): 227–37.

Houlden, J.L.
1983 'A Response to J.D.G. Dunn', in *JSNT* 18: 58–67.

Hubbard, M.V.
2002 *New Creation in Paul's Letters and Thought* (SNTSMS, 119; Cambridge: Cambridge University Press).

Hutchinson, J., and A.D. Smith (eds.)
1996 *Ethnicity* (Oxford: Oxford University Press).

Jenkins, R.
1997 *Rethinking Ethnicity: Arguments and Explorations* (London: Sage).

Jervell, J.
1972 *Luke and the People of God: A New Look at Luke–Acts* (Minneapolis: Augsburg Publishing House).
1980 'Mighty Minority', *ST* 34: 13–38.
1991 'The Letter to Jerusalem' in K. Donfried (ed.), *The Romans Debate* (Peabody, Mass.: Hendrickson): 53–64.

Jewett, R.
1971 *Paul's Anthropological Terms: A Study of their Use in Conflict Settings* (Leiden: E.J. Brill).
1981 *Letter to Pilgrims. A Commentary on the Epistle to the Hebrews* (New York: Pilgrim Press).
1982 *Christian Tolerance: Paul's Message to the Modern Church* (Philadelphia: Westminster).
1985 'The Law and the Co-Existence of Jews and Gentiles in Romans', *Int* 39: 341–56.
1988 'Paul, Phoebe and the Spanish Mission', in J.Neusner *et al.* (eds.), *The Social World of Formative Christianity and Judaism: Essays in Tribute to Howard Clark Kee* (Philadelphia: Fortress Press): 142–61.
1993 'Tenement Churches and Communal Meal in the Early Church: The Implications of a Form-Critical Analysis of 2 Thessalonians 3:10', *BR* 38: 23–42.

Johnson, E. E.
1989 *The Function of Apocalyptic and Wisdom Traditions in Romans 9–11* (SBLDS; Atlanta, GA: Scholars Press).

Johnson, E.E. (ed.)
1997 *Pauline Theology IV: Looking Back, Pressing On* (Atlanta: Scholars Press).

Judge, E.A.
    1972   'St. Paul and Classical Culture', *JAC* 15.
    2005   'The Roman Base of Paul's Mission', *TynBul* 56.1: 103–17.
Judge, E.A., and G.S.R. Thomas
    1966   'The Origin of the Church at Rome: A New Solution', *Reformed Theological Review* 25/3: 81–94.
Kahl, B.
    1999   'Gender Trouble in Galatia: Paul and the Rethinking of Difference', D.F. Sawyer and D.M. Collier (ed.), *Is There a Future for Feminist Theology?* (Sheffield: Sheffield Academic Press): 57–73.
Käsemann, E.
    1969a   *New Testament Questions of Today* (London: SCM Press).
    1969b   'Paul and Israel', in *New Testament Questions for Today* (London: SCM Press): 183–7.
    1969c   'The Righteousness of God in Paul', in *New Testament Questions for Today* (London: SCM Press): 168–82.
    1969d   'On the Subject of Primitive Christian Apocalyptic', *New Testament Questions for Today* (London: SCM Press): 108–37.
    1971a   *Perspectives on Paul* (London: SCM Press).
    1971b   'The Faith of Abraham in Romans 4', *Pauline Perspectives* (London: SCM Press): 79–101.
    1971c   'Justification and Salvation History in the Epistle to the Romans', *New Testament Questions for Today* (London: SCM Press): 60–78.
    1980   *Commentary on Romans* (ET; London: SCM Press).
Keck, L.
    2005   *Romans* (Abingdon New Testament Commentaries; Nashville: Abingdon Press).
Kee, H.C.
    1989   *Knowing the Truth: A Sociological Approach to New Testament Interpretation* (Philadelphia: Fortress Press)
Kelley, S.
    2002   *Racializing Jesus: Race, Ideology and the Formation of Modern Biblical Scholarship* (London/New York: Routledge).
Kertelge, K.
    1967   *Rechtfertigung bei Paulus* (Münster: Aschendorff).
Klein, G.
    1969   'Römer 4 und die Idee der Heilsgeschichte', *Rekonstruktion und Interpretation* (München: Kaiser): 145–79.
Kloppenborg, J.S., and S.G. Wilson (eds.)
    1996   *Voluntary Associations in the Graeco-Roman World* (London: Routledge).
Krauss, W.
    2005   'Gottes Gerechtigkeit und Gottes Volk. Oekumenisch-ekklesiologische Aspekte der New Perspective on Paul', in M. Bachmann (ed.), *Lutherische und Neue Paulusperspektive* (Tübingen: Mohr Siebeck, 2005): 329–48.
Kugel, J.
    1997   *The Bible as it Was* (Cambridge MA: The Belknap Press of Harvard University).
Kümmel, W.G.
    1972   *The New Testament: The History of its Problems* (Nashville: Abingdon Press).
LaGrande, J.
    1996   'Proliferation of the "Gentile" in the NRSV', *BR* 41: 77–87.
Lampe, P.
    2003   *From Paul to Valentinus: Christians at Rome in the First Two Centuries* (New

York and London: T&T Clark) ET by M. Steinhauser, *Die stadtrömischen Christen in den ersten beiden Jahrhunderten* (Tübingen: Mohr Siebeck 1989).

Langton, D.R.
2005a 'The Myth of the "Traditional View of Paul" and the Role of the Apostle in Modern Jewish-Christian Polemics', in *JSNT* 28.1: 69–104.
2005b 'Modern Jewish Identity and the Apostle Paul: Pauline Studies as an Intra-Jewish Ideological Battleground', *JSNT* 28.2: 217–58.

Lee, J.W.
2005 'Justification of Difference in Galatians', paper presented at the SBL Annual Meeting Philadelphia.

Leenhardt, F.J.
1961 *The Epistle to the Romans* (London: Lutterworth).

Leon, H.J.
1995 *The Jews of Ancient Rome* (Peabody, Mass.: Hendrickson, updated edn).

Levinas, E.
1969 *Totality and Infinity: An Essay on Exteriority*. ET by A. Lingis (Pittsburgh, PA: Duquesne University Press).

Levine, L.
2003 'The First Century C.E. Synagogue in Historical Perspective', in B. Olsson and M. Zetterholm (eds.), *The Ancient Synagogue from its Origins until 200 CE* (Stockholm: Almqvist & Wiksell International): 1–24.

Lieu, Judith M.
1996 *Image and Reality: The Jews in the World of the Christians in the Second Century* (Edinburgh: T&T Clark).
1998 'The "Attraction of Women" in/to Early Judaism and Christianity: Gender and the Politics of Conversion', *JSNT* 72 (1998): 5–22.
2002 ' "Impregnable Ramparts and Walls of Iron": Boundary and Identity in Early "Judaism" and "Christianity" ', *NTS* 48.3 (July): 297–313.
2002 *Neither Jew Nor Greek: Constructing Early Christianity* (London and New York: T&T Clark).

Lim, T.H. (ed.)
2000 *The Dead Sea Scrolls in Their Historical Context* (Edinbrugh: T&T Clark).

Lodge, J.G.
1996 *Romans 9–11: A Reader-Response Analysis* (University of South Florida: Scholars Press).

Longenecker, B. (ed.)
2002 *Narrative Dynamics in Paul: A Critical Assessment* (Louisville, KY: Westminster/John Knox Press).

Lyons, G.
1985 *Pauline Autobiography: Toward a New Understanding* (SBLDS, 73; Atlanta: Scholars Press).

Magonet, J.
1992 'The Biblical Roots of Jewish Identity: Exploring the Relativity of Exegesis', *JSOT* 54: 3–24.

Malina, B.
2002 'Social-Scientific Methods in Historical Jesus Research', in W. Stegemann, B.J. Malina and G. Theissen (eds.), *Jesus and the Gospels* (Minneapolis: Fortress Press): 3–26.

Manson, T.W.
1948 'Paul's Letter to the Romans and Others', *BJRL* 31: 224–40.

Marcus, J.
1989 'The Circumcision and Uncircumcision in Rome', *NTS* 35: 67–81.
2001 ' "Under the Law": The Background of a Pauline Expression', *CBQ* 63: 72–83.
Martin, D.M.
1990 *Slavery as Salvation* (New Haven, London: Yale University Press).
2001 'Paul and the Judaism/Hellenism Dichotomy: Toward a Social History of the Question', in Engberg-Pedersen Troels (ed.), *Paul Beyond the Judaism/Hellenism Divide* (Louisville, KY: Westminster/John Knox Press): 29–62.
Martin, T.W.
2003 'The Covenant of Circumcision (Genesis 17:9–14) and the Situational Antithesis in Galatians 3:28', *JBL* 122/1: 111–25.
Martyn, J.L.
1997a *Theological Issues in the Letters of Paul* (Nashville: Abingdon Press).
1997b *Galatians: a New Translation with Introduction and Commentary* (New York: Doubleday).
Matlock, R.B.
1996 *Unveiling the Apocalyptic Paul: Paul's Interpreters and the Rhetoric of Criticism* (Sheffield: Sheffield Academic Press).
Meeks, W.A.
1983 *The First Urban Christians: The Social World of the Apostle Paul* (New Haven: Yale University Press).
1987 'Judgment and the Brother: Romans 14:1–15:13', in G. Meeks W.A. (ed.).
1972 *The Writings of St. Paul* (New York and London: Norton).
1990 'On Trusting an Unpredictable God: A Hermeneutical Meditation on Romans 9–11', in J.T. Carroll, C.H. Cosgrove and E.E. Johnson (eds.), *Faith and History: Essays in Honor of Paul W. Meyer* (Atlanta, GA: Scolars Press): 105–24.
1993 *The Origins of Christian Morality: The First Two Centuries* (New Haven: Yale University Press).
1998 'The Circle of Reference in Pauline Morality', in D. Balch, E. Ferguson and W.A. Meeks (eds.), *Greeks, Romans, Christians: Essays in Honour of Abraham Malherbe* (Minneapolis, MN: Fortress Press): 305–317.
2001 'Judaism, Hellenism, and the Birth of Christianity', T. Engberg Pedersen (ed.), *Paul Beyond the Judaism/Hellenism Divide* (Louisville, KY: Westminster/John Knox Press): 17–28.
Meeks, W.A., and R.L. Wilken
1978 *Jews and Christians in Antioch: In the First Four Centuries of the Common Era* (Missoula, MT: Scholars Press).
Meyer, P.
1995 'Pauline Theology: Some Thoughts for a Pause in its Pursuit', *SBLSP* (ed. E.H. Lovering Jr; Atlanta: Scholars Press).
Michel, O.
1976 *Der Brief an die Römer* (Göttingen: Vandenhoeck & Ruprecht).
Mitternacht, D.
2002 'Foolish Galatians? – A Recipient-Oriented Assessment of Paul's Letter to the Galatians', in M.D. Nanos (ed.), *The Galatians Debate: Contemporary Issues in Rhetorical and Historical Interpretation* (Peabody, MA: Hendrickson): 408–33.
2003 'Current Views on the Synagogue of Ostia Antica and the Jews of Rome and Ostia', in B. Olsson and M. Zetterholm (eds.), *The Ancient Synagogue: From its Origins until 200 C.E.* (Stockholm: Almqvist & Wiksell International): 521–71.

Mitchell, M.
2000   *The Heavenly Trumpet: John Chrysostom and the Art of Pauline Interpretation* (Tübingen: Mohr Siebeck).

Moore, G.F.
1921   'Christian Writers on Judaism', *HTR* 14: 197–254.

Munck, J.
1959   *Paul and the Salvation of Mankind* (London: SCM Press, 1954).
1967   *Christ and Israel: An Interpretation of Romans 9–11* (Philadelphia: Fortress Press).

Nagata, J.A.
1974   'What is a Malay? Situational Selection of Ethnic Identity in a Plural Society', *American Ethnologist* 1.
1984   *The Reflowering of Malaysian Islam: Modern Religious Radicals and Their Roots* (Vancouver: University of British Columbia Press).

Nanos, M.D.
1996   *The Mystery of Romans: The Jewish Context of Paul's Letter to the Romans* (Minneapolis: Fortress Press).
1999   'The Jewish Context of the Gentile Audience Addressed in Paul's Letter to the Romans', *CBQ* 61.2 (April).
2000   'The Inter- and Intra-Jewish Political Context of Paul's Letter to the Galatians', in R.A. Horsley (ed.), *Paul and Politics: Ekklesia, Israel, Imperium, Interpretation* (Harrisburg, PA: Trinity Press International): 146–59.
2002a   *The Irony of Galatians: Paul's Letter in First-Century Context* (Minneapolis: Fortress Press).
2002b   'Introduction' in M.D. Nanos (ed.), *The Galatians Debate: Contemporary Issues in Rhetorical and Historical Interpretation* (Peabody, MA: Hendrickson): xi–xli.
2002c   'What Was at Stake in Peter's "Eating with Gentiles" at Antioch?', M.D. Nanos (ed.), *The Galatians Debate: Contemporary Issues in Rhetorical and Historical Interpretation* (Peabody, MA: Hendrickson): 282–318.
2002d   'The Inter- and Intra-Jewish Political Context of Paul's Letter to the Galatians' in M.D. Nanos (ed.), *The Galatians Debate: Contemporary Issues in Rhetorical and Historical Interpretation* (Peabody, MA: Hendrickson): 396–407.
2005   'How Inter-Christian Approaches to Paul's Rhetoric Can Perpetuate Negative Evaluations of Jewishness-Although Proposing to Avoid that Outcome', *BibInt* 13.3: 255–67.

Nanos, M.D. (ed.)
2002e   *The Galatians Debate: Contemporary Issues in Rhetorical and Historical Interpretation* (Peabody, MA: Hendrickson).

Nickelsburg, G.W.E., and G.W. MacRae (eds.)
1986   *Christians Among Jews and Gentiles: Essays in Honor of Krister Stendahl on His Sixty-fifth Birthday* (Philadelphia: Fortress Press).

Nickelsburg, G.W.E.
2003   *Ancient Judaism and Christian Origins Diversity: Continuity and Transformation* (Minneapolis: Fortress Press).

Nobs, A.
2004   '"Beloved Brothers" in the New Testament and Early Christian World', in P.J. Williams, A.D. Clarke, P.M. Head and D. Instone-Brewer (eds.), *The New Testament in Its First Century Setting: Essays on Context and Background in Honour of B.W. Winter on His 65th Birthday* (Grand Rapids, MI: Eerdmans): 143–50.

Olsson, B., and M. Zetterholm (eds.)
2003   *The Ancient Synagogue: From its Origins until 200 C.E.* (Stockholm: Almqvist & Wiksell International).

Olsson, B.
2003   'The Origins of the Synagogue: An Evaluation', in B. Olsson and M. Zetterholm (eds.), *The Ancient Synagogue: From its Origins until 200 C.E.* (Stockholm: Almqvist & Wiksell International): 132-8.

O'Sullivan, O. (ed.)
2000   *The Bible as Book: The Reformation* (London: British Library).

Painter, J.
2005   'James and Peter: Models of Leadership and Mission', B. Chilton and G. Evans (eds.), *The Missions of James, Peter, and Paul: Tensions in Early Christianity* (Leiden: E.J. Brill): 143-209.

Park, E.C.
2003   *Either Jew or Gentile: Paul's Unfolding Theology of Inclusivity* (Louisville, KY: Westminster/John Knox Press).

Parkes, J.
1979   *The Conflict of the Church and the Synagogue: A Study in the Origins of Antisemitism* (New York: Atheneum, 4th reprint).

Patte, D.
1975   *Early Jewish Hermeneutic in Palestine* (SBLDS, 22; Missoula, MT: Scholars Press).
1983   *Paul's Faith and the Power of the Gospel: A Structural Introduction to the Pauline Letters* (Philadelphia: Fortress Press)

Patte, D., and E. TeSelle (eds.)
2003   *Engaging Augustine in Romans: Self, Context, and Theology in Interpretation* (Romans Through History and Cultures Series; Harrisburg, PA: Trinity Press International).

Pauck, W.
1961   *Luther: Lectures on Romans* (Library of Christian Classics, 15; London: SCM Press).

Peerbolte, L.J.L.
2003   *Paul the Missionary* (Leuven: Peeters).

Plietzsch, S.
2005   *Kontexte der Freiheit: Konzepte der Befreiung bei Paulus und im rabbinischen Judentum* (Stuttgart: W. Kohlhammer).

Polaski, S.H.
1999   *Paul and the Discourse of Power* (Sheffield: Sheffield Academic Press).

Rader, W.
1978   *The Church and Racial Hostility: A History of the Interpretation of Ephesians 2:11-22* (Tübingen: Mohr).

Räisänen, H.
1980   *Die paulinische Literatur und Theologie* (Aarhus: Forlaget Aros).
1983   *Paul and the Law* (WUNT; Tübingen: Mohr Siebeck).

Rambo, L.R.
1993   *Understanding Religious Conversion* (New Haven /London, Yale University Press).

Reasoner, M.
1999   *The Strong and the Weak in Romans: 14:1-15:13 in Context* (Cambridge: Cambridge University Press).

Richardson, P.
2003 'An Architectural Case for Synagogue as Associations', in B. Olsson and M. Zetterholm (eds.), *The Ancient Synagogue: From its Origins until 200 C.E.* (Stockholm: Almqvist & Wiksell International): 90–117.

Ricoeur, P.
1984 *Time and Narrative*, vol. 1 (Berkely: University of California Press).

Rock, I.E.
2004 *Paul's Letter to the Romans and Roman Imperialism* PhD thesis submitted to the University of Wales Lampeter, forthcoming with Paternoster Press.

Roetzel, C.
1999 *Paul, the Man and the Myth* (Minneapolis: Fortress Press).

Rohrbaugh, R.L.
2002 'Ethnocentricism and Historical Questions about Jesus', in W. Stegemann, B.J. Malina and G. Theissen (eds.), *Jesus and the Gospels* (Minneapolis: Fortress Press): 27–44.

Rohrbaugh, R.L. (ed.)
1996 *The Social Sciences and New Testament Interpretation* (Peabody, Mass.: Hendrickson).

Rosner, B.
1994 *Scripture and Ethics: A Study of 1 Corinthians 5–7* (Leiden: E.J. Brill).

Runesson, A.
2003 'Persian Imperial Politics, the Beginnings of Public Torah Reading and the Origins of the Synagogue', in B. Olsson and M. Zetterholm, *The Ancient Synagogue: From its Origins until 200 C.E.* (Stockholm: Almqvist & Wiksell International): 63–89.

Rutgers, L.V.
1998 *The Hidden Heritage of Diaspora Judaism* (Leuven: Peeters).

Sabou, S.C.
2005 *Between Horror and Hope: Paul's Metaphorical Language of Death in Romans 6:1–11* (Milton Keynes: Paternoster Press).

Sampley, J.P.
1994 'The Weak and the Strong: Paul's Careful and Crafty Rhetorical Strategy in Romans 14:1–15:13', in L.M. White and O.L. Yarbrough (eds.), *The Social World of the First Urban Christians: Studies in Honour of Wayne A. Meeks* (Minneapolis: Fortress Press): 40–52.

Sampley, J.P. (ed.)
2003 *Paul in the Greco-Roman World: A Handbook* (Harrisburg, PA: Trinity Press International).

Sanders, E.P.
1973 'Patterns of Religion in Paul and Rabbinic Judaism: A Holistic Method of Comparison', *HTR*, 66: 455–78.
1977 *Paul and Palestinian Judaism: A Comparison of Patterns of Religion* (Philadelphia: Fortress Press).
1983 *Paul, the Law, and the Jewish People* (Philadelphia: Fortress Press).

Sanders, J.T.
1993 *Schismatics, Sectarians, Dissidents, Deviants: The First One Hundred Years of Jewish-Christian Relations* (Valley Forge, PA: Trinity Press International).

Schäfer, P.
1997 *Judeophobia: Attitudes Toward the Jews in the Ancient World* (Cambridge, MA: Harvard University Press).

Schelke, K.H.
 1956 *Paulus, Lehrer der Väter: Die altkirchlichliche Auslegung von Römer 1–11* (Düsseldorf: Patmos).

Schiffman, L.H.
 1985 *Who Was a Jew? Rabbinic and Halakhic Perspectives on the Jewish-Christian Schism* (Hoboken, NJ: Ktav).

Schmithals, W.
 1960 *The Office of an Apostle* (Nashville: Abingdon Press).

Schütz, J.H.
 1975 *Paul and the Anatomy of Apostolic Authority* (Cambridge: Cambridge University Press).

Schwartz, S.
 2001 *Imperialism and Jewish Society, 200 BC to 640 CE* (Princeton and Oxford: Princeton University Press).

Schweitzer, A.
 1951 *Paul and His Interpreters: A Critical History* (New York: Macmillan).

Scott, J.M.
 1995 *Paul and the Nations: The Old Testament and Jewish Background of Paul's Mission to the Nations with Special Reference to the Destination of Galatians* (WUNT, 84; Tübingen: Mohr/Siebeck).

Segal, A.F.
 1990 *Paul the Convert: The Apostolate and Apostasy of Saul the Pharisee* (New Haven and London: Yale University Press).
 1990 'Paul's Experience and Romans 9–11', *The Church and Israel: Romans 9–11, The Princeton Seminary Bulletin*, Suppl.Issue 1: 56–70.

Seifrid, M.
 2000 'The New Perspective on Paul and Its Problems', *Themelios* 25: 4–18.

Senior, D.
 1996 *What Are They Saying About Matthew?* (New York: Paulist Press).

Shkul, M.
 2005 'Religious Identity and the Power of Naming', paper presented at the Pauline Epistles Section, SBL/AAR Annual meeting, Philadelphia.

Siker, J.S.
 1991 *Disinheriting the Jews: Abraham in Early Christian Controversy* (Louisville, KY: Westminster/John Knox).

Smith, C.W.
 1992 *The Meaning and End of Religion* (Minneapolis: Fortress Press [1962]).

Smith, J.A.
 2005 *The Marks of an Apostle: Deconstruction, Philippians, and Problematizing Pauline Theology* (Atlanta, GA: Society of Biblical Literature).

Soderlund, S., and N.T. Wright
 1999 *Romans and the People of God: Essays in Honor of Gordon D. Fee* (Grand Rapids: Eerdmans).

Soulen, R.K.
 1996 *The God of Israel and Christian Theology* (Minneapolis: Fortress Press).

Spilsbury, P.
 1998 *The Image of the Jew in Flavius Josephus' Paraphrase of the Bible* (Texte und Studien zum antiken Judentum, 69; Tübingen: Mohr Siebeck).

Stanley, C.
 1992 *Paul and the Language of Scripture: Citation Technique in Pauline Epistles and Contemporary Literature* (Cambridge: Cambridge University Press).

2003 *Arguing with Scripture: The Rhetoric of Quotations in the Letters of Paul* (New York, London: T&T Clark International).

Stanton, G.N., and G.G. Strousma (eds.)
1998 *Tolerance and Intolerance in Early Judaism and Christianity* (Cambridge: Cambridge University Press).

Stanton, G.N., B.W. Longenecker and S.C. Barton (eds.)
2004 *The Holy Spirit and Christian Origins. Essays in Honour of James D.G. Dunn* (Grand Rapids, MI: Eerdmans).

Stark, R.
1996 *The Rise of Christianity: A Sociologist Reconsiders History* (Princeton: Princeton University Press).

Stegemann, E.W.
2005 *Paulus und die Welt. Aufsätze* (Zürich: Theologischer Verlag).

Stegemann, E.W., and W. Stegemann
1999 *The Jesus Movement: A Social History of its First Century* (Edinburgh: T&T Clark).

Stegemann, W.
2002 'The Contextual Ethics of Jesus', in W. Stegemann, B.J. Malina and G. Theissen (eds.), *The Social Setting of Jesus and the Gospels* (Minneapolis: Fortress Press): 45–61.

Stegemann W., B.J. Malina and G. Theissen (eds.)
2002 *The Social Setting of Jesus and the Gospels* (Minneapolis: Fortress Press).

Stendahl, K.
1976 *Paul Among Jews and Gentiles and Other Essays* (Philadelphia: Fortress Press).
1995 *Final Account: Paul's Letter to the Romans* (Minneapolis: Fortress Press).

Stowers, S.K.
1989 'Ἐκ πίστεως and διὰ τῆς πίστεως in Rom 3:30', *JBL* 108: 665–74.
1994 *A Rereading of Romans: Justice, Jews and Gentiles* (New Haven & London: Yale University Press).

Stuhlmacher, P.
1986 'Der Abfassungszweck des Römerbriefes', *ZNW* 77: 180–93.
1988 'The Theme of Romans', *Australian Biblical Review* 361: 31–44.

Talbert, C.H.
1995 'Freedom and Law in Galatians', *Ex Auditu* 11: 17–28.
2001 'Paul, Judaism, and the Revisionists', *CBQ* 63/1: 1–22.

Taubes, J.
2004 *The Political Theology of Paul* (ET by D. Hollander; Stanford, CA: Stanford University Press).

Taylor, M.S.
1995 *Antijudaism and Early Christianity: A Critique of the Scholarly Consensus* (Leiden: E.J. Brill).

Taylor, N.H.
1992 *Paul, Antioch, and Jerusalem: A Study in Relationships In Early Judaism and Christianity* (JSNTSup, 66; Sheffield: Sheffield Academic Press).
1995 'The Social Nature of Conversion in the Early Christian World', in P.F. Esler (ed.), *Modelling Early Christianity: social-scientific studies of the New Testament in its context* (London/New York Routledge): 128–36.

Tellbe, M.
2001 *Paul Between Synagogue and State: Christians, Jews and Civic Authorities in 1 Thessalonians, Romans, and Philippians* (Stockholm: Almqvist & Wiksell International).

Theissen, G.
  1992 *Social Reality and the Early Christians: Theology, Ethics, and the World of the New Testament* (ET M. Kohl; Minneapolis: Fortress Press).
Thiselton, A.C.
  2000 *The First Epistle to the Corinthians: NITC Greek Testament Commentary* (Grand Rapids: Eerdmans).
Thompson, M.
  1991 *Clothed With Christ: The Example and Teaching of Jesus in Romans 12.1–15.13* (Sheffield: Sheffield Academic Press).
Tomson, P.J.
  1990 *Paul and the Jewish Law: Halakha in the Letters of the Apostle to the Gentiles* (Minneapolis: Fortress Press).
  1996 'Paul's Jewish Background in View of His Law-Teaching in 1 Corinthians 7', in J.D.G. Dunn (ed.), *Paul and the Mosaic Law: The Third Durham-Tübingen Research Symposium on Earliest Christianity and Judaism*, Durham September 1994 (Tübingen: Mohr Siebeck): 251–70.
Tomson, P.J. and D.L. Lambers-Petry (eds.)
  2003 *The Image of the Judeo-Christians in Ancient Jewish and Christian Literature* (WUNT, 158; Tübingen: Mohr Siebeck).
Tyson, J.B.
  1999 *Luke, Judaism and the Scholars: Critical Approaches to Luke–Acts* (Columbia, SC: University of South Carolina Press).
Wagner, J.R.
  2002 *Heralds of Good News: Isaiah and Paul 'In Concert' in the Letter to the Romans* (Leiden: E.J. Brill).
Walters, J.C.
  1993 *Ethnic Issues in Paul's Letter to the Romans: Changing Self Definitions in Earliest Roman Christianity* (Valley Forge, PA: Trinity Press International).
Wan, Sze-kar
  2000 'Collection for the Saints as an Anticolonial Act: Implications of Paul's Ethnic Reconstruction', in R.A. Horsley (ed.), *Paul and Politics: Ekklesia, Israel, Imperium, Interpretation. Essays in Honour of Krister Stendahl* (Harrisburg, PA: Trinity Press International): 191–215.
Watson, F.W.
  1989 *Paul among Jews and Gentiles. A Sociological Approach* (Cambridge: Cambridge University Press).
  1997 'The Scope of Hermeneutics', in C. Gunton (ed.), *The Cambridge Companion to Christian Doctrine* (Cambridge: Cambridge University Press): 65–80.
Watt, J.
  2003 'Language Pragmatism in a Multilingual Religious Community' in B. Olsson and M. Zetterholm (eds.), *The Ancient Synagogue from its Origins until 200 CE* (Stockholm: Almqvist & Wiksell International): 277–97.
Weber, F.
  1897 *Jüdische Theologie auf Grund des Talmud und verwandter Schriften* (Leipzig: Dörffling & Franke, 2nd edn).
Weber, M.
  1968 *Economy and Society: An Outline of Interpretative Sociology* Vol. 1 (ed. G. Roth and C. Wittich; New York: Bedminster Press).
Wedderburn, A.G.M.
  1988 *The Reasons for Romans* (Edinburgh: T&T Clark).

White L.M., and O.L. Yarbrough (eds.)
    1994   *The Social World of the First Urban Christians: Studies in Honor of Wayne A. Meeks* (Minneapolis: Fortress Press).

Wilckens, U.
    1978   *Der Brief an die Römer* (3 vols.; Düsseldorf: Benziger; Neukirchen–Vluyn: Neukirchener Verlag, 1978 [1980. 1982]).

Williams, P.J., A.D. Clarke, P.M. Head and D. Instone-Brewer (eds.)
    2004   *The New Testament in Its First Century Setting: Essays on Context and Background in Honour of B.W. Winter on His 65th Birthday* (Grand Rapids, MI: Eerdmans).

Wilson, B.
    1970   *Religious Sects: A Sociological Study* (London: Weidenfeld and Nicholson).

Wilson, S.
    1992   'Gentile Judaizers', *NTS* 38: 605–16.

Wright, T.
    1991   *The Climax of the Covenant: Christ and Law in Pauline Theology* (Minneapolis: Fortress Press).
    1992   *The New Testament and the People of God* (Minneapolis: Fortress Press).
    1995   'Romans and the Theology of Paul', in D.M. Hay and E.E. Johnson (eds.), *Pauline Theology* 3 (Minneapolis: Fortress Press): 30–67.
    2000   'Paul's Gospel and Caesar's Empire', in R. Horsley (ed.), *Paul and Politics: Ecclesia, Israel, Imperium, Interpretation: Essays in Honour of Krister Stendahl* (Harrisburg, PA: Trinity Press International): 160–83.

Wyschogrod, M.
    2004   *Abrahams's Promise: Judaism and Jewish-Christian Relations* (ed. R. Kendall Soulen; Grand Rapids: Eerdmans).

Yee, T.L.N.
    2005   *Jews, Gentiles, and Ethnic Reconciliation: Paul's Jewish Identity and Ephesians* (SNTSMS, 130; Cambridge: Cambridge University Press).

Young, I.M.
    1990a   *Justice and the Politics of Difference* (Princeton, NJ: Princeton University Press).
    1990b   'The Ideal of Community and the Politics of Difference', in L. Nicholson (ed.), *Feminism/Postmodernism* (New York: Routledge): 300–23.

Zetterholm, M.
    2002   *The Formation of Christianity at Antioch: A Social-Scientific Approach to the Separation Between Judaism and Christianity* (London, New York: Routledge).

INDEXES

INDEX OF ANCIENT SOURCES

OLD TESTAMENT

Numbers
19	117

Deuteronomy
32.19–21	120
32.43	120

Joshua
24.2–3	63

Isaiah
2.2–4	59
49	64
56	122
56.3–7	95

Jeremiah
31.33	131

Daniel
1.3–1.7	117

Micah
4.1	95

Zechariah
2.11	95
8.23	95

Habakuk
2.4b	30

Deuterocanonical Books (Apocrypha)

Judith
	118

2 Maccabees
10.5	118

Tobit
13.11	95

NEW TESTAMENT

Mark
1.5	2
7.9–13	107

John
3.22	2
4.22	102

Acts
15	39, 40
28.2	118

Romans
1	107, 108, 109
1–3	122
1.2–3	110
1.3–4	113
1.4	124, 154
1.5	124
1.5–7	38
1.5–10	75
1.12	75
1.14	122
1.16	109, 122
1.18–3.20	126
1.24	109
1.26	109
1.28	109
1–8	15
2	107, 108, 115,
2.1	107, 108, 109, 119
2.9–10	122
2.17	108, 109, 122
2.17–20	108
2.17–29	108
2.28	104
2.29	107
3	63
3–4	112
3.1–2	112
3.2	58
3.3–7	145
3.21	110, 142
3.21–6	109
3.25b–26	135
3.31	168
4	62, 63, 112, 118, 128, 161
4.1–22	63
4.9	63

Romans (cont.)					
4.11–12	113, 124	9.1–5	88, 135	11.11	58, 110, 123
4.11–16	113, 128	9.3	122	11.11–24	24
4.12	124	9.4	58, 87, 106, 122, 171	11.13	123, 141
4.13–16	130			11.13–16	129
4.16	63, 90, 127, 133, 151	9.5	171	11.13–24	105, 106, 129
		9.6	113, 122, 131	11.15	172
4.17	63	9.6b	124	11.16f.	52
6	154, 163	9.6–13	24	11.17	59
6.3	60	9.6–15	145	11.17–18	137
6.12	154	9.7	130	11.17–24	54, 79, 101, 136, 164
6.14	154	9.8	124, 126, 145		
6.16	154				
6.18	154	9.8–9	171	11.18	38, 117
6.20	154	9.22	49	11.20	150
6.22	154	9.22–4	130	11.23	124, 133, 171, 172
7	109, 118	9.23	171		
7.1	60, 106, 113	9.24	100, 122, 124, 126, 127, 131	11.25	3. 123
				11.25–32	170
7.3	113			11.26	123
7.7–23	110	9.25	130	11.27	123
7.13–20	110	9.26	130	11.28	171
7.14	60	9.27	126, 128	11.28–9	137
7.17–19	113	9.27–8	110	11.33–6	172
7.18	60	9.27–9	129	11.34–5	133
8.1	109	9.30	122, 123	12	164
8.4	90	9.30–1	3	12–15	77
8.15	106	10.2–3	110	12.1–15.13	94
8.29	154	10.3	30	12.2	164
8.31–9	165	10.4	109, 111	12.5	36
8.32	134	10.12	122	12.10	36
8–11	24	10.19	122	13	78
9–11	15, 21, 22, 24, 49, 55, 100, 109, 110, 114, 120, 121, 122, 124, 127, 128, 129, 131, 143, 162, 170, 171	10.21	122, 123	13.1–7	71
		11	49, 79, 114, 124, 127, 131, 169, 170, 171, 172	13.8	36, 78, 90
				13.14	164
				14	118
				14.1	161
				14.1–15.6	115, 121
		11.1	58, 87, 110, 157	14.1–15.13	162, 169
				14.2–3	115
9–15	105	11.1–2	123	14.4	118
9	98, 114, 124, 126, 129, 131, 137	11.2	123	14.5	76, 79, 115, 117
		11.4–5	129		
		11.5	129	14.5–6a	117
		11.5–6	162	14.5–6	38
		11.5–12	110	14.5–13	76
		11.7	38, 123	14.6b	117
9.1–23	147			14.10	117

14.13	117	7.17–24	91, 118, 130	3.16	62, 63
14.15–20	67			3.28	48, 92, 149
14.21	115	7.17	92	3.29	62
14.22–15.3	76	7.18	91	4.12	37
14.23	94	7.19	1, 91	5.6	93
14–15	7, 38, 60, 67, 76, 93, 109, 110, 113, 114, 115, 116, 161	7.20	91	5.13	36
		7.24	91	5.14	90
		7.31	91	6.2	36
		9.19	37	6.15	91, 93, 149
		9.19–23	96	6.16	49, 52
		11.1	37, 167		
15	171	12.20	165	*Ephesians*	
15.1	37, 94, 161	15	141	2.11–22	97, 136
15.5	36	15.24	172	2.19–20	59
15.7	36, 90	15.58	172	4.24	164
15.7–12	115	16.25	36		
15.8	112, 121, 133, 171			*Philippians*	
		2 Corinthians		3.2	20
15.8–9	17	1.5	87	3.4–8	88
15.8–12	171	1.20	133	3.5–6	157
15.9	171	1.21	90	3.7–9	149
15.10	119, 120	1.24	37	3.9	30
15.12	124, 154	3.1ff.	39		
15.14	76	5.17	91, 104	*Colossians*	
15.14–21	75	6.10	107	3.9–10	164
15.19	41, 87, 134	10–13	167	4.16	45
15.20	86	10.1	167		
15.23–4	77	10.13–16	39, 45, 86	*1 Thessalonians*	
15.25–7	129	11.22	87	1.4	70
15.26	123	12.10	166, 167	1.9–10	149, 168
15.32	77	13.12	36	2.12	70
16	77, 107			2.14	38, 72
16.4	87	*Galatians*		2.16	134
16.5	106	1–2	39, 46, 87	3.12	36
16.10	77	1.19	40	4.7	70
16.10–11	118	1.22	72	4.9	36
16.16	36	2	3, 39, 40	4.12	70
		2.1–14	40	4.18	36
1 Corinthians		2.2–8	40	5.3	70
1.7–8	172	2.8	39	5.11	36
2.3	167	2.11–14	39	5.15	36
3.10	86	2.11–18	39	5.24	70
4.8	134	2.14	88, 107		
4.8–21	167	2.20	164	*Philemon*	
4.10	166	3	112	1.8	37
4.11	167	3–4	112		
4.15	86	3.11	112	*Revelation*	
6.20	154	3.13–14	129	21.5	90
7	91	3.14	61		

OTHER ANCIENT SOURCES

Qumran
4QMMT   30
4QMMT 111–118 30

Magnesians
10.3   51, 81, 151

Philadelphians
6.1   151

Pseudo–Philo
Biblical Antiquities 61

Josephus
Antiquities
             61

Jubilees
             47, 61

Psalms of Solomon
7.31–41   95

Sybilline Oracles
3.616   95
3.724f.   95

Letter to Aristeas
1.81–4   117

INDEX OF MODERN AUTHORS

Aasgaard, R. 36, 37, 162
Adams, E. 86
Alexander, P. 8
Anderson, H. 143
Avemarie, F. 30

Badenas, R. 110
Baird, W. 2, 17
Banks, R. 36, 37, 74
Barclay, J.M.G. 88, 90, 94, 116, 117, 147, 148, 149, 152, 168
Bartchy, S.S. 37, 86, 166, 167
Barth, F. 3, 4, 5
Barth, K. 22, 25, 92, 127, 142
Barth, M. 94
Barton, S.C. 46
Baur, F.C. 13, 15, 17, 18, 19, 20, 21, 23, 31, 51, 97, 121
Beker, J.C. 71, 99, 110, 112, 133, 140, 152, 154, 155, 156, 160, 172
Bell, R.H. 170
Berger, P. 143
Bockmuehl, M.N.A. 34, 35, 40, 41, 47, 48, 50, 57, 58, 60, 81, 83, 93, 110, 117, 119, 173
de Boer, M.C. 144
Bourdieu, P. 168
Bousset, W. 17, 32
Boyarin, D. 45, 51, 52, 53, 64, 89, 94
Brooke, G.J. 30
Brown, R.E. 75
Buell, D.K. 5
Bultmann, R. 18, 24, 26, 102, 110, 143
Burrowes, B. 142

Calvert-Koyzis, N. 61, 62
Campbell, D.A. 33, 112, 144
Campbell, W.S. 27, 34, 38, 46, 49, 52, 65, 66, 70, 71, 72, 75, 76, 94, 99, 100, 104, 105, 110, 114, 115, 117, 123, 127, 130, 132, 141, 142, 153, 156, 158
Cartlidge, D.R 92
Castelli, E.A. 37, 86
Clarke, A.D. 76
Cohen, S.D. 2, 3, 65, 78, 111
Collins, J.J. 180
Cornell, S. 5, 6
Cosgrove, C. 96, 98, 127, 128, 137
Crüsemann, F. 126

Dahl, N.A. 29, 42, 135
Davies, W.D. 17, 18, 32, 96, 104, 105, 131, 135
Deming, W. 89, 93
Derrida, J. 157
Donaldson, T.L. 21, 23, 32, 42, 48, 54, 55, 59, 63, 121, 129, 134, 152, 168
Dodd, C.H. 128, 134, 135
Donfried, K.P. 118
Dunn, J.D.G. 2, 3, 7, 13, 18, 20, 26, 27, 28, 29, 33, 39, 42, 45, 46, 49, 51, 52, 59, 90, 107, 118, 127, 138, 147, 151, 153, 160, 172

Ehrensperger, K. 11, 24, 44, 61, 72, 115, 118, 119, 127, 158, 161
Eisenbaum, P. 43, 47, 48, 61, 63, 86
Elliott, N. 13, 50, 72, 73, 77, 84, 97, 105, 113, 125, 135, 162
Engberg-Pedersen, T. 160, 173
Eskola, T. 30
Esler, P.F. 2, 3, 4, 5, 6, 12, 38, 39, 47, 76, 77, 94, 95, 101, 106, 107, 109, 115, 116, 117, 118, 119, 157, 169

Feldman, L. 62, 104, 105, 107
Fitzmyer, J. 30, 118
Fredriksen, P. 95, 133
Furnish, V. 160

Gager, J.G. 29, 131
Garlington, D. 30
Gathercole, S.J. 30, 46
Geertz, C. 157
Georgi, D. 77, 78, 135
Gorday, P. 108
Gorman, M. 73
Goulder, M. 33
Gundry-Volf, J. 9, 30, 52, 164

Haacker, K. 77
Hall, J.M. 4
Harink, D. 43, 127, 135, 137, 138, 141, 144, 145, 146, 150, 154, 162, 169
Hartmann, D. 5
Harvey, A.E. 55
Hay, D.M. 34, 94
Hays, R. 103
Hodgson, P. 15
Holmberg, B. 83, 161
Hooker, M.D. 29
Horowitz, D.L. 115
Horrell, D.G. 86, 89, 90, 91, 97, 98, 102, 148, 152
Horsley, R.A. 4, 53, 77, 135
Houlden, J.L. 51
Hutchison, J. 5

Jenkins, R. 4
Jervell, J. 78, 137
Jewett, R. 45, 74, 115, 118, 119, 134
Johnson, E.E. 94
Judge, E.A. 75, 77, 106, 107, 167

Kahl, B. 53
Käsemann, E. 18, 21, 22, 23, 24, 25, 26, 55, 83, 110, 111, 121, 123, 124, 129, 131, 136, 137, 143, 144, 145, 146, 148, 150, 163
Keck, L. 149, 168, 170
Kee, H.C. 112
Kelley, S. 16
Kertelge, K. 24
Klein, G. 150
Krauss, W. 172
Kugel, J. 63
Kümmel, W.G. 18, 105

LaGrande, J. 13
Lampe, P. 77, 94, 104, 106, 107, 119
Lee, J.W. 9
Leenhardt, F.J. 113
Leon, H.J. 107
Levinas, E. 9, 74
Levine, L. 5
Lieu, Judith M. 72
Lightfoot, J.B. 18
Lim, T.H. 30
Longenecker, B. 64
Lyons, G. 39

Malina, B. 150, 153, 156
Manson, T.W. 20
Marcus, J. 115
Martin, D.M. 92
Martyn, J.L. 43, 143, 144
Matlock, R.B. 144
Meeks, W.A. 47, 73, 74, 84, 96, 115, 128, 153
Meier, J.P. 75
Meyer, P. 160
Michel, O. 62, 113
Mitchell, M. 2
Mitternacht, D. 66, 77, 174
Montefiore, C. 18
Moore, G.F. 17, 32
Müller, C. 24
Munck, J. 10, 13, 17, 18, 19, 20, 21, 22, 23, 114, 121, 129

Nagata, J.A. 157
Nanos, M.D. 6, 10, 20, 38, 39, 42, 43, 47, 56, 60, 65, 67, 75, 76, 79, 95, 110, 111, 112
Newlands, G. 153
Nickelsburg, G.W.E. 43, 44, 47, 140, 141

Painter, J. 40
Patte, D. 60
Pauck, W. 72
Peerbolte, L.J.L. 34, 163
Plietzsch, S. 165, 169
Polaski, S.H. 33, 37, 39

Rader, W. 49, 97
Räisänen, H. 72
Rambo, L.R. 66
Reasoner, M. 106, 117, 161

Richardson, P. 106
Ricoeur, P. 89
Rock, I.E. 79
Roetzel, C. 160
Rohrbaugh, R.L. 147
Rosner, B. 93, 142
Runesson, A. 106

Sabou, S.C. 154
Sanders, E.P. 9, 13, 17, 18, 25, 26, 27, 28, 29, 30, 31, 32, 43, 47, 48, 55, 96, 97, 101, 102, 114, 134, 135, 140, 149
Schelke, K.H. 107
Schiffmann, L.H. 8
Schmithals, W. 40
Schürer, E. 17, 32
Schütz, J.H. 37, 38, 39
Schwartz, S. 47
Schweitzer, A. 18, 52
Segal, A.F. 34, 66, 147, 149, 165, 166, 168
Seifrid, M. 30
Shkul, M. 165
Smith, A.D. 5
Smith, C.W. 12
Smith, J.A. 160, 161
Soulen, R.K. 145
Spilsbury, P. 62
Stanley, C. 60
Stark, R. 34, 35, 44
Stegemann, W. 143, 150
Stendahl, K. 13, 15, 19, 21, 22, 23, 24, 25, 26, 66, 74, 112, 143
Stowers, S.K. 63, 77, 107, 108, 120
Stuhlmacher, P. 24, 112, 143
Sundkler, B. 10

Tajfel, H. 115
Talbert, C.H. 30
Taylor, M.S. 65
Taylor, N.H. 41
Tellbe, M. 69, 70, 71, 74, 75, 77, 78, 79, 80, 112, 113, 153
Thiselton, A.C. 49, 89, 90, 91, 92, 93
Thomas, G.S.R. 106
Thorsteinsson, R. 105, 107, 108
Tomson, P.J. 38, 42, 60, 93, 117, 119, 142, 160
Travisano, R. 66
Tyson, J.B. 15, 16, 134

Von Wahlde, U. 2

Wagner, J.R. 35, 37, 63, 64, 120, 123, 135, 159, 168, 170, 171, 172, 173
Walters, J.C. 78
Watson, F.W. 46, 47, 148
Watt, J. 4
Weber, F. 17, 32
Weber, M. 36
Wedderburn, A.G.M. 75, 78, 113
Wilckens, U. 41
Wilson, B. 46
Wrede, W. 25
Wright, T. 59, 63, 87, 127, 135, 137, 149, 150, 152, 154, 169, 170, 172
Wyschogrod, M. 6, 65

Yoder, J.H. 170

Young, I.M. 9, 10

Zetterholm, M. 44, 50, 57, 58, 65, 74, 75, 79, 80, 81, 82, 83, 138, 151